War and Stereotypes

War (Hi) Stories

Edited by

Frank Jacob, Sarah K. Danielsson
Hiram Kümper, Sabine Müller, Jeffrey M. Shaw

Vol. 7

Scientific Board

Frank Jacob, Sepp Linhart (eds.)

War and Sterotypes

The Image of Japan's Military Abroad

BRILL | Ferdinand Schöningh

Bibliographic information published by the Deutsche Nationalbibliothek

The Deutsche Nationalbibliothek lists this publication in the Deutsche Nationalbibliografie;
detailed bibliographic data available online: http://dnb.d-nb.de

© 2020 Verlag Ferdinand Schöningh, an Imprint of the Brill-Group
(Koninklijke Brill NV, Leiden, Netherlands; Brill USA Inc., Boston MA, USA; Brill Asia Pte Ltd, Singapore;
Brill Deutschland GmbH, Paderborn, Germany)

www.schoeningh.de

Cover design: Nora Krull, Bielefeld
Production: Brill Deutschland GmbH, Paderborn

ISSN 2511-5154
ISBN 978-3-506-70293-7 (paperback)
ISBN 978-3-657-70293-0 (e-book)

Contents

Introduction: Japan's Military as Seen from Abroad

Frank Jacob and Sepp Linhart

Japan's modern history is defined by its wars. Related to them is the image of the Japanese, especially that of the Imperial Army's soldiers abroad. When taking a look at the different perceptions during these wars, a transformation from almost Western-like "gentlemen-soldiers" during the Russo-Japanese War (1904-05), when "Asia's Prussians" defeated the Czarist Army in every battle of the war, to demon-like monsters and perpetrators during the Pacific War (1941-1945), who tortured POWs and raped women by the thousands, can be emphasized.[1] The image of the Japanese soldiers changed similarly to the role of Japan within international politics. After the forceful opening of Japan in 1853 by an American diplomatic mission under the leadership of Commodore Matthew C. Perry (1794-1858), the Asian country, which was often described as militarily antiquated by Western visitors,[2] decided its future course after an internal power struggle and the reinstallation of the Emperor as the real political power in Japan: the Meiji Restoration.[3]

The new leadership realized rather fast that it needed reforms in two areas to prevent a colonial, or semi-colonial, fate, as could have been observed to be coming into existence in China. The agenda was consequently clear: rich country, strong army (*fukoku kyōhei*). Foreign specialists (*o-yatoi gaikokujin*) were hired to train Japan's future elite in almost every sector, but especially its military and economic leaders of the next generation.[4] The Japanese Imperial Army was trained by French and later Prussian officers, while the Navy was following the British model. Both would show the country's achievements five

---

1 For a discussion of the Japanese Army and its war crimes see: Frank Jacob, *Japanese War Crimes During World War II: Atrocity and the Psychology of Collective Violence* (Santa Barbara, CA: Praeger, 2018). For the perception of these crimes see: Barak Kushner, *Men to Devils - Devils to Men: Japanese War Crimes and Chinese Justice* (Cambridge, MA: Harvard University Press, 2015). For the reasons for this "War without Mercy" see: John W. Dower, *War Without Mercy: Race and Power in the Pacific War* (New York: Pantheon Books, 1986).

2 Many early Western visitors later published their impressions of the Asian country. One example would be: Gustav Spiess, *Die preussische Expedition nach Ostasien während der Jahre 1860-1862. Reise-Skizzen aus Japan, China, Siam und der indischen Inselwelt* (Berlin: Otto Spamer, 1864).

3 A classic read on the Meiji Restoration is Tōyama Shigeki, *Meiji ishin* (Tokyo: Iwanami Shoten, 2018).

4 Umetani Noboru, *O-yatoi gaikokujin: Meiji Nihon no wakiyaku-tachi* (Tokyo: Nihon Keizai Shinbunsha, 1965).

decades later, when the island nation was able to defeat the "Russian bear" in a war over influence in Korea and north-eastern China.[5] Nevertheless, the new course for the country after 1868 was not accepted uncontested by all subordinates of the Emperor. The old warrior elite, the *samurai*, whose image would dominate the stereotypes about the Japanese army even after their disappearance, would not tolerate all the reforms, especially general conscription, the abolishment of the right to wear swords in public, or the transformation of the feudal into a stipend system.[6] In the later 1870s, the Japanese government had to use force to settle its internal conflicts first. A discourse about the invasion of Korea (*seikanron*) in 1873[7] had shown two things: 1) the government was not willing to send the *samurai* abroad to invade a foreign territory, and 2) Korea would become a target of Japanese expansionism in later years. The impoverished *samurai*, however, remained a factor of instability, and a conflict seemed inevitable, eventually causing the Satsuma Rebellion in 1877[8] and its suppression by the Japanese Imperial Army, a conscript army established and trained according to Western standards.

The age of the *samurai* ended before Nitobe Inazō (1862-1933), with his work *Bushido: The Soul of Japan* (1900),[9] described a long gone time, but he thereby stimulated the continuation of Japanese stereotypes abroad for decades to come. In the meantime, Japanese soldiers had shown the value of their military education during the Sino-Japanese War, when the Emperor's army defeated the Chinese. Not many military observers had expected such a result,[10] but the victory proved that Japan was more important in the region. It consequently demanded not only financial reparations, but also Chinese territory as a token of victory. However, the so-called Triple Intervention by Russia, France,

---

5   On the Russo-Japanese War and its Impact see: Frank Jacob, *The Russo-Japanese War and Its Shaping of the Twentieth Century*, Paperback edition (London/New York: Routledge, 2019).

6   For a more detailed discussion see: Frank Jacob, "Die Meiji-Restauration und die Neuordnung Japans. Umverteilung und sozialer Wandel," *Traverse: Zeitschrift für Geschichte* 22 (2015), 79-92.

7   On the *seikanron* see Andō Hideo, *Saigō Takamori – Hyōden*, 2nd edition (Tokyo: Shirakawa Shoin, 1977), 158-168; Sakamoto Takao, *Meiji kokka no kensetsu 1871-1890* (Tokyo: Chūō Kōronsha, 1999), 165-178; Suzuki Hideo and Yoshii Akira, *Rekishi ni miru: Nihon to Kankoku – Chōsen* (Tokyo: Akashi Shoten, 1999), 64-65; Tōyama Shigeki, *Meiji ishin to gendai*, 19th edition (Tokyo: Iwanami Shoten, 1986), 205-208.

8   On the Satsuma Rebellion see Olavi K. Fält's chapter in this volume.

9   Nitobe Inazō, *Bushido: The Soul of Japan* (Philadelphia: The Leeds & Biddle Co, 1900).

10   Erich Ludendorff (1865-1937) was acutally one of the German military thinkers and planners, who was not surprised by the Japanese victory. Frank Jacob, "General der Infanterie Erich Ludendorff," in *Des Kaisers militärische Elite*, ed. Lukas Grawe (Darmstadt: WBG, 2019) (forthcoming).

and Germany prevented the Japanese government from taking the Liaodong Peninsula from China to extend Japan's influence on the mainland. As Russia was the initiator of this humiliation of the island country and had thereby also emphasized that Japan was not considered to be an equally great power, the enemy for a future war had already been chosen in 1895.[11]

A decade later, during the Russo-Japanese War, the Japanese Army and Navy, now allied with Britain in the Anglo-Japanese Alliance,[12] showed the world that they were equals on the battlefield with Western soldiers and sailors. The Czar was surprised by Japan's decision to go to war, and probably even more surprised by the defeats of his own army, which was driven further back battle by battle by the Japanese forces. Around the world, interest in Japan and its army continued to grow, especially since it had to be taken to be a serious factor in future war plans on a global scale or even solely within the Pacific. Nevertheless, the tradition to caricature the Japanese in Western print media or on picture postcards continued, and no Japanese victory seemed to change that.[13] While the observers highlighted the effectiveness of the military performance of Japan's army and navy, many military planners continued to pay almost no attention to the developments in that region during the years to come. It seemed like many lessons with regard to the war between Russia and Japan had simply been ignored.

It was very often emphasized that the spirit of the soldiers was decisive in winning the battle for Port Arthur, although reports, like the one later published by Sakurai Tadayoshi, highlighted that it was by the use of "human bullets" and not by spirit that the Russian fortress was eventually won.[14] The war also further stimulated the idea of a Yellow Peril,[15] and had tremendous global implications. However, the Portsmouth Peace Treaty was considered a humiliation for the Asian country, whose soldiers and sailors had died on the battlefields, and who now again felt betrayed by the Western Powers, especially the United States, whose President, Theodore Roosevelt (1858-1919), had helped to forge

---

11   George Alexander Lensen, "Japan and Tsarist Russia: The Changing Relationships, 1875-
        1917," *Jahrbücher für Geschichte Osteuropas* 10:3 (1962), 338-339.
12   Ian Nish, *The Anglo-Japanese Alliance: The Diplomacy of Two Island Empires, 1894-1907*
        (London: Athlone, 1966).
13   Sepp Linhart, *"Dainty Japanese" or Yellow Peril? Western War Postcards 1900-1945* (Vienna:
        LIT, 2005).
14   Sakurai Tadayoshi, *Human Bullets: A Soldier's Story of Port Arthur* (Boston/New York:
        Houghton, Mifflin and Company, 1907).
15   John Kuo Wei Tchen and Dylan Yates, *Yellow Peril!: An Archive of Anti-Asian Fear* (London/
        New York: Verso, 2014).

this treaty. The Hibiya Park Riots in Tokyo expressed these feelings of anger about a supposed betrayal of the last war within the Meiji period (1868-1912).

The First World War saw Japan as an allied power of the Entente, providing some of its naval power to secure British transports in the Mediterranean and fighting a short war against the German troops in China. The fact that Japan was an allied power stimulated further interest in the country and its people, especially since the Japanese soldiers and sailors, as during the Russo-Japanese War, were praised as gallant and chivalrous.[16] During the war, Japan was a topic of interest, and this was displayed in multiple ways. To name just one example, the Panama-Pacific Exposition in 1915 in San Francisco offered its visitors an insight into the Asian country that lacked "no detail of landscape, trees, plants, flowers and pretty native women presiding in its shops and tea houses needed to make the illusion complete."[17] The successes on the battlefield eventually caused an interest in Japan and its culture, making the "land of cherry blossoms and geisha girls"[18] more popular among Westerners around the globe. The growing interest in Japan, however, was not enough to overcome stereotypes or to accept the idea of "racial equality" as one of the preconditions for the League of Nations, which was to secure peace in the aftermath of the "war to end all wars."

While Japan had gained from the First World War financially and was also transformed by its events in many ways,[19] the socio-economic impact of the war eventually led to a crisis.

The radicalization of the Japanese Army in the 1930s, especially visible through the acts of the Kwantung Army in Manchuria, the May 15 incident in 1932, and the February 26 incident in 1936, was a process related to the growing ambition to extend Japan's influence in China as well as the increasing antagonism with the United States. At the same time, a battle within the military leadership about the course of a future war, either against the Soviet Union or to increase Japan's influence in the Pacific, led to further trouble within Japan's army and navy. The war against China since 1937, and eventually the Pacific War that would globalize the Second World War (1939-1945), witnessed a new kind of Japanese soldier, one who had been unknown in the years before: the violent and aggressive Japanese. These soldiers would be known for

---

16   Famous scenes from the Russo-Japanese War were also re-printed during the First World
      War. One example would be "A Japanese Charge, From Famous Picture," *The Day Book*
      (Chicago, IL), May 10, 1915, 7.

17   "Japan at the Big San Francisco Exposition," *Richmond Times Dispatch*, June 13, 1915, 51.

18   Ibid.

19   Inoue Toshikazu, *Dai-ichiji sekai taisen to Nihon* (Tokyo: Kōdansha, 2014), 174-211 (society)
      and 214-251 (culture).

Fig. 0.1   "Geisha Girls" at the Panama-Pacific Exposition in 1915 in San
            Francisco. The subheading says: "Three Types of Japanese
            Comeliness Now Living in 'Japan Beautiful' [the Japanese section
            of the exhibition, F.J.] Who Assist in the Welcome of Visitors to
            the Exposition." Image taken from: "Japan at the Big San Francisco
            Exposition," *Richmond Times Dispatch*, June 13, 1915, 51.

many things during and after the war, especially their acts of violence and in-humanity, their willingness to fight until death and to sacrifice themselves, if not on the ground[20] or at sea then as *kamikaze* pilots, and their inability to show human emotions towards their victims or the defeated enemy. It also seemed unlikely to ever be able to engage with a Japanese POW, because as the US *Intelligence Bulletin* reported in July 1945, "[w]hen surrounded by an Allied force, Japanese soldiers were either to break through the encirclement or com-mit suicide."[21] If, however, a rare chance for an interrogation appeared, it was reported that only two types of Japanese POWs existed:

> There will be those who surrendered voluntarily because they couldn't take it, and those taken against their wills because of wounds or shock. The first are mostly stupid animal-slaves who have been drilled and drilled until they know how to handle a piece or wield a knife and kill. Otherwise they know absolutely nothing about anything. They have no minds of their own and act only when a superior presses a button.
>
> The second type is something else again. They are fanatic, shrewd and possessed of an amazing singleness of purpose that is the direct result of just one thing – their sheeplike subservience to their superiors and to the Emperor. They're slick and well trained and live only to obey their superiors' orders to kill as many of us guys as possible. Otherwise they're just like the first type – mindless automatons who move when the button is pressed.
>
> There's a third type, too, but you won't see many of them in any pris-on camp because they're almost never captured. They're the killers who fight like madmen until they're wiped out. You can realize how many of these bastards there are when you consider the small number of prison-ers we've taken compared with Jap casualties.[22]

---

20   Japanese ground forces were repeatedly involved in raids that targeted key personnel of the enemy. The US *Intelligence Bulletin* reported that "these attacks may vary from con-certed raids by trained units to small suicide assaults executed by ordinary Jap service or combat foot soldiers." "Combat Methods of Small Raiding Parties," *Intelligence Bulletin* 3:2 (July 1945), 6-14, quote from 7.

21   Ibid., 10. Some Japanese soldiers were even reported to have committed suicide after read-ing US propaganda leaflets about the US victory in the war. "Jap Reactions to Propaganda," *USAF Intelligence Bulletin* 12 (March 23, 1945), 20.

22   Sgt. H. N. Oliphant, "A Talk with Some Japs," *Yank: The Army Weekly* 3:34 (February 9, 1945), 2-4, quote on p. 2.

In contrast to the Japanese soldiers, who resisted being taken prisoner because they considered it as a shame for their whole family, many US soldiers became POWs during the war, and, due to being despised by Japan's army, suffered from countless forms of violence, most visible due to the Bataan Death March,[23] or the famous building of the Burma-Thailand Railway.

Those prisoners, who were supposed to build the latter, were instructed as follows in the often quoted speech by Col. Nagatama, who was responsible for the railway's construction from the Burmese side: "He told [the POWs that they] were the remnants of a beaten nation and should weep with gratitude that the Imperial Japanese Army had spared [their] lives. 'But,' he finished, 'your lives are worth nothing if they can't serve us. I intend to build that railroad – if it is over your dead bodies.'"[24] For the Japanese soldiers, it was not a question of guilt[25] when the British and American POWs were treated badly, especially since it was considered more honorable to commit suicide than to become a prisoner of the enemy.

All in all, the war was one "without mercy," which on both sides was based on racial stereotypes that had preconditioned the mind and the attitude towards the enemy. These stereotypes were also expressed by US POWs, as the following statement by a survivor of the Bataan Death March highlights:

> In all prison camps, we nicknamed the Japanese in attendance. These names were chosen primarily because of physical characteristics. Here are some of those names ...: Creepy, Sportsu, Humpy, Paddlefoot, The Snake, The Squirrel, Goldtooth, Bundle of Love, Gobo, The Wine Merchant, Bushido, One Armed Bandit, The Kendo Kid, Fat Stuff, Peg Leg, Gimpy, Duck Butt, Horse Face, Leather Wrist, White Fist, Iron Fist, Shufflefoot, Smiling Jack.[26]

Those who continued the fight would gather souvenirs on the battlefield, often taken from dead soldiers, sending them home to highlight their success in fighting the Japanese devils. These souvenir collections, very well described for US troops by Mark D. Van Ells, took strange forms. Some soldiers would send Japanese plane parts to the radio broadcasting stations of the War Department

---

23   Jacob, *Japanese War Crimes*, 94-108.

24   Bill Reed, "Prisoner of the Japs," *Yank: The Army Weekly* 4:11 (August 31, 1945), 2-4, quote on p. 3.

25   Frank Jacob, "Narratives Without Guilt: The Self-Perception of Japanese Perpetrators," in *Genocide and Mass Violence in Asia: An Introdutory Reader*, ed. Frank Jacob (Berlin: De Gruyter Oldenbourg, 2019), 101-116.

26   Ernest B. Miller, *Bataan Uncensored* (Long Prairie, MN: Hart Publications, 1949), 322.

in exchange for a tune,[27] while others would cook the heads of dead Japanese soldiers and send the skull home by mail to keep as a trophy.

All in all, as this short survey shows, the image of the Japanese soldiers and sailors depended on many things. While the initial image of the *samurai* was rather a fantasy, since its perception began after the ancient warriors of Japan had already disappeared, the allied soldiers of the Asian country were naturally much better perceived than the enemy. The image of the Japanese enemy during the Pacific War was full of stereotypes, and the racial antagonism on both sides found its reproduction on the battlefields, where soldiers were trying to survive while killing an Other that was described to both parties as violent, morally inferior, and racially unworthy. This was one factor that led to extreme forms of violence during the Pacific War, and an extreme change to the image of the Japanese Imperial Army and Navy. This transformation also shows that historical perceptions tend to change in the same way as alliances and military necessities change. The eight chapters of the present volume, however, want to further trace the reasons and ways Japan's military personnel were perceived abroad between 1868 and 1945.

Olavi K. Fält, in the first two chapters, discusses the image of the Japanese military due to the Formosan Expedition in 1874 and the Satsuma Rebellion in 1877. He focuses on the perception of the events and the Japanese forces by the local Anglophone press and therefore provides an early insight into the perception of Japan's modern army by the English reading community in Japan and abroad. Henna-Riikka Pennanen then shows how Japan was step by step considered a military threat for the United States at the end of the 19th century as the Pacific became a contested ocean between the two imperialist powers. The further development of the martial image of Japan, especially during the Boxer Uprising (1899-1901) and its suppression in China, will be analyzed in Joe Fonseca's chapter. The above-mentioned impact of the Russo-Japanese War on the perception of the Japanese Army and Navy abroad will then be discussed by Frank Jacob, whose chapter deals with this war and the extent to which a third power, in this case Imperial Germany, was perceiving the events in East Asia in general, and its military consequences in particular. How and why the image of the Japanese soldiers changed from the Russo-Japanese War (1904-05) to the Pacific War (1941-1945) will then be taken into closer consideration by Sepp Linhart, who will compare this image in American popular songs.

The final two chapters will then specifically deal with the period of the Pacific War and its aftermath. Adam S. Rock discusses the popular perceptions of Japanese POWs in the United States to show how the question about their

---

27   "Among My Souvenirs," *Air Force* 26:4 (Apriil 1943), 3.

identity as monsters or men was answered by the US public. The image of the Japanese perpetrators and war criminals in particular, however, were not only shaped during the Pacific War, but were established, further discussed, and eventually solidified by postwar events. Aiko Otsuka discusses this process as it relates to the mass killings of civilians in British Malaya during the war. All in all, the volume only offers a first survey of different images of Japanese soldiers and sailors at different times, and the editors hope that it will stimulate further research related to the overall topic discussed here, namely the changing images and perceptions of Japan's military forces abroad.

Works Cited

"A Japanese Charge, From Famous Picture." *The Day Book* (Chicago, IL), May 10, 1915, 7.

"Among My Souvenirs." *Air Force* 26:4 (Apriil 1943), 3.

Andō Hideo. *Saigō Takamori - Hyōden*, 2nd edition. Tokyo: Shirakawa Shoin, 1977.

"Combat Methods of Small Raiding Parties." *Intelligence Bulletin* 3:2 (July 1945), 6-14.

Dower, John W. *War Without Mercy: Race and Power in the Pacific War*. New York: Pantheon Books, 1986.

Inoue Toshikazu. *Dai-ichiji sekai taisen to Nihon*. Tokyo: Kōdansha, 2014.

Jacob, Frank. "Die Meiji-Restauration und die Neuordnung Japans. Umverteilung und sozialer Wandel." *Traverse: Zeitschrift für Geschichte* 22 (2015), 79-92.

———. *Japanese War Crimes During World War II: Atrocity and the Psychology of Collective Violence*. Santa Barbara, CA: Praeger, 2018.

———. "Narratives Without Guilt: The Self-Perception of Japanese Perpetrators" in *Genocide and Mass Violence in Asia: An Introductory Reader*, ed. Frank Jacob, 101-116. Berlin: De Gruyter Oldenbourg, 2019.

———. *The Russo-Japanese War and Its Shaping of the Twentieth Century*, Paperback edition. London/New York: Routledge, 2019.

"Jap Reactions to Propaganda." *USAF Intelligence Bulletin* 12 (March 23, 1945), 20.

"Japan at the Big San Francisco Exposition," *Richmond Times Dispatch*, June 13, 1915, 51.

Kushner, Barak. *Men to Devils - Devils to Men: Japanese War Crimes and Chinese Justice*. Cambridge, MA: Harvard University Press, 2015.

Lensen, George Alexander. "Japan and Tsarist Russia: The Changing Relationships, 1875-1917." *Jahrbücher für Geschichte Osteuropas* 10:3 (1962), 337-348.

Linhart, Sepp. *"Dainty Japanese" or Yellow Peril? Western War Postcards 1900-1945*. Vienna: LIT, 2005.

Miller, Ernest B. *Bataan Uncensored*. Long Prairie, MN: Hart Publications, 1949.

Nish, Ian. *The Anglo-Japanese Alliance: The Diplomacy of Two Island Empires, 1894-1907*. London: Athlone, 1966.

Nitobe Inazō. *Bushido: The Soul of Japan*. Philadelphia: The Leeds & Biddle Co, 1900.

Oliphant, Sgt. H. N. "A Talk with Some Japs." *Yank: The Army Weekly* 3:34 (February 9, 1945), 2-4

Sakamoto Takao. *Meiji kokka no kensetsu 1871-1890*. Tokyo: Chūō Kōronsha, 1999.

Sakurai Tadayoshi. *Human Bullets: A Soldier's Story of Port Arthur*. Boston/New York: Houghton, Mifflin and Company, 1907.

Spiess, Gustav. *Die preussische Expedition nach Ostasien während der Jahre 1860-1862. Reise-Skizzen aus Japan, China, Siam und der indischen Inselwelt*. Berlin: Otto Spamer, 1864.

Suzuki Hideo and Yoshii Akira. *Rekishi ni miru: Nihon to Kankoku – Chōsen*. Tokyo: Akashi Shoten, 1999.

Tōyama Shigeki. *Meiji ishin* (The Meiji Restoration). Tokyo: Iwanami Shoten, 2018.

Umetani Noboru. *O-yatoi gaikokujin: Meiji Nihon no wakiyaku-tachi* (Tokyo: Nihon Keizai Shinbunsha, 1965).

Wei Tchen, John Kuo and Dylan Yates. *Yellow Peril!: An Archive of Anti-Asian Fear*. London/New York: Verso, 2014.

CHAPTER 1

The Changing Image: The Formosan Expedition in 1874 in the Eyes of the Local Anglo-Saxon Press

Olavi K. Fält

Introduction

The present topic, the views of the Anglo-Saxon press in Japan on the Formosan expedition in 1874[1], is closely connected with the general problem of relations between Japan and the Western world and of interaction between the Japanese and Western cultures. The group of Westerners who probably felt the impact of this interaction most intimately, especially since it impinged on their own interests, was the community actually living in Japan, the views of whom were represented best by the newspapers and magazines published by them.

The present work represents above all an attempt at studying the interpretation given by the papers: what their attitude was to the expedition, what image they conveyed of Japan and the Japanese, and why. By studying an image one can also form a picture of the creator of that image, the observer or subject, to the extent that an image can tell us at least as much about its creator as about its object.[2]

The material to be studied here comprises the main foreign English-language newspapers and magazines published in Yokohama and Tokyo: *The Japan Daily Herald* (Yokohama), *The Japan Gazette* (Yokohama), *The Japan Weekly Mail* (Yokohama), *The Tokei Journal* (Tokyo), *The Far East* (Yokohama) and the satirical magazine *Japan Punch* (Yokohama).[3]

---

1   Based principally on Olavi K. Fält, *The Clash of Interests: The Transformation of Japan in 1861-1881 in the Eyes of the Local Anglo-Saxon press* (Rovaniemi: Societas Historica Finlandiae Septentrionalis 1990), 111-142; Olavi K. Fält, "The Western Views on the Japanese Expedition to Formosa in 1874," *Asian Profile* 13:3 (1985), 201-219.

2   Olavi K. Fält, "Introduction", in *Looking at the Other: Historical Study of Images in Theory and Practise* (Acta Universitatis Ouluensis: Humaniora, vol. 42), eds. Kari Alenius, Olavi K. Fält and Seija Jalagin (Oulu: University of Oulu 2002), 7-12.

3   For a discussion of the Western press in Japan see Fält, *The Clash of Interests*, 13-23.

© VERLAG FERDINAND SCHÖNINGH, 2020 | DOI:10.30965/9783657702930_002

The appearance of English-language newspapers in Asia has been seen as a part of both building the British Empire and Christian mission work.[4] Foreign newspapers functioned in Asia as a link between the East and the West in joining these two worlds to each other.[5] In addition, English-language newspapers are thought to have played a significant role in shaping Western readers' conceptions of the East.[6] Among the first English-language newspapers in East Asia were the *Canton Register* established in China 1827[7], *the Pinang Gazette* established in Malaysia in 1833, the *Observer* established in Ceylon in 1834, the *Times of India* established in India in 1838 and the *China Mail* established in Hong Kong in 1845[8].

The "father" of the English-language press[9] in Japan was Albert W. Hansard, who had moved from England to New Zealand, where he had acquired newspaper experience by publishing a paper called the *Southern Cross*. Furthermore, he had also bought a printing press while there, which he then brought with him to Japan.[10] Initially he established a newspaper in Nagasaki called *The Nagasaki Shipping List and Advertiser*, which came out twice a week in 22.6.–1.10.1861. Hansard was also the *London and China Telegraph's* representative in Nagasaki. However, he was not satisfied with the low number of readers in Nagasaki, and in addition, Yokohama – opened to foreigners in 1859 – had already displaced Nagasaki as a commercial centre and was much closer to Edo (Tokyo), the seat of the Tokugawa government, so he moved the newspaper to Yokohama. There Hansard began publishing the paper once a week as *The Japan Herald.*[11]

In its first issue on November 23, 1861, the newspaper, like its predecessor, defined as its goal satisfying the rapidly increasing need for information about Japan in England and elsewhere in the world. The newspaper hoped to be a significant addition to the "Eastern Press" as Japan's only newspaper which would

---

4   John Lee, "English-Language press in Asia," *The Asia Newspapers' Reluctant Revolution*, ed. John A. Lent (Iowa: Ames 1971), 13.

5   Harry Emerson Wildes, *Social Currents in Japan: With Special Reference to the Press* (Chicago: University of Chicago Press, 1927), 253.

6   Peter O'Connor, *The English-Language Press Networks of East Asia, 1918-1945* (Folkestone: Global Oriental, 2010), 1.

7   Ibid., 32.

8   Lee, *English-language Press in Asia*, 15-16.

9   The first non-English newspaper in Japan was *L'Echo du Japon*, which appeared in 1870-1885. J.E. Hoare, *Japan's Treaty Ports and Foreign Settlements: The Uninvited Guests, 1858-1899* (Folkestone: Japan Library, 1994), 145.

10   Grace Fox, *Britain and Japan 1858-1883* (Oxford: Oxford University Press, 1969), 416.

11   Fox, *Britain and Japan 1858-1883*, 416-417; Fält, *The Clash of Interests*, 14; Wildes, *Social Currents in Japan*, 260-261.

affect "much good" and would spark interest not only locally, but also back home in England and in China, India and everywhere in the world.[12] By conveying news from both Japan and elsewhere in the world *The Japan Herald* and later other English-language papers functioned as an information link which joined two worlds.

The Expedition

The expedition to Formosa in 1874 was the most critical episode of the decade as far as Japan's foreign policy was concerned, especially her policy towards China. Relations between the two countries at the beginning of the decade were governed by the Treaty of Tientsin, signed on 13th September 1871 and ratified at the end of April 1873. This included a declaration of eternal friendship and a non-aggression agreement. The most disturbing point in it for the western powers, particularly Britain, was its second clause: "now that friendly relations subsist between the two countries this friendship shall without fail, be of an intimate and reciprocal character. Should either State experience at the hands of another country injustice or slighting treatment, on communication being made to the other state the latter shall give assistance or shall use her good offices in mediating between the two countries."[13]

After the signing of the treaty, however, the greatest threat to China did not come from the Western world but from the east. The obligations of the treaty did not discourage Japan's ambitions towards China, and the nationalist group in the government in particular tried to allay the rising discontent of the samurai class by calling for the annexation of the Ryūkyū and Bonin Islands and the mounting of punitive expeditions to Korea and Formosa.[14]

The Japanese expedition to Formosa represented a compromise between the militarists and the moderates, although the supporters of the most active policy resigned from the Council of the State in protest. Those who supported the expedition believed that sympathy could also be expected from the West. The expedition may be attributed to the weakness of China. Although the Beijing

---

12   *The Japan Herald* 1:1, November 23, 1861; Fox, *Britain and Japan 1858-1883*, 416.
13   Ibid., 276.
14   Akira Iriye, "Japan's Drive to a Great-Power Status," in *The Cambridge History of Japan*, vol. 5: *The Nineteenth Century*, ed. Marius B. Jansen (Cambridge: Cambridge University Press, 1989), 741-744; Norihito Mizuno, "Qing China's Reaction to the 1874 Japanese Expedition to the Taiwanese Aboriginal Territories," *Sino-Japanese Studies* 16 (2009), 100-125; G.B. Sansom, *The Western World and Japan: A Study in the Interaction of European and Asiatic Cultures* (Tokyo: Charles E. Tuttle Company, 1977), 332.

government professed to administer Formosa as a prefecture of the province of Fukien, it had not incorporated the eastern and south-western areas of the island into the administration of the prefecture. The aborigines who lived in that part of Formosa caused great damage to trade in the Far Eastern Seas by murdering the crews of ships wrecked on the eastern and southern coasts of the island, and the Beijing government had generally ignored these brutalities. When a Ryūkyūan ship was wrecked on the south cost of the island on December 1871, the Botan tribe murdered fifty-four of its crew, a further twelve escaping to reveal the crime to the world at large. This gave Japan her excuse to invade Formosa. The dispute involved relations between the Ryūkyūan people, Japan, and China. Ryūkyū had paid tributes to both China and the Daimyō of Satsuma, and the wrecked ship had been carrying such tributes to China. The Meiji government nevertheless annexed the islands in 1873 and its naval and military forces demanded the right to punish the tribes, which had murdered the Ryūkyūan castaways.[15]

After complicated discussions, a punitive expedition initially consisting of 3,000 men was sent to Formosa in May 1874, and the Japanese also appointed some American advisors to the mission, including general Charles Le Gendre (1830-1899), who had first-hand knowledge of the island and who wholeheartedly encouraged the operation. The troops quickly accomplished their purpose, and by the end of July all the hostile tribes in the south of the island had submitted to the Japanese. During the Formosa Operation itself, to the foreign representatives in the two countries war between China and Japan seemed a more probable outcome than peace, but after long, difficult negotiations and through the good offices of the British, the Beijing Agreement was eventually signed on 31 October 1874. Under the terms of this document China accepted Japan's action in Formosa as an endeavour to provide security for her own subjects and promised to pay 750,000 Mexican Dollars in compensation to the families of the Japanese killed on the island and for the roads and buildings erected there by the Japanese, which China would retain for her own use.[16] The Japanese government was satisfied with the treaty, but it was no more than marginally acceptable to the Chinese.

---

15   Fox, *Britain and Japan*, 282; Iriye, "Japan's Drive", 741-744; Mizuno, "Qing China's Reaction," 100-125.

16   Fox, *Britain and Japan*, 282-308; Iriye, "Japan's Drive", 741-744; Mizuno, "Qing China's Reaction," 100-125.

First Critical Comments

The Japan Daily Herald criticized the Formosan expedition from the very beginning, claiming in its edition of 7 April 1874 that a vast number of influential people looked upon the whole affair with great disfavor and regarded it as a useless and hazardous experiment, which could do much harm, but gain the country little practical advantage.[17] The considerable sum of money, which it would cost, could have been much more usefully spent.[18] The paper also had other reasons for regarding it as a dangerous venture: "China by force of circumstances may have to submit, with the best grace she may, to Russian encroachment upon her territory, but she will not tolerate nibbling like a mouse at a cheese, on the edge of her empire, on the part of a petty state like this."[19] The paper did not believe that China would be altogether indifferent to the projected Japanese operations within her territory,[20] but thought that the Japanese would be elbowed out of the island. The whole Japanese plan was highly questionable.[21]

When it seemed that Japan planned to abandon the expedition, the *Herald* was highly sarcastic. In its opinion there were no statesmen in Japan but only "statesmen", and this expedition, which had begun in a muddle, seemed to be destined to end in a mess.[22] The paper thought it a misfortune for Japan that no mature statesmen had arisen to guide her steps in the path of progress. It confidently expected China to demand reparations for the insult of a threat to invade and annex part of her territory. The paper naturally declared that it sincerely wished Japan well, but still did not consider the intentions of the Japanese leaders to be honorable, wise or patriotic.[23] It believed that the government's action had been childish and that the affair would end in a fiasco.[24]

---

17   *The Japan Daily Herald*, April 7, 1874.

18   "The Expedition to Formosa," *The Japan Daily Herald*, April 11, 1874.

19   Ibid. The problem that Japan was experiencing in the northern part of her territory in the early 1870's was that of securing her own sphere of interest against the expansionist designs of Russia, which had gained possession of the area between the Ussuri and the Pacific ocean as a result of a treaty signed with China in 1860. John K. Fairbank, Edwin O. Reaischauer, Albert M. Graig, *East Asia: Tradition and Transformation* (Tokyo: Charles E. Tuttle Company, 1976), 479.

20   "The Japanese Expedition to Formosa," *The Japan Daily Herald*, April 17, 1874.

21   "The Expedition to Formosa," *The Japan Daily Herald*, April 1, 1874.

22   *The Japan Daily Herald*, April 2, 1874. See also "The Collapse of the Formosan Project," *The Japan Daily Herald*, April 28, 1874.

23   "Wanted, Patriotic and Able Statesmen for Japan," *The Japan Daily Herald*, April 28, 1874.

24   "The Collapse of the Formosan Project," *The Japan Daily Herald,* April 28, 1874.

Through the Japanese leaders, the *Herald* also leveled its stringent criticism at the whole nation: "As the rulers are, so are the governed: and it is impossible to resist the conclusion that a people that permits its affairs to be so maladministered can be but low in the scale of intelligence, deficient in political knowledge, and wanting in courage and patriotism."[25] The paper particularly blamed Japan's diplomacy, picturing her envoys as mere babes and sucklings. In view of her unfavorable position as compared with China, she would be better off confining herself within her own boundaries.[26]

It was a great surprise to the *Herald* that, after some delay, the Japanese government really did send the expedition to Formosa. At first the paper thought that the Japanese warships had violated government orders, and regarded their commanders as mutineers and pirates because their own government was not responsible for the acts that they might commit,[27] but later it explained that the government had given its post facto sanction to the affair.[28] It is very difficult to find any real cause for the *Herald*'s criticism of the government, but perhaps part of the explanation may lie in the paper's conservatism. It blamed Japan for being too hasty in her development; the advantages of what was called progress would be lost by excessive haste. Instead, the paper promoted the notion of slow, steady innovation.[29] This way of thinking may be a heritage from the Western culture and its slow but steady growth towards modernization. It would then be quite logical to think that no other possibilities existed for alien countries but to follow the Western example. This view left no place for a military expedition by a country, which was just about to reap her first fruits of Western culture. It also seems that the paper did not really appreciate the Japanese people and their actions.

The Japan Gazette was similarly quite critical of the Formosan expedition at first, believing that it had been entered into unwisely and that the expeditionary force had departed without government sanction. It expected the government to declare it piratical in order to wash its hands of the whole affair, but was afraid that even though disowned by their government, the troops would have the sympathy of the samurai behind them. In the eyes of the Gazette there seemed to be only two alternatives, war with China or civil war. At least this would be the case in a similarly muddled situation in Europe. The only chance of escaping one or the other of these alternative fates, it claimed, lay

---

25   Ibid.
26   Ibid.
27   "The Formosan Fleet very much at Sea," *The Japan Daily Herald*, May 7, 1874.
28   *The Japan Daily Herald*, May 13, 1874.
29   "Wanted, Patriotic and Able Statesmen for Japan," *The Japan Daily Herald*, April 28, 1874.

in the extraordinary way in which easterners acted on such occasions. China might remain inactive, for instance.[30] Compared with the opinions of the *Herald*, the *Gazette*, however, was neither so biting nor so critical. In a way it tried to understand the difficult situation in which the Japanese government found itself in this affair, and seemed to believe that there were some chances of Japan escaping from the predicament.

The Japan Weekly Mail understood the government's motives much better than did the *Gazette* at first. It believed that the Chinese would disclaim all jurisdiction over the southern trip of Formosa and all responsibility with regard to the actions of the tribes occupying it.[31] In accordance with this understanding approach, the paper wished the expedition success in spite of its misgivings as to the outcome of the affair.[32] One week later, however, the tone of the paper became more critical. Japanese government policy appeared to be more and more perplexing, and was from the European point of view little short of madness. The paper did not believe that Japan could gain anything if her policy led to war with China. It particularly emphasized the progress made by China in the field of military equipment and army discipline, which had made its empire stronger than it had been in any previous period of the nineteenth century.[33] It seemed as if the government would disown the expedition, why the paper did not speak out against Japan as such but took the attitude of a friend of the country. Notes of the operation would nevertheless damage her reputation and fortunes to an extent from which it would not be easy to recover: "No words are too strong to characterize the heedless manner in which this transaction has been – we will not say, managed – but muddled, the humiliation to which it had led, or the sorrow it causes to those who wish well to the country."[34]

The Weekly Mail hoped that this humiliating experience would awaken Japanese statesmen to the serious sense of responsibility than they apparently possessed, and that it would teach them that it was folly to enter upon serious enterprises without sufficient consideration of what the probable consequences would be.[35] The paper feared that the events could arouse suspicion among the public as to the wisdom of the policy pursued by the country.[36] The departure of the Formosan Expedition seemed to come as a bombshell to the

30 *The Japan Gazette*, May 11, 1874.
31 "Notes of the Week," *The Japan Weekly Mail*, April 4, 1874.
32 "Notes of the Week," *The Japan Weekly Mail*, April 11, 1874.
33 "Notes of the Week," *The Japan Weekly Mail*, April 18, 1874.
34 "Notes of the Week," *The Japan Weekly Mail*, April 25, 1874.
35 "The Formosan Expedition," *The Japan Weekly Mail*, April 25, 1874.
36 "Notes of the Week," *The Japan Weekly Mail*, May 2, 1874.

Western residents. *The Japan Weekly Mail* did not understand the policy of the Japanese government at all. It regarded the departure as a mathematical problem, the solution of which demanded a higher calculus than it itself was in possession of.[37]

In fact British and American opposition did cause the Japanese to pause, and they resolved to explain to China that Japan had no hostile intentions towards her, but the commander of the expedition, Lieutenant-General Saigō Jūdō (1843-1902), forced the government to give its support, and the decision to dispatch troops to Formosa was officially announced on 19 May.[38] Western residents did not know exactly how the Japanese had come to this decision, and assumed that the troops were acting in defiance of government orders. According to the *Weekly Mail*, the rest of the world would regard them as filibusters, if not as pirates. In an opinion that carried a tinge of racial discrimination with it, the paper admitted that it was difficult to predict the results of the expedition, as the surprises of Asia were beyond the European powers of prediction: "... where [in the Western world] the working of men's minds are controlled by more definite and better known laws, and where cause and effect have relations which do not seem to belong to them here."[39]

The paper was nevertheless quite sure that the expedition would be a prelude to a series of disasters for Japan.[40] Although the opinions of the *Weekly Mail* were not so biting as those of the *Herald*, the paper was pessimistic regarding Japan's chances of extricating herself from the mess. This tendency to view the Japanese policy initially as folly was perhaps due to an underestimation of the power of the "new" Meiji Japan, which has harked back to the teacher-student relationship between the Western world and Japan. The opinions of the paper changed quite quickly, however, for just one week after prophesying disaster it was inclined to view the government's endorsement of the expedition as the right course of action, although it still could not predict a favorable outcome for Japan.[41]

The Far East similarly did not understand the Japanese policy. It was a mystery even for the country's closest friends. In particular, the paper wondered why the government was unwilling to give even the foreign representatives any precise information on its real intentions at the time when the expedition was already being prepared.[42] When it was reported that the expedition would be

---

37   "Notes of the Week," *The Japan Weekly Mail*, May 9, 1874.

38   Fox, *Britain and Japan*, 292-293.

39   "The Formosan Expedition," *The Japan Weekly Mail*, May 9, 1874.

40   Ibid.

41   "Notes of the Week," *The Japan Weekly Mail*, May 16, 1874.

42   *The Far East* 5:4 (1874), 234.

recalled, the paper conjectured that after reconsideration the government had at least come to regard it as folly.[43] In the same way *Japan Punch* was critical towards the venture. One cartoon depicted a solid Chinese looking at the amusing, childish preparations of the Japanese. The Japanese navy was by no means pictured as comparable with that of the Chinese, for instance, and one of the main aims seems to have been to ridicule the person of General Le Gendre.[44]

Negotiations – Little Trust for the Japanese

The Herald still believed in the strength of the Chinese even after the landing of the Japanese troops on Formosa. They were probably playing a waiting game, and when the climate and various diseases had decimated and disgusted the Japanese the Chinese would take offensive action. The paper regarded the Formosan expedition as an expensive and unsatisfactory undertaking for the Japanese government.[45] When the government dispatched an envoy to China for negotiations after sending their fleet to Formosa, the *Herald* took this as a reversal of the usual procedure and blamed the Japanese "statesmen" for seldom doing things in the ordinary way. But a quite new feature entered the paper's statements at this point, for at the end of May 1874 it began criticizing the Chinese for the first time: "Japanese policy, as well as Chinese, is so tortuous and crooked, – so involved and so illogical –, that there is no telling what the new Envoy might find it convenient to say, or what the Chinese foreign officials may deny."[46] Obviously these opinions reflected a general contempt for the eastern people on the part of the Western world, and also a certain difficulty in understanding procedures in a foreign culture. The fact that the East had to borrow arms from the West was in itself evidence of the superior genius of the Western peoples, but the paper did not really appreciate the borrowing of Western ways by the Japanese, regarding it from the Chinese point of view as too facile an abandonment of national habits, customs and procedures. China was too solid and self-possessed to be moved to take such steps. Perhaps the paper did not set any very profound value on the existence of the Japanese nation and regarded it simply as a gift from the western countries, since it was dependent on the sufferance of others. Russia alone was strong

---

43   Ibid., 235.
44   *Japan Punch* 4 (1874), 89-90.
45   *The Japan Daily Herald*, May 19, 1874.
46   *The Japan Daily Herald*, May 21, 1874.

enough to possess herself of Japan, and Japan could not expect sympathy or assistance from other nations.[47]

The paper regarded the position of the Japanese government in the Formosan affair as a weak one and expected the troops to quit without delay.[48] It nevertheless had to accept gradually that China was not being particularly active in resisting the Japanese advance into Formosa. It claimed that the Chinese did not think there would be any necessity for being in a hurry to interfere, and consequently the local authorities had refrained from taking any active measures against the intruders. The Chinese were content to look on while the Japanese expended their own wealth and the lives of their soldiers and regarded them as mosquitoes without stings. Although it was not quite sure of the policy being observed by the Chinese government, the paper believed that it was being insensitive to this violation of its territory.[49]

The opinions of the *Herald* as far as Japan was concerned did not change at all. On 18 June 1874 it advised the Japanese to return more quickly than they had gone, if possible, and suspected that after evacuating Formosa they would also have to pay a good round sum to the Chinese in compensation. It also waited for the leading actors in the affair to be hissed off the stage in Japan.[50] Opinions concerning China gradually seemed to be changing, however the paper believed that the governments of both countries had exhibited low moral standards and a disregard for their ordinary responsibilities in relation to the Formosan affair. China had never fulfilled her obligations towards Formosa, the Chinese settlers there, or towards the foreigners who had been cast upon the island by shipwreck or some other cause, losing their property, and their lives in some cases, at the hands of barbarians, as it called them. The paper regarded the actions and attitudes of the Chinese as despicable and those of the Japanese as tortuous and dishonest.[51] The paper did not rate the determination of the Japanese government very highly, and expected the Japanese to leave the island before the Chinese delivered any crushing blow.[52] It advised them to abandon this attempt to acquire additional territory,[53] but if they wanted to fight, they should engage more talented leaders than the

---

47   *The Japan Daily Herald*, May 26, 1874.
48   *The Japan Daily Herald*, May 22, 1874.
49   *The Japan Herald*, June 4, 1874.
50   "The Formosan Performance," *The Japan Daily Herald*, June 18, 1874.
51   "The Action of China and Japan in regard to Formosa," *The Japan Daily Herald*, June 26, 1874.
52   *The Japan Daily Herald*, June 2, 1874.
53   *The Japan Daily Herald*, July 4, 1874.

so-called generals in charge of their forces at that time.[54] The paper believed that the Chinese were underestimating their own strength and overestimating the prowess of their opponents. Before long Japan would be withdrawing her troops from the island, thankful to have escaped confrontation with her powerful neighbor,[55] for the Chinese had no intention of permitting them to remain to colonise any part of Formosa.[56]

The Herald believed that the Japanese would retreat very soon, as the attitude of passive waiting adopted by the Chinese had completely frustrated their desire to acquire the territory, and the troops had become sick of their task on account of their dislike for the discomforts they had to experience and the general evaporation of their martial enthusiasm.[57] In accordance with its anti-Japanese opinions, the paper distrusted the advancing civilization of Japan, and referred to people who believed in it as sanguine and ill informed.[58] Japan's position was not a promising one: "Altogether, the prospects for Japan appear to be dark. She stands to gain neither territory nor indemnity for the expenses already incurred, with the prospect of becoming embroiled with China in a war which must prove most disastrous to the interests and prosperity of Japan."[59] An issue around the middle of August also regarded the Japanese negotiating prospects as dismal, claiming that the government was seeking to make good its retreat from the affair with the best grace it could.[60] The paper gradually became also more and more disappointed with the actions taken by the Chinese, which manifested a very craven disposition, it said, in contrast to the patriotism and bravery exhibited by the Japanese.[61] The paper nevertheless regarded Japan as having insufficient resources to meet her goals and referred to her people as being poised on an airy pedestal of self-conceit.[62]

The *Herald*'s viewpoint seemed to change occasionally, but this depended on the news it received, of course. Usually it was opposed to the policies of the Japanese government, but sometimes it was inclined to look impartially on the two countries. On 12 September, for instance, it claimed that neither side wished to engage in actual hostilities, China being apprehensive of the courage of the Japanese and Japan of the resources of China. The paper suggested

54   *The Japan Daily Herald*, July 10, 1874.
55   "The Japanese Navy," *The Japan Daily Herald*, July 10, 1874.
56   *The Japan Daily Herald*, July 11, 1874.
57   *The Japan Daily Herald*, July 22, 1874.
58   *The Japan Daily Herald*, August 4, 1874.
59   *The Japan Daily Herald*, August 14, 1874.
60   *The Japan Daily Herald*, August 15, 1874.
61   *The Japan Daily Herald*, August 26, 1874.
62   *The Japan Daily Herald*, September 4, 1874.

arbitration by friendly powers, which would enable both parties to extricate themselves without further expense or any loss of national prestige or honor.[63] But some days later it was again calling the conduct of the Japanese government inconsiderable and foolish and speaking of a war with China as one of the greatest follies, which the rulers of Japan could commit.[64] From September onwards the paper seemed to be advocating peaceful foreign intervention to make China and Japan come to terms, the basic motives behind this being western commercial interests: "Even from a purely selfish point of view, foreign nations having commercial dealings with these people cannot assume the position of indifferent spectators of the fight."[65] The paper feared the prospect of revolution, and suspected that these weak governments might no longer possess the power to protect either the persons or the property of their foreign residents. At the very least, potential customers would become greatly impoverished and the money usually spent in purchasing foreign imports would be wasted on war.[66]

A rumor that the Japanese were preparing to break off diplomatic relations with China at the beginning of November led the paper to recall its own statements at the beginning of the crisis and to emphasize that China would refuse to recognize any Japanese occupation of Formosa or to pay any indemnity to the Japanese. In its opinion, China had been playing cat and mouse with Japan prior to devouring it. It regarded Japan's future as very bleak. The best thing that could possibly be done was to evacuate Formosa, which might placate the Chinese and prevent them from making reprisals.[67] Japan did not have the money with which to go to war with her wealthy neighbor, whose resources, both human and economic, were practically limitless. The paper tried to appeal to the Japanese rulers to foster peace: "All the money Japan can raise or borrow is needed for the works of internal improvement, and the education and the amelioration of the condition of her people. There is no one wishing [not] well to the country, but must regret to find that any of her rulers should be bent on war, – instead of sedulously cultivating peace, and all attendant blessings which peace alone can confer."[68]

Obviously the basic motives behind the appeal were the commercial interests of the foreign residents in Japan, as noted above, and it may be that the

---

63   *The Japan Daily Herald*, September 12, 1874.
64   *The Japan Daily Herald*, September 22, 1874.
65   *The Japan Daily Herald*, September 26, 1874.
66   Ibid.
67   "Cessation of Diplomatic Relations with China," *The Japan Daily Herald*, November 5, 1874.
68   "Japan Cannot Afford to Go to War," *The Japan Daily Herald*, November 6, 1874.

Herald was the leading organ for those interests at the time. Like the *Herald*, the *Gazette* also criticized the policy of the Japanese government. It was unable to approve of the expedition at the end of May, and did not believe that Japan could prevent Russia from taking "Yeso" [Hokkaido] whenever she wanted.[69] The opinions of the paper regarding the expedition changed very rapidly, however, and by the beginning of June its comments were encouraging. According to information received, everything connected with the expedition was progressing most satisfactorily.[70] The Gazette confessed that it had underestimated Japanese potential, and that the things did look far more favorable for Japan than it had first anticipated. But it believed that this was due to the weak course pursued by the Chinese. If any other nation had been concerned, Japan's position would have been more serious. The Gazette did not want to blame the Japanese, and would rejoice openly if they succeeded in putting a stop to a great evil.[71]

Although the paper anticipated that after the Formosan expedition a Korean conflict would be a mere question of time, it did not criticize such an expansive policy. Its main worry seemed to be the lack of discipline in the naval and military forces during the expedition, and it called for a stricter command before the outbreak of the Korean crisis came: "It will be a great thing if, when that time comes, the naval and military forces have attained to greater perfection of obedience: and we hope that the government will not again 'let loose the dogs of war' until both services approximate in some measure to the foreign models they have selected for their soldiers and sailors."[72] The Gazette's attitude became progressively more favorable towards Japanese government policy, avowing now that the Japanese were not so badly in the wrong as if it had first thought to be. In adopting a non-interference policy, without restraining the savages or establishing any authority over them, China had neglected her obligations, and had no right whatsoever to complain about the measures taken by Japan.[73] But the opinions of the paper changed quickly when it received information that Japan intended to colonize the south-eastern part of Formosa, deeming such a policy folly. It was a sure of spoiling the splendid progress she had made and of squandering the results and efforts, which had earned the admiration of all people. Japan needed all her resources for the development on her own soil, it maintained, and failed to see the logic behind

69   *The Japan Gazette*, May 29, 1874.
70   *The Japan Gazette*, June 4, 1874.
71   *The Japan Gazette*, June 8, 1874.
72   *The Japan Gazette*, June 22, 1874.
73   *The Japan Gazette*, June 25, 1874.

the Japanese plans as it regarded the climate of Japan as exceptionally good and the land promising as compared with Formosa, which was hot and generally unhealthy.[74]

The opinions of the paper against the colonization of the south-eastern part of Formosa did not mean a general hostility towards the expedition, however, and according to the Gazette, the foreign press, with the exception of the *Herald* and the *Japan Mail*, did not lean in that direction. It saw the real cause of the criticism as lying in the determined opposition of the present members of the government to the desires of the foreigners in Japan. But this did not mean that they should declare sympathy for China. On the contrary, if it became necessary for foreigners to take sides, everybody would instantly support Japan. If war were to break out Japan would see that she had the sympathy of all the foreigners on her soil. The paper also indicated its favorable view of Japan's chances in the event of war.[75]

The Gazette was glad to see that the government was making preparations to meet the Chinese with arms if negotiations failed, but was worried that if China engaged foreigners in her armies the Japanese forces would never be able to measure up to her strength,[76] even though generally speaking the paper had confidence in the chances of the Japanese. The paper also criticized the *Herald* for carrying its affected contempt a little too far by speaking frivolously of the Japanese navy.[77] The Gazette obviously served as a mouthpiece of the Western commercial interests in Japan to some extent, but its outlook was different from that of the Herald. What was good for Japan from the Japanese point of view was also good for the *Gazette*. In other words, the paper wanted to share in the destiny of the Japanese, perhaps, because of its commercial interests, just as the *Herald*, paradoxically, criticized Japan out of commercial interest.

The Tokei Journal spoke up for Japan from the very beginning. It believed that she had a perfect right to send a mission to Formosa because of the atrocities committed by the aboriginals there, that as soon as China was fully aware of the objects of the mission correspondence between the two nations would cease, in Japan's favor.[78] Its view was that in terms of relative position and power Japan had little or nothing to fear from China, and that it was in fact China that ought to fear Japan. The Chinese would learn that the adoption of

---

74   *The Japan Gazette*, June 27, 1874.
75   *The Japan Gazette*, August 3, 1874.
76   *The Japan Gazette*, August 12, 1874.
77   *The Japan Gazette*, September 14, 1874.
78   "The Formosan Mission," *The Tokei Journal*, June 27, 1874.

modern civilization by Japan meant something more than comical external features such as "long-faced" hats.[79] The paper criticized the *Mail*, which it saw as being in opposition to the Japanese government, and likened the policy of Japan to the actions of Western nations: "There is one point in connection with this which has puzzled us much. If England had a right to send an expedition to southern Formosa, to take up someone else's quarrel; if America had the right to do the same thing on her own behalf, why not Japan? She has but copied the example of England and America."[80] By comparing the actions of Japan with English and American behavior and by demanding an equal position for her alongside the major Western countries, the paper was trying to argue against Western views of the world and against the dominant position of these countries.

The Tokei Journal was disturbed by the opposition to the Japanese government shown by one of the Yokohama journals, which had called it an organ of the government, and wished to leave its readers to form their own opinion on whether the government was only a subscriber (150 copies) or whether it really was a government organ.[81] This invective appears to have been aimed at either the *Herald* or the *Mail*. In August *The Tokei Journal* found that the other papers, especially the *Mail*, were beginning to support the Formosan expedition more and more, using the same arguments. The paper then set out to emphasize that it had been the innovator in this respect: "... but we were the first, and, for long, the only supporter of the Japanese, and we used the very same arguments that find an exponent in the writer in the Mail."[82] It praised the achievements of the Japanese expedition by claiming that a region, which for years had spelled terror to all eastern navigators, would, through the action of Japan, be free of peril in the future.[83] At the end of September the paper regarded war between Japan and China almost inevitable,[84] but a week later it was predicting peace, on terms in every way "honorable" to Japan[85]. The use of the word "honorable" represented a typical attitude of the paper towards Japan, whereas when speaking of the Chinese it would frequently adopt the opposite tone: it, for example, spoke of "support given to the Chinese system of falsehood."[86] In the same vein the paper felt if war were to break out the Japanese would conduct

---

79   "China and Formosa," *The Tokei Journal*, July 4, 1874.
80   "The Japan Mail on Mission," *The Tokei Journal*, July 11, 1874.
81   "Subventions," *The Tokei Journal*, July 25, 1874.
82   "Ratting," *The Tokei Journal*, August 8, 1874.
83   "Formosa," *The Tokei Journal*, August 15, 1874.
84   "Our Position in Japan," *The Tokei Journal*, September 26, 1874.
85   "Is It Peace?" *The Tokei Journal*, October 3, 1874.
86   "The London Press on the Formosan Mission," *The Tokei Journal*, October 17, 1874.

their affairs better than the Chinese, and thus the latter would be more anxious to avoid war.[87] It may be that the *Tokei Journal* was at least in part strongly pro-Japanese from the very beginning precisely because the government was a major subscriber, even though it tried to pre-empt such a conclusion by encouraging its readers to form their own opinion on the matter. It should also be recalled, of course, that the Journal's proprietor, John R. Black, was usually inclined to view Japan in a favorable light.[88]

The Weekly Mail, on the other hand, was against Japan. It showed itself on 23 May to be strictly opposed to the plans for a Japanese colonization of Formosa, which, it noted, bore no analogy to the subjugation by England of the barbarous tribes on the frontiers of her territories. The expedition was not the fruit and outcome of a vigorous national life, and it would be much better to spend millions of dollars on roads, railways and telegraph services to improve the internal organization of the country than to waste that money on such a useless expedition. The paper admitted that it was considering this problem from the selfish point of view, but asked what foreigners could expect from the transfer of Formosa to Japanese ownership. They could not expect more freedom of trade, the benign influence of a new and higher civilization on the island, or even a reversion from savagery to peace, progress and cultivation. The point of view of the *Weekly Mail* represented a European-centred way of thinking. Japan had deliberately entered on a course of progress along European lines, but had not yet reached her goal by any stretch of imagination:

> Japan may possibly coerce a race of savages and make slaves of them; but she has not the moral or intellectual force to do more than this, and it is wicked folly in those who know it to delude her into the belief that she possesses it. As to commercial freedom, and the large liberality which, like a beneficent shadow, has followed the conquests of England in the East ... Such blessings only come in the fullness of time.[89]

The paper saw that Japan could not bring such blessings to any colony it might acquire, and to talk of this in connection with her was sheer nonsense.[90]

The Weekly Mail was persuaded that China regarded the Formosan expedition with a hostile eye and announced that it had mistrusted the adventure from the very first and hoped at best for some stroke of good luck to rescue

---

87   "The Week," *The Tokei Journal*, November 7, 1874.
88   Fält, *Clash of Interests*, 21 and 57.
89   "The Daily Press on Japan," *The Japan Weekly Mail*, May 23, 1874.
90   Ibid.

the Japanese from the entanglement into which they had been led. Although the paper had been quite strongly against the expedition, it sometimes looked more sympathetically upon the difficulties, by which the Japanese were beset,[91] and in Japan's favor, it wondered greatly at the attitude assumed by China, which was not at all compatible with the reaction to be expected from a European power.[92] The paper recognized that Japan's position was a very difficult one, and one from which she would require every ounce of good fortune and courage to extricate herself. Her action could not be defended on any moral grounds, only selfish ones. If there had been sufficient cause for punishing the aborigines, the great powers could at any time have accomplished with five hundred blue-jackets what the Japanese were attempting with a force of two thousand men.[93] It advised the Japanese to consider their mission to Formosa fulfilled once they had punished those who had murdered their shipwrecked sailors.[94]

Since China had more than half of the right on her side, it regarded the payment of indemnities or compensation to the Japanese as an absurd notion. Japan's real work lay within her own boundaries, not in Formosa. She needed to consolidate her government, reform her financial system and administrative machinery, educate her people, and develop her natural and industrial resources. There would be time to talk about armed expeditions when legitimate demands against outrages had been legitimately preferred and when there was a good balance in the treasury.[95] The paper was quite sure of its own course, and announced in July that it was sadly afraid that it had been entirely right in its view of the affair, concluding that the Japanese had no firm ground to stand on in the question.[96] At the beginning of August there were some signs of a change in attitudes concerning Japanese policy. At first the paper argued that there was a strong patriotic feeling in the Japanese and a complete absence of such in the Chinese.[97] More important omens, however, were two articles about the Formosan question, which were strongly angled in favor of Japan. One of these claimed that although the press and foreign residents in general were practically unanimous in condemning the action of the Japanese government. "... Japan is justified in sending her troops to Formosa, and keeping them there for a reasonable time ... that China, by her supineness or weakness, has

91   "Notes of the Week," *The Japan Weekly Mail*, June 6, 1874.
92   "Notes of the Week," *The Japan Weekly Mail*, June 13, 1874.
93   "The Formosan Expedition," *The Japan Weekly Mail*, June 20, 1874.
94   "Notes of the Week," *The Japan Weekly Mail*, July 4, 1874.
95   "Notes of the Week," *The Japan Weekly Mail*, July 11, 1874.
96   "Notes of the Week," *The Japan Weekly Mail*, July 18, 1874.
97   "Notes of the Week," *The Japan Weekly Mail*, August 1, 1874.

invited the invasion of territory to which she has, at best, but a doubtful claim; and that the European powers ... have no right to object to Japan's interference in Formosa to protect her own subjects, and in the general interest of humanity."[98]

The Weekly Mail could not accept all these statements, however. It argued that the indifference of China could not be pleaded to justify the unannounced, unexpected and violent action of Japan, and that the example of the European powers did not justify the Japanese action. Japan had only herself to blame.

> But when all has been said in favour of the Japanese side of the argument, they will not be acquitted by the world of having acted with an entire want of reflection in undertaking an expedition of so grave a nature against so powerful an antagonist, and a want of foresight and prudence altogether inexplicable on an occasion demanding the most solid qualities which men entrusted with the welfare of States should possess.[99]

It nevertheless seemed that the attitudes of the paper had become more pro-Japan than before. It prophesied in August that if war was declared, rebellion would break with China, while warmth and martial feeling throughout Japan would, with equal probability, weld together such discontented masses as that country might contain and contribute to the greater security of the government.[100] Just as the paper had announced three months earlier that it hoped at best for some stroke of good luck to save the Japanese,[101] so it now argued that if the Japanese had only been content to go down to Formosa, punish the savages and come away, these lessons would have ensured the safety of the coast for years to come[102]. The tone of the argument in August was no longer so strictly in opposition to Japan as it had been earlier.

The Weekly Mail accused LeGendre of taking a mere book view of the question and of having misled Japan into a radically false position, but the paper felt the amount of unquestionable right on the Japanese side to be such that they could afford to abandon it without disgrace or humiliation. Since neither side wished to go to war, a way should be found to accommodate the disagreement that had arisen.[103] One clear proof of the new course charted by the paper was its argument that there was about the same proportion of right and

---

98   "A New View of the Formosan Question," *The Japan Weekly Mail*, August 15, 1874.
99   "The Formosan Question," *The Japan Weekly Mail*, August 22, 1874.
100   "Notes of the Week," *The Japan Weekly Mail*, September 12, 1874.
101   "Notes of the Week," *The Japan Weekly Mail*, June 6, 1874.
102   "Notes of the Week," *The Japan Weekly Mail*, August 12, 1874.
103   "Why War?," *The Japan Weekly Mail*, September 26, 1874.

wrong on both sides, neither being blameless and neither entirely in the right. The honor of both should therefore be satisfied by a friendly arrangement of the matter, and the interests of both could be protected by the same means. Since it seemed that the basic motives for the attitudes of the foreigners were their own interests, the *Weekly Mail* pointed out that the interests of foreigners were also largely bound up in the maintenance of peace.[104] Since the paper did not doubt the fighting spirit of the Japanese, it saw that if war did break out it might continue for a long while, and the cost would be very great for both the Japanese and the foreign residents "Then will come a distress such as this generation in this country has no knowledge of, and our merchants will be the great sufferers by it. Every one of their customers may find his wealth disappearing day by day, fear may become panic, and panic universal ruin."[105]

Although the paper frankly admitted that the interests of the foreigners were its first consideration in hoping that war might be avoided, it was also worried about progress in Japan, about how almost everything that had been begun would be thrown back. It hoped that the ministers of foreign powers could interpose a friendly and conciliatory presence between the contending parties and prevent war. A requested and friendly intervention could not fail to have the desired effect.[106] Further proof of the new course followed by the paper comes from an article in which it speaks very sympathetically about the patriotism of the Japanese people and their readiness to die for the honor of their country.[107] Since the *Weekly Mail* spoke so much about the mercantile interests of foreigners, it is possible that those interests were also the underlying causes for the change in its opinions concerning the expedition. It was better for those living and working in Japan to find some way of understanding Japanese policy than to criticise it.

Punch was also critical at first. In June it published a cartoon in which a Japanese envoy was meeting a representative of the Chinese government. The Chinese was a tall, magnificent figure dressed in characteristic clothes, whereas the Japanese envoy was a tiny, comical man dressed in western clothes and with a silk hat. He was telling the Chinese "we mean nothing only joke".[108] The tone was slightly ironical when the journal argued that the object of the Formosan expedition was to destroy the Botans because these savages were the forefathers of the Japanese race. In the same tone, it reckoned that the

---

104   "A Possible Solution," *The Japan Weekly Mail*, September 26, 1874.
105   Ibid.
106   Ibid.
107   "Notes of the Week," *The Japan Weekly Mail*, October 3, 1874.
108   *Japan Punch* 6 (1874), 117.

expedition was the most complete ever fitted out in any country in the world. It announced that it wished the Japanese, a noble and highly gifted race, every success in all their undertakings, and regarded Japan as a guiding star in the east.[109] *Punch* also criticized the Chinese, however. It pointed to the weakness of their preparations for action, taking its metaphor in one cartoon from the Chinese farmer with his pigs.[110] Although the economic resources behind Japan in the prospective war with China were represented as poor, neither side, in the journal's view, really wanted to go to war.[111] It also seemed that the opinions of *Punch* became more pro-Japanese during the negotiation period. It may be that the general interests of the foreigners in Japan and the weakness displayed by China on the Formosan question provided the basic motives for this.

The Treaty and the Changing Image

Even after the eventual signing of a peace treaty, the *Herald* was critical towards Japan, claiming that she had reason to congratulate herself upon the narrow escape she had had from a calamitous and impoverishing war. The paper regarded the conquest of China, with its wealth and resources, as an impossible achievement for Japan because of her own poverty and internal weakness. If the Japanese had had as their only purpose the punishing of the savages they would have been praised by the civilized world, but it was the mixture of motives, which withheld sympathy from the Japanese. The paper felt that China was paying an indemnity to the Japanese because of impending difficulties with other nations. Her fault lay in her unpreparedness for war and her childish and ludicrous terror of Japanese arms. The paper regarded bowing the knee to Japan as a humiliation for China, and did not see Japan as a victor but as a considerable loser from a financial point of view. She had to thank her lucky stars that she had escaped so cheaply, for it was only due to Chinese pusillanimity that she had managed to retreat from her false and untenable position.[112] The paper argued that the settlement of the Formosan question with China had been a great relief to the official mind of Japan because of the country's poor economic position.[113] After a preliminary evaluation of the

---

109   Ibid., 125.
110   *Japan Punch* 7 (1874), 135.
111   *Japan Punch* 9 (1874), 155.
112   "End of the Japanese and Chinese Imbroglio," *The Japan Daily Herald*, November 10, 1874.
113   *The Japan Daily Herald*, November 19, 1874.

treaty, the *Herald* saw for the first time that the Japanese position was not so bad after all, and that the results were quite impressive:

> Unwittingly, no doubt, the Chinese have drifted into a position which is dishonouring, and, therefore, lowering to the nation, which enables the Japanese by contrast, to make a comparatively respectable figure before the world ... Japan has got much the best of the negotiation ... something in money, and an admission, however of little value in the eyes of civilized nations, from the Chinese that she was right in fitting out the expedition.[114]

The paper hoped that the government, after escaping from the great peril, would undertake to build up the country, because there were thousands of things that needed to be done within Japan itself, which would take up all the resources and energy the rulers had their disposal.[115] It may be due to the goof offices of the British in concluding the treaty that the paper was more pro-Japanese than before. It attacked the *Tokei Journal*, which it claimed had belittled those who actually brought about the result. One might say that due to its Europe and, or British, point of view the *Herald* wanted to emphasize the role of the British in concluding the treaty, for it treated with amusement those who assigned all the praise for conducting the negotiations with China to the Japanese alone.[116]

The *Gazette* rejoiced at the success of Japan, stating that all except those whose sympathies were utterly chilled by selfishness or prejudice must be delighted at the assurance of peace, while at the same time the honor and dignity of the Japanese government had been sustained. All the Japanese demands had been recognized and acceded to, in spite of the fact that there were foreign commentators, who had hoped for the failure of Japan and others, who doubted whether the Japanese statesmen would prove competent to meet and defeat the Chinese on their own ground of argument and discussion. The paper took Japan's success as a new proof of her position as the foremost nation in the east. The indemnity received by Japan would stand against any attempt to show that her claims had been successfully resisted or contemptuously overlooked. The paper welcomed the immediate result of the Formosan question: "... with its attendant consequences of a new accession of credit and repute to a nation which, in vindicating its own self-respect, has also commanded the

---

114   "The Chinese and Japanese Convention," *The Japan Daily Herald*, November 21, 1874.
115   Ibid.
116   *The Japan Daily Herald*, December 4, 1874.

respectful attention of the world. The congratulations of Foreign Powers will be unanimous and unfeigned."[117]

The *Gazette* criticized the comments of the *Herald* concerning the treaty, and accused it of having made up its mind that the sufferer must and should be Japan alone. It argued that by condemning a peaceful solution as being humiliation, because it had predicted the failure of the negotiations and had confidently stated that the Chinese would refuse to pay any indemnity. The paper suggested the following amendments to the words of the *Herald*: "The intelligence, though humiliating to China *and to us*, was received with general satisfaction. The conduct of China is here, *in this office*, unanimously condemned, *as proving directly the reverse of what we said it would be*."[118]

The Tokei Journal, which had been pro-Japan from the outset, argued after the signing of the treaty that Chinese promises were like the proverbial pie, made to be broken. China had never kept a treaty and never honourably fulfilled any obligation. It was fully convinced that as soon as the attention of the world had been diverted elsewhere, the Chinese would neglect their duties. *The Tokei Journal* regarded the treaty as a good one from the Japanese point of view. China had been compelled to acknowledge the soundness of the Japanese arguments and Japan could stand forth before the world as the champion of humanity. Japan had emerged triumphant from a contest, which only few who knew her powers thought she could win. The image of the island nation would consequently be quite different from that time on:

> Henceforth Japan cannot but be looked on with more respectful eyes than before. She diplomatists as ability; is not afraid of threats; and despite the reports which prejudiced Ministers may send to their respective Government, has earned for herself a reputation in the public mind – and it is public opinion which governs most enlightened nations – which hereafter will do her infinite service.[119]

In its description of the arrival of the victorious troops in Tokyo, the paper referred to their triumph as a new jewel in the crown of Potentate, during whose reign so many milestones in the history of the east had already been achieved. As if by way of a demonstration of the paper's identification with Japan, this leading article ended with the words "The Love of Country" set apart from the

117   *The Japan Gazette*, November 9, 1874.
118   *The Japan Gazette*, November 11, 1874.
119   "The China–Japan Treaty," *The Tokei Journal*, November 28, 1874.

rest of the column.[120] Later, in its review of the year's events, *The Tokei Journal* praised the victory as an achievement which had "raised Japan many hundred-fold in the eyes of the world".[121]

The *Weekly Mail* emphasized at first how important the friendly offices of the British Minister in Beijing had been for the concluding of the treaty.[122] As before, the paper argued that there was much that was right and wrong on both sides. It was astonished at the indemnity paid by the Chinese, and had to confess that the Formosan expedition had been a great success for Japan:

> It would be unjust to this country to deny that, apart from the grounds of the quarrel, which have found in us firm and consistent opponents, she comes out of it with credit, and may legitimately experience much satisfaction at the manner in which it had been terminated. She undoubtedly owes this to the firm attitude assumed and maintained by the Government, the active measures taken to defend herself in case of attack, and the posture of her nobles and military class.[123]

The Weekly Mail felt that through the indemnity the Japanese had obtained an acknowledgement from China of their right to send such an expedition to Formosa. The success of Japan seemed to be something of a problem for the paper, as it wished to restrain the Japanese by warning that they should preserve the memories of the danger through which they had come and should maintain an attitude of moderation: "Modesty in victory is the truest dignity, and Japan will show a real wisdom if she now orders her conduct by this maxim."[124]

Nevertheless, the paper had to congratulate Japan on her substantial victory, which would undoubtedly affect the country's image in the Western world. The paper felt that her spirit of patriotism would increase European esteem for the Japanese character: "... in her hour of peril and trial, the country stood firmly in support of her government, and evinced a spirit of the existence of one tithe of which in China would have plunged the two nations into war."[125] The paper's way of thinking was Euro-centric, or perhaps it would better to say British-centred. *The Weekly Mail* wished to remind its readers that Japan must

---

120   "10 Carmen Triumphale," *The Tokei Journal*, December 19, 1874.

121   "The Past Year," *The Tokei Journal*, January 2, 1875.

122   "Peace," *The Japan Weekly Mail*, November 14, 1874.

123   Ibid.

124   Ibid.

125   "The Recent Convention between China and Japan," *The Japan Weekly Mail*, November 21, 1874.

not forget in her hour of triumph that it was also an hour of escape from great peril. She could not have averted such calamity without the influence of one power, England: "England is great, if not greatest of the Asiatic Powers, and though it is little to our humour to descant on the fact in any spirit of national vanity, it is well at times to recall and even to insist on it."[126] The paper argued that the union of justice and good sense exhibited by Britain was one of the most efficient causes of the advances made by the Asiatic nations. Under her vast influence peaceful trade flourished, national enmities disappeared and wars were avoided. The English character could combine the highest and most humane purposes with the most ordinary routine of duty.[127]

The Weekly Mail nevertheless backed down a little on its opinions concerning the contribution of the Japanese themselves to the gaining of this good result, and reminded its readers that the new-born life of Japan, with its hopes, aspirations and even the errors and failings which Western people were so ready to criticize, had a Western parentage. It would therefore be unjust to deny the firmness of the government, the attitude of the nation and the skill of its envoy were also causes of the success that had been achieved. The basic source of this attitude would again seem to have been a Europe-centric way of thinking, because the paper believed it quite conceivable that the advances made by the Japanese during the past five years had given them some of that same feeling of superiority over the Chinese which Western people felt towards the Asiatic races. This superiority was a source of moral force both in negotiations and on the battlefield. Finally the paper regarded the Japanese success as being for the most part fairly earned.[128]

After receiving news about the conduct of the Japanese troops in Formosa, the *Weekly Mail* began to convey a still more favourable image of Japan, even though its European-centred approach was still very obvious: "... the persons and prosperity of the peaceable natives have been respected, outrages of every kind were rare, if indeed any occurred, while supplies drawn from the country have been paid for the punctuality and exactness. These are unusual features in Asiatic warfare."[129] In its annual review, the newspaper defended its earlier critical stance by explaining that it had been anxious about the dangers posed by the expedition for peace and affluence in Japan. It reiterated the opinion that both sides had been both right and wrong in the dispute and that the British representative in Beijing had played an important role in the

---

126   "One Lesson," *The Japan Weekly Mail*, November 21, 1874.
127   Ibid.
128   "The Return of Okubo," *The Japan Weekly Mail*, November 28, 1874.
129   "Notes of the Week," *The Japan Weekly Mail*, December 5, 1874.

negotiations. It did not deny the strong political line pursued by the Japanese government, however, nor the contribution of its people's patriotic spirit or the skills of the Japanese negotiator in ensuring a favorable outcome. The annual review ends with an admission of the paper's own limitations as an interpreter of affairs in Japan, which reflects well the moderate tone characteristically adopted by it: "... the foreign critic has his own errors and should learn from them by how dim a light he walks in his attempts to judge truly, and with the generous consideration we all demand for our shortcomings".[130]

Punch radically changed its attitude towards Japan after the signing of the treaty. In a cartoon in which "Young Japan" is receiving a prize of 500,000 Tael from a Chinese woman as the winner of a horse race, the Japanese soldiers are depicted as handsome and stately figures bearing no resemblance to the comical Japanese envoy of some months earlier.[131] There is also another cartoon, with the text: "The corrupt and venial press of Yokohama having written against the Formosan Expedition makes the amende honorable to The Japanese Government."[132] Three figures, caricatures of three papers, obviously *Punch*, the *Mail* and the *Herald*, are seen committing harakiri (*seppuku*).[133]

Conclusions

Although these two cartoons provide very clear proof of the change in the attitudes of these newspapers towards Japan, they are still better evidence of the change, which came over the country's image in the course of the Formosan Expedition. Obviously Japan's success, which supplied the first evidence of her new power, influenced her image among the Western residents. Both the country and her people had to be taken much more seriously than before. Where earlier the Japanese efforts at modernizing their society sometimes seemed curious to the western eyes, the expedition smashed this image and replaced it with one of new, modern "Young Japan". For example by the mid-1870s Japan had become a means by which the British journalism could express unrestricted opinions about Britain.[134] Just as the main consideration for the Western residents during the Formosan episode was a commercial one, so the new position, which Japan assumed in the east after the expedition meant that political

---

130   "1874," *The Japan Weekly Mail*, January 2, 1875.
131   *Japan Punch* 11 (1874), 181.
132   Ibid., 182.
133   Ibid.
134   Toshio Yokoyama, *Japan in the Victorian Mind, 1850-1880: A Study of Stereotyped Images of a Nation 1850-1880* (London: Palgrave Macmillan, 1987), 175.

interests gained greater importance. Similarly the event did much to increase the self-esteem of the Japanese themselves.[135]

The image of the Japanese army and navy was also at first quite negative. They were not comparable with that of the Chinese and the Japanese generals were not talented as leaders. The quality of the troops was not high because they had become sick of their task on account of their dislike for the discomforts they had to experience and they lacked discipline. The great powers could do with five hundred blue-jackets what the Japanese have attempted with a force of two thousand men. However also in this case in the end of the Expedition the image changed more positive. It emphasized the patriotism of the Japanese people and their readiness to die for the honor of their country. Victorious troops and their triumph were referred to as a new jewel in the crown of the Emperor. This favorable image was however a very Europe-centric way of thinking because it was believed that the advances made by the Japanese during the past five years had given them some of that same feeling of superiority over the Chinese which Western people felt towards the Asiatic races. As already mentioned the *Weekly Mail* conveyed a very positive Europe-centric image of the activities of the Japanese troops: "... the persons and prosperity of the peaceable natives have been respected, outrages of every kind were rare, if indeed any occurred, while supplies drawn from the country have been paid for the punctuality and exactness. These are unusual features in Asiatic warfare."[136]

The Formosan Expedition also served to highlight the sharp contrasts between the papers in their attitude towards Japan. *Punch*, the *Weekly Mail* and the *Herald* entertained the most anti-Japanese sentiments at that stage, the last of these have taken an extremely critical view of the expedition throughout. Very much greater understanding had been shown by the *Gazette*, and especially *The Tokei Journal*, which had supported government policy over Formosa from the beginning. The expedition marked a crisis which inevitably served to reveal the whole range of public opinion regarding attitudes towards Japan, towards her modernisation policy, towards her interests in general and of course also towards the interests of the Westerners themselves. The attitudes and images presented by the papers told especially about strong existence of a western view of the world coloured by acceptance of British hegemony, the

---

135   See John R. Black, *Young Japan: Yokohama and Yedo 1858-79*, vol. 2, Reprint, With an Introduction by Grace Fox (Tokyo: Oxford University Press, 1968 [1883]), 426.

136   "Notes of the Week," *The Japan Weekly Mail*, December 5, 1874.

associated emphasis placed on the superiority of western world and the prosperity of the local merchant class.

Works Cited

Newspapers and magazines

The Far East 1874

The Japan Daily Herald 1874

The Japan Gazette 1874

Japan Punch 1874

The Japan Weekly Mail 1874

The Tokei Journal 1874

Cited Secondary Literature

Black, John R. *Young Japan. Yokohama and Yedo 1858-79*, vol. 2, Reprint, With an Introduction by Grace Fox. Tokyo: Oxford University Press, 1968 [1883].

Fairbank, John K., Reaischauer, Edwin O., Albert M. Graig, Albert M. *East Asia: Tradition and Transformation*. Modern Asia Edition. Tokyo: Charles E. Tuttle Company, 1976.

Fox, Grace. *Britain and Japan 1858-1883*. Oxford: Oxford University Press, 1969.

Fält, Olavi K. *The Clash of Interests: The transformation of Japan in 1861-1881 in the Eyes of the Local Anglo-Saxon Press*. Rovaniemi: Societas Historica Finlandiae Septentrionalis, 1990.

Fält, Olavi K. "The Western Views on the Japanese Expedition to Formosa in 1874." *Asian Profile* 13:3 (1985), 201-219.

Fält, Olavi K. "Introduction", in *Looking at the Other: Historical study of images in theory and practis*, Acta Universitatis Ouluensis. Humaniora B 42, eds. Kari Alenius, Olavi K. Fält & Seija Jalagin, 7-12. Oulu: University of Oulu, 2002. http://herkules.oulu.fi/isbn9514266331/isbn9514266331.pdf

Hoare, J.E. *Japan's Treaty Ports and Foreign Settlements: The Uninvited Guests, 1858-1899*. Folkestone: Japan Library, 1994.

Iriye, Akira. "Japan's Drive to a Great-Power Status." In *The Cambridge History of Japan*, vol. 5, *The Nineteenth Century*, ed. Marius B. Jansen, 741-744. Cambridge: Cambridge University Press, 1989.

Lee, John. "English-Language Press in Asia". *In The Asia Newspapers' Reluctant Revolution*, ed. John A. Lent, 13-16. Iowa: Ames, 1971.

Mizuno, Norihito. "Qing China Reaction to the 1874 Japanese Expedition to the Taiwanese Aboriginal Territories." *Sino-Japanese Studies* 16 (2009), 100-125

O'Connor, Peter. *The English-Language Press Networks of East Asia, 1918-1945*. Folkestone: Global Oriental, 2010.

Sansom, G.B. *The Western World and Japan: A Study in the Interaction of European and Asiatic Cultures*. Tokyo: Charles E. Tuttle Company, 1977.

Wildes, Harry Emerso. *Social Currents in Japan: With Special Reference to the Press*. Chicago: University of Chicago Press, 1927.

Yokoyama, Toshio. *Japan in the Victorian Mind: A Study of Stereotyped Images of a Nation, 1850-1880*. London: Palgrave Macmillan, 1987.

CHAPTER 2

The Stabilization of the Image:
The Satsuma Rebellion in 1877 in the Eyes of the Local Anglo-Saxon Press

Olavi K. Fält

Introduction

The present topic, the views of the Anglo-Saxon press in Japan on the Satsuma Rebellion in 1877,[1] is closely connected with the general problem of relations between Japan and the Western world and of interaction between the Japanese and Western cultures. The group of Westerners who probably felt the impact of this interaction most intimately, especially since it impinged on their own interests, was the community actually living in Japan, the views of whom were represented best by the newspapers and magazines published by them.

The present work represents above all an attempt at studying the interpretation given by the papers: what their attitude was to the rebellion and what image they conveyed of Japan and the Japanese, and why. By studying an image one can also form a picture of the creator of that image, the observer or subject, to the extent that an image can tell us at least as much about its creator as about its object.[2]

The material to be studied here comprises the main foreign English-language newspapers and magazines published in Yokohama and Tokyo: *The Japan Daily Herald* (Yokohama), *The Japan Gazette* (Yokohama), *The Japan Weekly Mail* (Yokohama), *The Tokio Times* (Tokyo), *The Far East* (Yokohama) and the satirical magazine *Japan Punch* (Yokohama).[3]

---

1 Based principally on Olavi K. Fält, *The Clash of Interests: The Transformation of Japan in 1861-1881 in the Eyes of the Local Anglo-Saxon Press* (Rovaniemi: Societas Historica Finlandiae Septentrionalis 1990), 223-248.

2 Olavi K. Fält, "Introduction," in *Looking at the Other: Historical Study of Images in Theory and Practise*, eds. Kari Alenius, Olavi K. Fält, and Seija Jalagin, Acta Universitatis Ouluensis. Humaniora B 42 (Oulu: University of Oulu 2002), 7-12. http://herkules.oulu.fi/isbn9514266331/isbn9514266331.pdf (Last access, March 6, 2017).

3 On the Western press in Japan see Fält, *The Clash of Interests*, 13-23; and the article on the Formosan Expedition in the present volume.

© VERLAG FERDINAND SCHÖNINGH, 2020 | DOI:10.30965/9783657702930_003

The Rebellion

The Meiji government found itself in the most serious crisis of its existence in 1877, threatened by an uprising led by Saigō Takamori (1828-1877). Saigō had been one of the original leaders of the Meiji Restoration, but had resigned from the government in 1873 on account of its failure to undertake the war on Korea, which he had advocated and had begun to set up private military schools in his own province of Satsuma for frustrated samurai. It is said that he had as many as 20 000 men in training by 1877. Minor revolts by samurai had been occurring in different parts of the country from 1873 onwards, but these were easily quashed. The situation began to look more dangerous for the government in 1876, however, when its actions began to meet with more resistance from the samurai. In March they were deprived of their right to carry swords, the last outward symbol of their status, and in August their allowances were paid off in a single lump sum either in cash or in bonds, which meant a considerable loss of income.[4]

This latter step aroused much ill feeling, and disturbances broke out in many parts of the country, although admittedly not in Satsuma at this stage. The government felt the situation in Satsuma to be highly critical, however, and decided in January 1877 to have the weapons and ammunition depot in the provincial capital Kagoshima moved elsewhere. Saigō's supporters were one move ahead, however, and took possession of the depot, claiming at the same time to have uncovered an attempt on his life being planned in government circles. This virtually forced Saigō to assume command of his supporters and to demand retribution by marching on the capital, a decision, which led to him being officially declared a renegade against the government on 20 February 1877.[5]

Unexpectedly solid resistance by the local government troops restricted the rebellion to the southern part of Kyushu, but even so the government needed all the forces it could muster, about 60 000 men, and a period of over six months to put the revolt down. The incident came to an end in 24 September 1877 with the overthrow of the rebels and Saigō's death, asssumed that he was taking his own life on the field of battle. It was only after that that the government was

---

4   William G. Beasley, *The Modern History of Japan*, 3rd revised edition (Tokyo: Charles E. Tuttle Company, 1982), 117-119; James H. Buck, "The Satsuma Rebellion: From Kagoshima Through the Siege of Kumamoto Castle," *Monumenta Nipponica* 28, no. 4 (1973): 427-446; John K. Fairbank, Edwin O. Reischauer and Albert M. Craig, *East Asia: Tradition and Transformation* (Tokyo: Charles E. Tuttle Company, 1976), 512; Stephen Vlastos, "Opposition Movements in Early Meiji, 1868-1885," in *The Cambridge History of Japan*, vol. 5: *The Nineteenth Century*, ed. Marius B. Jansen (Cambridge: Cambridge University Press, 1989), 393-402.

5   Ibid.

entirely free to carry forward its programme of reform without the fear that it would be undermined by internal opposition.[6]

Early Stages – an Unstable Image

When Saigō returned to the province of Satsuma in 1873 it was like a state within the state, as all central government decisions concerning the region required his approval in practice before they became law.[7] The *Weekly Mail* looked on the hegemony of this clan in autumn 1875 as a real barrier in the way of national unity,[8] and claimed that the vast majority of the people were opposed to the samurai class and the power enjoyed by the Satsuma clan[9]. The paper warmly welcomed the government's move in spring 1876 to ban the carrying of swords, and regarded it as a major step forward in the country's development, although this view undoubtedly reflected to some extent the fears entertained by the foreigners, who had suffered brutal attacks from time to time.[10] It was inclined to link the decision with the success of the Korean negotiations, perceiving that the government had been inspired by the episode to take this step, which had done more to strengthen the social and intellectual revolution than any other single government decision.[11]

The *Weekly Mail* was very much more critical in autumn 1876, however, pointing out that the unrest that had followed the government's decision to 'capitalize' the incomes and pensions of the samurai class was an indication how much the Japanese still had to learn before they could safely tread the path which had led Europe to the peak of civilization. The disturbances caused the paper to look suspiciously,[12] and even critically, on the decision itself, regarding it as unjust in a sense and questioning its wisdom, as reflected in a fresh insistence on the importance of an aristocracy and of pressing forward slowly but surely:

> What aristocracy in the world was ever called on to stand, or even stood, such a shower of blows? Why be in such a hurry to transform the whole country? Why over-govern so much? Is there not, first drawn, then

---

6   Ibid.
7   Beasley, *Modern History*, 118.
8   "The Cabinet," *The Japan Weekly Mail*, October 30, 1875.
9   "The Conscription," *The Japan Weekly Mail*, November 13, 1875.
10   "Notes of the Week," *The Japan Weekly Mail*, April 1, 1876.
11   "The Sword Proclamation," *The Japan Weekly Mail*, April 8, 1876.
12   "The Insurrection," *The Japan Weekly Mail*, November 4, 1876.

twilight, then perfect day? It is light in the valleys because the sun has risen on the mountain tops?[13]

A little later the paper was nevertheless very much more understanding in its appraisal of the government, regarding the criticism put forward by foreigners as mechanical and unjustified. It looked on the last attempt at rebellion as merely part of final agony of a dying feudalism. As these death throes of an outdated system gradually became weaker, the government was correspondingly gaining in strength.[14]

Contrary to the *Weekly Mail*'s expectations, these death throes did not weaken, but rather the last of them, in 1877 proved so threatening that it was difficult for the Western press to find an appropriate approach from which to evaluate it. The *Herald* hoped at the outset that the government would succeed in putting the rebellion down as soon as possible, alluding humane factors, the preservation of general law and order and also the cessation in trade brought about by the state of alert which directly impinged on the Westerners' interests.[15]

On the other hand, it did not show much respect for the government, which had ruled with an iron hand, so that no one would care if it had to resign. It even regarded it as being within the bounds of possibility that the government might not prove capable of defending either the foreign population or itself, as had been the fate of its predecessor [the Tokugawa government].[16] The alternative, a victory for Saigō, did not inspire the paper with much confidence in the future, however, for he had not announced himself to be in support of the notion of a free press or of progressive institutions of other kinds. It believed that samurai hegemony would be predominantly a mishap for the country rather than the time of good fortune that some looked forward to. It pointed to the merits of the government as lying in the many reforms that it had brought about, which although they had aroused opposition among those of the Japanese who held on grimly to their traditions, had earned much praise from the civilized world.[17]

Saigō's position was strengthened somewhat by the fact that the claims of a conspiracy against him had probably aroused much sympathy for him amongst foreigners, as the *Herald* suggested when it expressed the hope that the government would exonerate itself as soon as possible.[18]

---

13   "The Insurrection," *The Japan Weekly Mail*, November 11,1876.
14   "The Late Insurrection," *The Japan Weekly Mail*, November 25, 1876.
15   *The Japan Daily Herald*, March 3,1877.
16   *The Japan Daily Herald*, March 9,1874.
17   "Saigō's Motives," *The Japan Daily Herald*, March 15, 1877.
18   Ibid.

The *Gazette* looked on the rebellion from a fairly neutral viewpoint at first, emphasizing that the foreign press had not shown any particular sympathy with either side,[19] although the paper had itself been rather dubious about the actions of the government troops just previously, accusing them of inefficiency and a propensity for wanton destruction.[20] In its own words, the paper could not believe without better evidence that a government minister was behind a plot against Saigō.[21] It was not long, however, before the same paper was regarding government policies as the cause of the revolt, asking first of all whether it was a consequence of too long a term in office. No outsider would be surprised at such a situation: "To the foreign mind the present aspect of affairs causes neither wonder nor surprise; how the voice of people has been stifled for so long is almost in comprehensible to men who would rather part with their lives than their liberty of speech, action and self-government ..."[22]

The *Gazette* told of the sympathy, which many Europeans felt for Saigō, and how his name was linked with the notion of progress. A system of government that forced such a man into the role of a rebel must have many faults in it. The paper thus pointed to the necessity for reforming the system and creating a legislative body represented all the classes in society, and interpreted Saigō's aim as being to create a system in which the aristocracy would play its own part alongside the other classes and communities within society.[23]

In other words, the *Gazette* looked on Saigō as a supporter of the progressive government with preservation of the aristocracy so much favored by the British newspapers, and in this way projected its own hopes and aspirations onto him, even though he did not in fact represent such views in spite of being highly regarded for his sincerity of purpose. His slogan "Reverence for Heaven and Love for Mankind" was indeed easily to link with whatever desires and expectations one liked, but in practice he was concerned most of all with the failing status of the lower samurai class as a consequence of the government's reform policies.[24]

The only way out of the predicament, which the *Gazette* could see at the end of March was to form a new government in order to ensure the country's

19 "Projected Asssassination of Saigo," *The Japan Gazette*, March 20, 1877.

20 "The Southern Difficulty," *The Japan Gazette*, March 3, 1877.

21 "Projected Asssassination of Saigo," *The Japan Gazette*, March 20, 1877.

22 "The Political Aspect of the Southern Difficulty," *The Japan Gazette*, March 21, 1877.

23 "A Compromise Desirable," *The Japan Gazette*, March 24, 1877. See also "Satsuma Insurrection," *The Japan Gazette*, April 9, 1877.

24 "Saigō Takamori," in *Biographical Dictionary of Japanese History*, ed. Seiichi Iwao, translator Burton Watson (Tokyo: International Society for Educational Information, 1982), 449-452.

future affluence and happiness. If the existing administration were to continue, it would only face new difficulties in the future. The future seemed quite
hopeless for the ministers who held power at that time, since it believed that
they would inevitably lose their positions if Saigō were to achieve his ends, and
if he failed they would have to flee the country for fear of assassination.[25]

At one point in April fortunes seemed to be turning in favor of the government forces, and the paper was ready to claim that the struggle would not have
been in vain if it meant that the people gained more progressive institutions
and a constitutional government, but if they were denied these things, the consequence would be a new rebellion before long.[26]

In spite of its critical attitude towards the government, the *Gazette* was
not ready in May to admit that the Yokohama press was pursuing an anti-
government course. It thought it natural that one should criticize the
government. Since the country had been so wonderfully successful in its modernization programme, it should also be capable of withstanding the stresses
of international interaction, which included criticism in the press, upon which
the civilized nations for practical purposes set no limits. The paper took the
opportunity to emphasize the importance of the foreign press by noting that
it was through it that Japan was best known to the world outside, and hoped
that the government would institute the same freedom of opinion for the
democratic press, since its limitations could only lead to further revolts.[27] This
implied in effect that the paper believed there was a direct causal connection
between censorship of the press and the Satsuma Rebellion.

In its own assessment of the revolt, the *Far East* dismissed the claim that
when the foreigners first came to Japan it had been a paradise in which life was
all sunshine, and that it was a pity that the Japanese had not been allowed to
remain in that state of innocence. The paper believed that the Japanese were
in fact no happier than any other people evidently wishing to avoid any accusation that the continual unrest in the country was a consequence of having
dealings with foreigners. The probable reason behind the revolt was dissatis-
faction among the samurai.[28]

To some extent the paper took a very understanding view of the rebellion,
and especially of Saigō as its leader. It believed that the best outcome would
be a compromise, which would lead to a cessation of bloodshed, save the life
and honor of a soldier, who had long been a national idol and guarantee for

---

25   "A Compromise Desirable," *The Japan Gazette*, March 24, 1877.
26   "The Effects of the Relief of Kumamoto," *The Japan Gazette*, April 19, 1877.
27   "The Japanese Position," *The Japan Gazette*, May 21, 1877.
28   "The Present Insurrection in Japan," *The Far East*, April 1877, 71-80.

the founding of a Deliberative Assembly. In the opinion of the *Far East* it was regrettable that some of those behind the revolt were people who wished to hold up the country's process of development and return it to its former condition. In spite of this the paper was not disturbed even at the prospects of eventual victory for the rebels, as it counted Saigō among the most sincere of all "progressists." He would obviously do justice to the samurai class, but he would not return the country to the state it had occupied in the past. It looked on him as an advocate of a Representative Assembly, for whom one of the reasons for departure from the government had been disagreement over precisely this issue.[29] In reality his resignation had arisen as a result of the dispute over Korea, as mentioned above.[30]

Punch tended to make light of the rebellion at first, with its caption "Schoolboys want to play at being government of Japan,"[31] as evident reference to the pupils at Saigō's military schools. The cartoon shows a teacher creeping up with a whip in his hand behind a schoolboy who is just about to cut off a chrysanthemum, the emblem of the Emperor, with his sword.[32] The government troops were depicted as a bunch of conscripts geared up in full armor and looking anything but convincing.[33] The paper ridiculed the fears of the Westerners by picturing them as children taking refuge in the laps of Japanese women from a "bogey" with a sword in its hand being directed by someone out of the picture.[34]

The magazine poked fun at the government troops and their lack of success by giving the rebels superhuman physical qualities and arming them with local products: "sweet potatoes for their artillery and gun cotton for power." Even so they were immensely superior to the government troops: "one insurgent armed with beans is equal to five Imperial soldiers armed with bullets."[35] The whole incident was referred to as the "sweet potato rebellion,"[36] as the province of Satsuma was renowned for its sweet potatoes. This led the paper to picture the imperial forces gathering round to taste them, but finding them too hot to manage.[37]

---

29   "The Present Insurrection in Japan," *The Far East*, May 1877, 93-96.
30   W.G. Beasley, *The Meiji Restoration* (Stanford, CA: Stanford University Press, 1981), 372-378.
31   *Japan Punch* 2 (1877), 16.
32   Ibid., 24.
33   Ibid., 19.
34   *Japan Punch* 3 (1877), 30.
35   Ibid., 3.
36   *Japan Punch* 4 (1877), 48.
37   *Japan Punch* 3 (1877), 38.

On the eve of the Satsuma Rebellion, in January 1877, the *Weekly Mail*, which had already criticized the government decision to capitalise the pensions and incomes of the samurai class at the end of 1876, once more stressed the great importance of conservative values and the aristocracy to society. It believed that a conservatism that permitted full discussion but was slow to make any movement was the safest form of government for the ruler and the best for his subjects. The paper pointed to the interference by the government with the incomes of the samurai class, which had brought it to power as a cautionary example to the westerners not to allow the Japanese legal jurisdiction over their affairs.[38]

Where the paper had earlier looked critically on the samurai and praised the government for such actions as the prohibition on carrying swords, it was inclined at the beginning of 1877 to view them as a valuable pillar of the social order and Japanese feudalism in general as in many ways a perfectly acceptable system:

> Ill advised, shortsighted, the councellors of the young Emperor failed to rise to the occasion. They might have surrounded him with an aristocracy, supported him with an army, strong in tradition, numbers, discipline, and long prescriptive title to the natural leadership of the nation. The feudal system, here, was no anachronism, and the influence of foreign commerce and foreign ideas should have been left to work its silent way towards its ultimate and inevitable victory.[39]

The newspaper's drift in a more conservative direction was evidently attributable to its change of proprietorship[40] and the shock aroused by government intervention in the financial affairs of the samurai. Infringement of the financial interests of any sector of the population whatsoever was obviously against the principles of a newspaper that lent its full support to the commercial interests of the merchant class. As if sensing the outbreak of a major revolt, the *Weekly Mail* suggested that appeasement of the injured samurai class was the only means of assuaging the endless stream of successful uprisings, and promised its support for such a policy.[41]

---

38   "Introductory," *The Japan Weekly Mail*, January 27, 1877.

39   Ibid.

40   W.G. Howell handed over control of the newspaper in January in 1877 to George Pearson, who is regarded as having been critical of the Japanese government. Fält, *Clash of Interests*, 19.

41   "Introductory," *The Japan Weekly Mail*, January 27, 1877.

When the first rumours of unrest in Satsuma came through in February, the paper judged that the government was about to be faced with its most serious problem ever and would bitterly regret its actions in alienating Saigō and his followers.[42] Once the fighting broke out, the paper was eager to emphasize the fact that Satsuma had never effectively been under the control of the Japanese government. It was now a question of who ruled the country, the government of the day or Satsuma. In terms of firepower there was no questioning the superiority of the government troops, but it suspected that if Saigō were to lead the rebels the final outcome would be very much in the balance, as his presence would add considerable weight to their efforts.[43]

The respect felt for Saigō is to be seen in the columns of the *Weekly Mail* in a number of ways. The paper recognized him as a man, who had raised the present government to power when leading the struggle against the power of the shogun. It also referred to the Satsuma rebels as the bravest men in the country, thus bearing witness to the magnitude of the task that faced the government. To the government, Saigō was a traitor, but for everyone else he was a hero: "As he was once the man not trusted, so now is he become the man most feared by those few who constitute a personal Government, but by the mass of people he still remains the man best beloved."[44]

The paper looked with horror on the accusation that the government was involved in a conspiracy to murder him, and trusted that it would prove its innocence as soon as possible.[45] Suspicions of that kind dispelled all hopes on the part of the Europeans of being able to relinquish their exterritorial rights in Japan in the near future. Referring to government discussions of this point, it used the term "Asian" of the country's legislation and constitution,[46] a clear indication of its anger over the matter, and its readiness to emphasize the superiority of Westerners over "Asians" at the slightest provocation.

The Weekly Mail did not believe that the government was capable of overthrowing Saigō, and was convinced that the outcome would be a compromise due to which some members of the government would have to resign and the changes that Saigō was calling for would be implemented.[47] The paper saw him having risen up against tyranny and centralization to call for a change of government. An inescapable change of policy lay ahead, and a government

---

42 "The Defection of Satsuma," *The Japan Weekly Mail*, February 17, 1877.
43 "The Present Crisis," *The Japan Weekly Mail*, February 24, 1877.
44 "Notes of the Week," *The Japan Weekly Mail*, March 3, 1877.
45 "Notes of the Week," *The Japan Weekly Mail*, March 24, 1877.
46 "Notes of the Week," *The Japan Weekly Mail*, March 31, 1877.
47 Ibid.

was needed that would heed the voice of the people.[48] The rebellion was an indication that the government had alienated itself from the people, and that administrative reform was called for.[49] In this sense the paper was virtually in support of the rebellion in spite of the bloodshed it had entailed: "… but the goal will assuredly be reached, and from out of all the suffering the nation will emerge, weakened it may be, for a time, but purified from many an abuse, and more fitted for accepting the sweeping changes that have been forced upon it by the events of the past few years."[50]

As a well-known spokesman on behalf of government policy, the *Tokio Times*, begun by the American Edward H. House in January 1877,[51] believed implicitly even before the outbreak of the revolt in the government's determination to achieve a permanent settlement to the crisis in Satsuma.[52] Once it transpired that the leader of the rebellion was Saigō, the paper was anxious to point out that it meant a loss of reputation for him and an end to the esteem he had enjoyed among the people. He was to be held responsible for the uprising.[53]

The paper criticized the Yokohama press for favoring the rebels and publishing blatantly unfounded reports of the fighting which heaped praise on them. For its own part, it believed that the imperial troops, although advancing slowly, would eventually surround the rebels, and did not doubt for a moment that they would be overthrown. The protracted nature of the campaign was due solely to the fact that it had come as something of a surprise and that Saigō had been looked on as a trustworthy person.[54] At the same time it justified the silence, which the government had maintained on the subject and did not believe that any events had occurred in the rebels' favor.[55]

The paper did not join the others in praising Saigō, but treated him only as a traitor with purely selfish motives. The virtues ascribed to him in public were no more than suppositions; he had proved in practice to be quite different, and had done his country nothing but harm:

> What has he done? Only – while shattering irretrievably his own renown – reopened the wounds that eight years of restored peace had begun to heal, set back the clock of the nation's progress, scattered her scanty treasure, strewn her soil with the dead bodies of his countrymen,

48   "Popular Government," *The Japan Weekly Mail*, April 28, 1877.

49   "The Pace that Kills," *The Japan Weekly Mail*, May 5, 1877.

50   "Is it Peace?" *The Japan Weekly Mail*, May 19, 1877.

51   Fält, *Clash of Interests*, 21-22.

52   "The Government and Satsuma," *The Tokio Times*, February 24, 1877.

53   "The Fall of Saigo," *The Tokio Times*, March 3, 1877.

54   *The Tokio Times*, March 17, April 7, April 14, May 26, 1877.

55   "The Insurrection," *The Tokio Times*, May 5, 1877.

and kindled a strife the baneful consequences of which will unhappily outlast this century.[56]

The *Tokio Times* thanked the European and American newspapers for the way in which they had reported the rebellion, regarding their approach as moderate and just. Earlier attitudes towards events in the East had been more frivolous, even among those responsible for shaping people's opinions and feelings, but a change had taken place over the last three or four years as a result of which more respect an goodwill was being shown towards Japan. This would imply that the change took place around the time of the Formosan expedition, thus supporting the conclusion that this event had a considerable influence on foreigners' impressions of Japan and the Japanese, persuading them to take the events more seriously. The paper mentioned as examples various English, French and American newspapers, noting in an "aside" how a systematic rejection of the entirely misleading conclusions published by the Yokohama press and an insistence on more reliable sources was detectable in the United States.[57]

Overthrow – Back to the Stabilized Image

As the rebellion dragged on, the *Herald* joined the camp of the opposition to the government, as may be seen in its claim in June that the reasons for the discontent lay in the lack of progressive institutions and the "gagging" of the press. These things could in turn be attributed to the scheming of unworthy advisors who kept the people in political slavery in order to further their own ends.[58]

When the government finally succeeded in putting down the rebellion in September, the paper moderated its criticism somewhat, although it still emphasized the importance of a progressive form of government, which it believed the general climate of the times favored. The paper expressed the hope that the government would capitalize on its victory by loosening the shackles which had bound the people, so that the rebellion could be said to have done some good and the blood spilled in overthrowing it would not have been shed in vain. It also believed that Saigō himself would remain respected in the minds of ordinary people for a long time to come in spite of his reputation as a rebel.[59]

---

56   "His Motives and His Deeds," *The Tokio Times*, May 12, 1877.
57   "Foreign Views of the Insurrection," *The Tokio Times*, June 2, 1877.
58   "The Rebellion," *The Japan Daily Herald*, June 4, 1877.
59   *The Japan Daily Herald*, September 25, 1877.

Following the overthrow of the revolt the paper again revealed its doctrine of the superiority of the Western culture over all others when it expressed surprise at the tolerance shown by the government towards the rebels, almost all of whom were pardoned, only 20 being sentenced to execution. The *Herald* remarked how unusual it was for an Asian government to adopt such a mild attitude. It was the best possible tribute to the rapid advance of civilization in Japan by comparison with China. The behavior of the Japanese deserved full praise, and the energy and endurance shown by the government in the course of the rebellion and its charitable attitude afterwards improved its image greatly in the eyes of the world in spite of the derision recently poured on it by that paper.[60]

The *Gazette* similarly felt the predicament of Japan in June to be indeed a dismal one. The country would face destruction if some radical change could not be brought about in government policy.[61] In the paper's view, the country's problems had become more difficult than ever when the news spread that torture had been reintroduced as part of the process of justice. The chances of the existing government ever gaining jurisdiction over citizens of the signatory countries to the exterritorial agreement residing in Japan were retreating fast.[62]

Where the *Tokio Times* had praised the European newspapers for their reporting on the rebellion, the *Gazette* regarded their reports as entirely erroneous. If the rebels had been victorious this would certainly not have meant a return to feudalism as the Europeans believed. On the contrary, Saigō was fighting on behalf of progressive institutions, and victory would most probably be followed by the full opening up of Japan to foreigners. The paper believed that progress would be better assured under the more conservative element of the aristocracy than under the government, which it regarded as irresponsible.[63]

In mid-September, just before the overthrow of the rebellion, it was of the opinion that the existing system had many defects and called for administrative reform and progressive institutions, for these steps alone could end the present general discontent with the government.[64] Once the government had emerged victorious the *Gazette* expressed its congratulations, but like the *Herald*, called for popular freedom so that the brave men who had suffered defeat would not have fought and shed their blood in vain. Only after that would the country be able to enjoy lasting peace and its rulers could cast aside their

60   *The Japan Daily Herald*, November 10, 1877.
61   "The Embarrassment," *The Japan Gazette*, June 13, 1877.
62   *The Japan Gazette*, August 1, 1877.
63   *The Japan Gazette*, August 3, 1877.
64   *The Japan Gazette*, September 15, 1877.

fears.[65] Even after the rebellion was over the paper was not able to abandon its critical attitude, but rejected accusations by the *New York Times* that the English newspapers in Yokohama were continually slandering the Japanese government, spreading falsehood about it and claiming that the country was on the verge of destruction. It replied that the papers were not hostile to the government, nor had they set out to encourage the rebels, but that they had in all honesty "fancied" that they could see faults in the way the country was run. The *Gazette* was ready to defend the general integrity of the approach adopted by the Yokohama press independent of the side, which it chose to support.[66]

The *Weekly Mail* regarded the rebels as being in an extremely strong position in June, and could not envisage the incident ended in anything other than a compromise solution or victory for Saigō.[67] It hoped for a quick end to the unrest, as it feared that the country was close to bankruptcy, and believed that only men of the calibre of Saigō were capable of releasing the people from despotism.[68] The paper's highly critical outlook emerges in the fact that it used the word "troops" of the government forces but felt itself unable to call them "men,"[69] in its reavowal in the midst of the rebellion of the extremely ill-conceived nature of the government's policy towards the samurai,[70] and in its call for the creation of a new system of government.[71]

With accusations of anti-government bias of the Yokohama press becoming increasingly common, the *Weekly Mail* ended up on 11 August by defining its policy quite openly, and in doing so restricted slightly on its earlier critical remarks. In the first place, it was quite obvious that a rebellion as such was an awful thing in the Englishman's mind, and that his sympathies would inevitably be with any government whose only aim the good of the nation. Evidently it believed that the Japanese government did not entirely meet up to this definition, although the paper did not deny outright that it had ever written about the government or its members in a hostile vein or supported the rebellion. Its only desire had been that the country should be successful in its strivings towards development and that it should become worthy of admiration which

---

65 "The Close of the Insurrection," *The Japan Gazette*, September 25, 1877.

66 *The Japan Gazette*, October 29, 1877.

67 "Notes of the Week," *The Japan Weekly Mail*, June 9, 1877.

68 "Notes of the Week," *The Japan Weekly Mail*, June 16, 1877.

69 "Notes of the Week," *The Japan Weekly Mail*, July 21, 1877.

70 "Notes of the Week," *The Japan Weekly Mail*, June 23, 1877.

71 "The Memorial of the Risshisha: First Notice", *The Japan Weekly Mail*, July 14, 1877; "The Memorial of the Risshisha. Second Notice," *The Japan Weekly Mail*, July 21, 1877.

had been accorded it elsewhere on account of its efforts in that direction, perhaps too readily in the paper's opinion.[72]

The *Weekly Mail* thus looked upon its criticism as no more than well-meaning advice offered to the government, looked down on the "false teachers ... who would have her believe that she is cheated and misled by everybody but themselves"[73] and did not view entirely with approval the praise heaped on Japan, which it regarded as excessive. The paper also admitted that when criticizing Japan it had failed to take account of the difficulties caused by the rapid changes its society was undergoing, as experienced by other nations in their time. The paper did not retract from its basic attitude, however, even though it found these things unpleasant to say. It still believed that the current conflict was in many ways a product of arbitrary government, but as if to clarify its own position it also noted that it did not regard rebellion as an appropriate means for achieving reform, nor did it believe that independence for Kyushu or hegemony for the Satsuma clan would bring the nation happiness and riches. Like the *Gazette* and the Herald, the *Weekly Mail* hoped that the blood spilled would not go unheeded, but that the future rulers of the country would benefit from these experiences.[74]

Although the paper denied hostility towards the government, it could not disguise the sympathy it felt for the rebels, and particularly their leader Saigō. It noted that not even his bitterest enemy could deny his heroic virtues, and no one could complain about his part in the uprising, since there were no constitutional means of altering national policies. On the other hand, the paper suspected that his policies had partly arisen out of personal motives, since the publicly affirmed reasons for it, Korea, Sakhalin and the restriction of the incomes of the samurai, did not constitute a sufficient cause. There could well be nobler reasons than these, which had not been mentioned openly. The paper, however, did not regard Saigō as a traitor, but a person who had chosen to launch an attack not on the Emperor but on a government which he believed was bad, in which case he was doing no more than following a tradition that had held good in the country in earlier times.[75]

Saigō's greatest mistakes, the paper claimed, had been to underestimate the government, to expect too much of the samurai in other areas and to have initiated the rebellion on inconsequential, largely personal grounds. Respecting Saigō at heart, the paper expressed the hope that he would not be treated too

---

72   "Notes of the Week," *The Japan Weekly Mail*, August 11, 1877.
73   Ibid.
74   Ibid.
75   "Saigo," *The Japan Weekly Mail*, August 25, 1877.

severely, referring to the possibility that he could become a very awkward martyr figure in the eyes of the people. There was much about him that the paper appreciated: "he still remains a gallant Japanese gentleman, a grand type of the old school that with all its failings has many claims to our admiration, and we felt sure that the Government would earn the gratitude of their people and the applause of the world, by extending to the unfortunate man a clemency ..."[76] The overthrow of the rebellion inevitably affected the paper's attitude towards the government, as if finally confirming its position. It congratulated the government and said that it did not believe such a rebellion would ever repeat itself. The power of the samurai had been crushed forever. Given this new situation, the paper was more convinced that the rebellion had not been justified. The aims of its perpetrators had been more local and personal than national or universal. It urged the government to apply itself in earnest to internal reforms, mentioning as the most important of these development of the national resources, lightening of the taxation burden, improvement of communications and education of the people, especially bearing in mind that the oligarchic system of government was bound to be replaced by a progressive one sooner or later.[77]

Clear evidence of the way the suppressing of this revolt strengthened the government's position and that of Japan in general in foreign eyes was provided by the paper's statement on the occasion of the Emperor's birthday on 3 November 1877:

> The present occasion of the birthday of the Mikado is the first time we believe that the anniversary has been acknowledged by the resident foreigners in any open manner ... and doubtless from the present time the 3rd of November will be kept by foreigners as by natives, as a general holiday.[78]

Similarly, the newspaper commented the overthrow of the rebels at the end of the year: "The dangers incident to the infancy of a new nation have been well won through, and the successful quelling of the Satsuma Rebellion has removed the last peril that beset the reconstructive effort of the Government."[79] The government victory was now turned into a victory for Western civilization, as the paper took the moderation shown towards the defeated rebels as

---

76 Ibid.
77 "The Political Situation," *The Japan Weekly Mail*, September 29, 1877.
78 "Notes of the Week," *The Japan Weekly Mail*, November 3, 1877.
79 "The New Year," *The Japan Weekly Mail*, December 29, 1877.

marking not merely a strengthening of its power, but also a form of wise government in the best western mould. In contrast to its judgements while the rebellion was still in progress, the whole history of the event now represented one of the brightest pages in the government's career and marked one strong claim on Japan's part to be able to enjoy full sovereign rights, as had already been granted to even the smallest and most stormy of the South American republics.[80]

Admittedly the *Weekly Mail* still entertained one hope in accordance with its earlier policy, namely that the government should not spoil the respect which it had gained from the whole world by unwisely embarking on restrictive policies but should base its actions on information gained from the foreign advisors and on its own estimations of the country's needs and interests.[81]

In its review of the year 1877, the *Weekly Mail* continued to praise the firmness and dignity shown by the government during the rebellion, which had gained the admiration of everybody.[82] The rebellion itself it now ascribed to a political plot hatched by a dissatisfied opposition within the oligarchy.[83] It continued to show respect for Saigō in a sense by referring to him as "the last of the samurai," but did not complain of his fate, which, in contrast to its opinion in June, admittedly under different management,[84] it regarded as having been entirely predictable. The rebellion had never had any chance of succeeding, but the humane treatment of the rebels by the government was unique in the history of civil wars and a tribute to the noble spirit of modern civilization which had entered the country in contrast to its earlier barbarism.[85]

Unlike the *Weekly Mail*, the *Tokio Times* never once flinched from the attitude it had expressed at the very beginning of the revolt, that of full support for the government. Thus when many newspapers were speaking of a compromise as one condition for ending the rebellion, the *Tokio Times* was never doubt regarding the eventual defeat of the insurgents. It criticized the Mail and Herald vociferously for supporting them and attacking the government, and suspected that a less tolerant government would not have put up with such writing for very long.[86] It could envisage no alternative to a government victory other than anarchy.[87]

---

80   Ibid.

81   Ibid.

82   "1877," *The Japan Weekly Mail*, January 26, 1878.

83   "1877," *The Japan Weekly Mail*, February 2, 1878.

84   George Pearson relinquished the paper in January 1878 to F.V. Dickins. Fält, *Clash of Interests*, 19.

85   "1877," *The Japan Weekly Mail*, February 9, 1878.

86   *The Tokio Times*, June 23, 1877.

87   "The Insurrection," *The Tokio Times*, June 23, 1877.

The paper foresaw the final outcome of the rebellion as being one that would at last remove all barriers to the country's development and safeguard the Empire's future wealth and happiness. All the country's true friends should congratulate the government on this, "while the avowed enemies of the government and clamorous supporters of the rebellion, of which the *Japan Mail* stands as the conspicuous type, will be compelled to bear their disappointments and mortification with such composure as they may command."[88] Unlike the other newspapers, the *Tokio Times* did not praise Saigō but treated him as a common insurgent who had not shown any "great military skill" at any time in his life and who did not deserve having his name used as a symbol of loyalty and devotion.[89]

Perhaps the most shameful thing about the attacks on the government by the Yokohama press in the eyes of the Tokio Times concerned their accusations that torture had been reintroduced during the rebellion. These were based purely on misunderstandings, rumors and imagination.[90]

At the end of August the paper forecast that the rebellion would soon be put down and congratulated the nation on having emerged from its ordeal so well. In its opinion the attitude of the government throughout the episode had been one, which inspired confidence at home and respect abroad, and in this sense there was no reason to doubt that it would be able to respond equally well to future challenges.[91]

Although the *Tokio Times* had not criticized the government's policy, it revealed through its discussion of what good this bloody conflict might have brought about, the same theme as taken up by the other papers, that it too believed that things could be better. It maintained that this stormy year would clear the way for mutual respect and wiser and broader policy directions. If this were to happen, the battle would not have been in vain. The paper also thought it important that this state of war had aroused public discussion and interest in affairs of government, which would enliven the whole of society.[92] In other words, the government's policies had not come up to the expectations of the *Tokio Times* in every respect, and it, too, would have liked the people to have the opportunity to participate in the management of public affairs on a broader front.

88　"The Approaching End," *The Tokio Times,* July 14, 1877.

89　*The Tokio Times,* August 11, 1877.

90　"The Latest Falsehoods Respecting Torture," *The Tokio Times,* August 11, 1877.

91　"The Last Hours of the Revolt," *The Tokio Times,* August 25, 1877.

92　"Some Hopeful Signs of the Times," *The Tokio Times,* September 1, 1877.

When, contrary to official announcements and the paper's predictions, the rebellion had not come to an end by the beginning of September, the *Tokio Times* returned to the criticism expressed by the Yokohama press, announcing that it was certain that foreign newspapers elsewhere would not sink to the same depths as these, the only purpose of which was to arouse mistrust in the government.[93] Once the conflict was over at the end of the month, it then stressed that the government had finally established its own position. Since Saigō had failed no other imitator of his could possibly succeed, evidence in itself that in spite of earlier claims to the contrary, the paper did entertain considerable respect for Saigō. It added that his personal qualities had evidently appealed to those who believed in his sincerity and impeccable character. It was this in part that explained the protracted length of the rebellion.[94]

It was naturally a highly significant thing for the paper that it had been the only foreign publication in Japan that had predicted the outcome of the rebellion successfully, although it did not regard this as evidence of its own clarity of vision as much as of either "dullness", "blindness" or "deliberate malice" on the part of the others. While expressing its great confidence in the country's rulers, it urged them to act more on their own initiative in future, without paying any heed to external protests.[95]

When considering the country's future in the wake of the rebellion, the paper attached particular importance to good will and mutual trust, a state of affairs, which had not yet been achieved. This remark again showed, as noted above, that the *Tokio Times* was in agreement with the others in perceiving the country's chief problem to lie in the excessive centralization of its administration, even though it did not say so in many words. It merely hoped that when those governing the country set about building its future they would show the appropriate tolerance, nobility of mind, avoidance of extremes and determination.[96]

Although the paper had criticized the other foreigners on many occasions for supporting the rebels, it returned to the same theme still in November, when, it claimed that they were so blind in their sympathy for the rebellion and its treacherous leader that they couldn't even believe that he was dead.[97] Taken all in all, the *Tokio Times* interpreted the overthrow of the rebels as marking the

---

93   "The Mishap of Kagoshima," *The Tokio Times*, September 8, 1877.
94   "Peace," *The Tokio Times*, September 29, 1877.
95   Ibid.
96   "Forbearance and Conciliation," *The Tokio Times*, October 13, 1877.
97   *The Tokio Times*, November 10, 1877.

end of feudalism. At last the Emperor was able to rule over a country that was whole and undivided.[98]

Apart from being an accepted manner of speaking, the paper's allusion to the Emperor as the ruler of the country rather than the government, the oligarchy or the like may also be a reflection of the government's specific aim of creating a form of nationalism in Japan that was centred around the Emperor. In this case the adoption and use of such a phraseology would seem natural in the columns of the *Tokio Times*, an acknowledged supporter of government policy, at least more natural than in the other newspapers.

Punch had also perceived the anti-government savor in the writings of the Yokohama papers during the rebellion, and had printed a cartoon showing the editor of the *Mail* in an aggressive pose carrying a sword and the banner of the *Mail* in his hand, with the caption "Saigo's official organ(ist)."[99] Once the rebellion had been put down it recommended seppuku[100] or harakiri[101] as one solution for the papers and ended up by picturing the editors of the Herald, Mail, Gazette and Echo du Japon each with a quill pen poised on his stomach, about to commit suicide in the Japanese style.[102] In other words, it was pursuing much the same theme as in 1874, following the Formosan expedition, during which the papers had similarly criticized the government's policy bitterly. Those to commit harakiri on that occasion had been representatives of the *Mail*, the *Herald* and *Punch* itself.[103] The 1877 cartoon was entitled "General view of Editors of the Foreign Press of Yokohama committing "Harakiri" on the Bund."[104]

Conclusion

The severity with which the papers spoke out against the government at times of crisis, as shown during the Formosan and Satsuma incidents, was one indication of the suspicion, which the foreigners felt towards the government, especially since it was chiefly gathered from those circles, which had looked on foreigners with disfavor or even hostility before the Meiji Restoration. A further probable consideration was the oligarchic form of the government, which

---

98   "The Tenth Year of Meiji," *The Tokio Times*, December 29, 1877.

99   *Japan Punch* 8 (1877), 91.

100   Ibid., 95.

101   *Japan Punch* 9 (1877), 112.

102   Ibid., 104.

103   *Japan Punch* 11 (1874), 182.

104   *Japan Punch* 9 (1877), 104.

was diametrically opposed to the progressive forms advocated by the British, and its interference in economic matters, which the majority of the papers believed should be allowed to proceed untrammelled by government control. It was also evidently highly important to satisfy the general need for security, as suggested by the reliance placed on the government in articles published at the beginning of the revolt, the notion of a compromise solution during the more confused middle phase, in order to bring the hostilities to an end, and the return to support for the government once it was over, the last mentioned situation being an essential prerequisite for successful trade, the principal motive behind the Westerners' presence in Japan. It would indeed seem that perhaps the chief aspect from which the British papers were led to view the situation even at times of crisis was anxiety at the potential damage which could be caused to trade.

The respect and deference shown for Saigō as leader of the rebellion was due partly to his general reputation, and partly, in the case of all the papers except for the *Tokio Times*, which represented for the British papers an American commercial competition,[105] and *Punch*, to a projection onto him of their own expectations and hopes for Japan. It would seem that the government's policy of modernization had not come up to the papers' expectations, and that they were working off the resulting frustration by coming down on the side of rebels. This could not have increased respect for the Western press, or for Westerners in general, amongst the Japanese, any more than did notion of the hereditary superiority of the white race over all others, which also gained still greater emphasis at the time of the rebellion. Of the individual newspapers, particular attention is attracted by the *Weekly Mail*'s departure from earlier traditions in the severity of its criticism, presumably attributable to the change in proprietorship at the beginning of 1877.

The image of the government forces was not also very good. They were looking anything but convincing and they were accused of inefficiency and a propensity for wanton destruction. Although the rebels were at first called schoolboys as evident reference to the pupils at Saigô's military schools they were immensely superior to the government troops: "one insurgent armed with beans is equal to five Imperial soldiers armed with bullets." The image of rebels reflected also memories of the old aristocracy with an army strong in tradition, numbers and discipline and therefore papers referred to the Satsuma rebels as the bravest men in the country. Although the government emerged victorious the papers still called the rebels the brave men who had suffered

---

105   Fält, *Clash of Interests*, 371.

defeat. Instead the government forces were called only troops but not "men". This tradition has been long because also the American historical war film *The Last Samurai* (2003) is reflecting the same image when the hero of the film US Army Captain Nathan Algren asks the Emperor to remember the traditions for which the rebels died.

However in spite of the criticism, the government victory was eventually hailed as a mark of a stabilization in society after the turmoil of the beginning of the Meiji period, and it strengthened the image and the position of government and of Japan in general in the eyes of the foreigners to such an extent that the government's moderate treatment of the rebels was even greeted as a victory in itself for Western civilization.

Works Cited

Newspapers and Magazines

The Far East 1877
The Japan Daily Herald 1877
The Japan Gazette 1877
Japan Punch 1877
The Japan Weekly Mail 1877-1878
The Tokio Times 1877

Cited Secondary Literature

Beasley, W.G. *The Meiji Restoration*. Stanford, CA: Stanford University Press, 1981.

Beasley, W.G. *The Modern History of Japan*. Third Revised Edition. Tokyo: Charles E. Tuttle Company, 1982.

Buck, James H. "The Satsuma Rebellion: From Kagoshima Through the Siege of Kumamoto Castle." *Monumenta Nipponica* 28:4 (Winter, 1973), 427-446.

"Saigō Takamori." In *Biographical Dictionary of Japanese History*, ed. Seiichi Iwao, translator Burton Watson, 449-452. Tokyo: International Society for Educational Information, 1982.

Fairbank, John K., Reischauer Edwin O. and Craig Albert M. *East Asia: Tradition and Transformation*. Tokyo: Charles E. Tuttle Company, 1976.

Fält, Olavi K. *The Clash of Interests: The transformation of Japan in 1861-1881 in the Eyes of the Local Anglo-Saxon press*. Rovaniemi: Societas Historica Finlandiae Septentrionalis, 1990.

Fält, Olavi K. "Introduction" in *Looking at the Other: Historical study of images in theory and practis*, Acta Universitatis Ouluensis. Humaniora B 42, eds. Kari Alenius,

Olavi K. Fält & Seija Jalagin, 7-12. Oulu: University of Oulu, 2002. http://herkules.
oulu.fi/isbn9514266331/isbn9514266331.pdf

Vlastos, Stephen. "Opposition Movements in Early Meiji, 1868-1885." In *The Cambridge History of Japan*, vol. 5, *The Nineteenth Century*, edited by Marius B. Jansen, 393-402. Cambridge: Cambridge University Press, 1989.

CHAPTER 3

Asia's Hope and Pacific Peril: Emergence of Japan as a Military Threat in the American Press at the End of the 19th Century

Henna-Riikka Pennanen

Writing under the pen name "Ex-Attache",[1] the retired British diplomat Frederick Cunliffe-Owen (1855-1926), who had settled in the United States, reminisced how (kaiser) Wilhelm II of Germany had in 1895 presented to (tsar) Nicholas II of Russia a lithograph[2] representing "Western civilization personified by Europe and the United States menaced by a dreadful Eastern specter formed by a fusion of China, Japan, and the other yellow races of Asia." At the time, Cunliffe-Owen continued, there had been "a disposition to scoff at his expense and to ascribe the fears expressed in his drawing to a disordered mind."[3] In contrast, when Cunliffe-Owen was writing in 1899, this "yellow peril"[4] was apparently realistic enough to feature as a serious topic in an American newspaper.

The present article examines this rise of the idea of Japan as a military threat, as well as the images of Japanese armed forces, in the United States press at the end of the nineteenth century. The sources mainly comprise of the established east coast newspapers and magazines, *The New York Times* (NYT), *North American Review* (NAR), and *The Atlantic Monthly* (AM). The critical juncture was the first Sino-Japanese War of 1894-1895. Before the war, the prevailing image of Japan in the United States was one of an enlightened and progressive nation. The war seemed to only confirm this image.[5] The press

---

1   "F. Cunliffe-Owen, Writer, Dies Here," *The New York Times*, July 1, 1926.
2   The lithograph, produced by painter Hermann Knackfuss, was titled "Völker Europas wahret eure heiligsten Güter" (Peoples of Europe, guard your most sacred possessions).
3   "Peril of Yellow Alliance," *The Washington Post*, August 20, 1899, 28.
4   Allegedly, also the phrase yellow peril was coined by Wilhelm II. Gregory Blue, "Gobineau on China: Race Theory, the 'Yellow Peril,' and the Critique of Modernity," *Journal of World History* 10:1 (1999), 121.
5   Arthur Dudden, *The American Pacific: From the Old China Trade to the Present* (New York: Oxford University Press, 1992), 143; Akira Iriye, *Across the Pacific: An Inner History of American-East Asian Relations* (New York: Harcourt, Brace & World, 1967), 32; William Neumann, *America Encounters Japan: From Perry to MacArthur* (Baltimore: Johns Hopkins Press, 1963), 104.

© VERLAG FERDINAND SCHÖNINGH, 2020 | DOI:10.30965/9783657702930_004

coverage of the war events affirmed that Japan was a civilized nation also in warfare, and that Japan was a sovereign state with a modernized army and navy capable of protecting this sovereignty.

However, after the war the admiring imagery of Japan was partly supplanted with more sinister "yellow perilist" images. Factions in both Japan and the United States were imbued with doctrines of nationalism and imperialism, and the two nations emerged as rivalling first-class powers in the Pacific region. The growth of Japanese military power caused concern in the United States, and resulted in views of Japan as a potential racial, commercial, political, and strategic threat.[6] As the century drew to a close, Americans advocating the Hawaiian annexation to the United States, both in the islands and the U.S., began claiming that these threats were about to materialize sooner than was expected. They alleged that Japan was planning to seize Hawaii, either through a political or military coup, with the help of the large number of Japanese contract laborers settling in the islands. Then, the Japanese would use Hawaii as a stepping stone for reaching the United States. This short-lived panic in the American papers toned down after the United States annexed Hawaii in 1898, but the idea of Japan as a threat lingered on.[7]

Harbinger of Modern Civilization in Asia

Korea was the setting for the first Sino-Japanese War. The immediate pretext was the Donghak (or Tonghak, Eastern Learning) Rebellion, an armed peasant insurrection that was half religious and half political and spread through Korea in 1893 and again in 1894. However, the Japanese preoccupation with Korea vastly preceded the uprising. Almost as soon as the Meiji Restoration of 1868 had been completed, the Japanese foreign policy makers concurred that Korea was strategically and militarily of prime importance for Japan, and hence the neighboring kingdom took a central place in Japanese geopolitical

---

6 Joseph Henning, *Outposts of Civilization: Race, Religion, and the Formative Years of American-Japanese Relations* (New York: New York University Press, 2000), 138; Iriye, *Across the Pacific*, 73-74; Rotem Kowner, "'Lighter than Yellow, but not Enough': Western Discourse on the Japanese 'Race', 1854-1904," *The Historical Journal* 43:1 (2000), 126; Daniel Metraux, "First Introduction," in *E. Warren Clark's Life and Adventure in Japan*, ed. Daniel Metraux et al. (San Jose: Writers Club Press, 2002), 15-16; Urs M. Zachmann, *China and Japan in the Late Meiji Period: China Policy and the Japanese Discourse on National Identity, 1895-1904* (New York: Routledge, 2009), 13.

7 Iriye, *Across the Pacific*, 78.

thinking.[8] In 1890, Prime Minister Yamagata Aritomo (1838-1922) elaborated on the question. He stated that the way to secure a nation's sovereignty and security lay in the defense of, first, the nation's "line of sovereignty", and second, of its "line of interest" against any and all foreign threats. With this he meant that Japan had to be prepared to defend not only its homeland, but also areas that had a bearing on the homeland security. Korea was such an area. Not only did Korea belong to the Japanese line of interest, but if Korea was controlled by a hostile power, it would directly threaten Japan's line of sovereignty. Geopolitically, the Korean Peninsula was a "dagger" pointing towards Japan. If Japan could not control Korea, the next best thing was to ensure that no other power did either.[9]

The main threats that seemed to compromise Korean independence were China and Russia. While the Chinese Qing Dynasty refused to relinquish its claim of ultimate sovereignty over Korea, its traditional vassal state, the Russians started constructing the Trans-Siberian Railway in 1891, which to the Japanese signaled only one thing: Russian expansion. The Japanese feared that Russia was out to invade parts of China first, then Korea, and finally perhaps even Japan. Because China had, in its own conflicts, proven to be no match for European powers, they could hardly be able to protect Korea against the Russian expansion. Thus, assuring the "independence" of Korea by blocking both Chinese and Russian attempts to wield control in the country became one of Japan's main foreign policy objectives. Korea was to be stemmed away from the Chinese Confucian world order and brought into the world order inhabited by sovereign states and defined and regulated by international law. To this end, Korea needed to be strengthened and modernized.[10]

From the Chinese perspective, Japan's contestation of the Qing dynasty's right to predominance in Korea appeared equally threatening to China's

---

8   Edward Chen, "Japan's Decision to Annex Taiwan: A Study of Ito-Mutsu Diplomacy, 1894-95," *The Journal of Asian Studies* 37:1 (1977), 62; Charles Schencking, *Making Waves: Politics, Propaganda, and the Emergence of the Imperial Japanese Navy, 1868-1922* (Palo Alto: Stanford University Press, 2004), 79.

9   Akira Iriye, *Japan and the Wider World: From the Mid-nineteenth Century to the Present* (London: Longman, 1997), 11, 14.

10   John Benson and Takao Matsumura, *Japan, 1868-1945: From Isolation to Occupation* (Essex: Pearson Education, 2001), 59; Akira Iriye, *From Nationalism to Internationalism: US foreign Policy to 1914* (London: Routledge, 1965), 117-118; Iriye, *Japan*, 12; Daniel Kane, "Each of Us in His Own Way: Factors Behind Conflicting Accounts of the Massacre at Port Arthur," *Journalism History* 31:1 (2005), 24; Junnan Lai, "Sovereignty and 'Civilization': International Law and East Asia in the Nineteenth Century," *Modern China* 40: 3 (2014), 297; Stewart Lone, *Japan's First Modern War: Army and Society in the Conflict with China, 1894-95* (New York: St. Martin's Press, 1994), 24.

security and interests. In 1879, Japan had already annexed the Ryukyu Kingdom, which had been simultaneously a tributary state to China and a vassal state of the Japanese Satsuma domain. Careful not to lose any more of its traditional sphere of influence, the Chinese sought to frustrate the reforms Japan was advocating in Korea and to reassert its claim to supremacy. They also urged the Korean court to open and maintain diplomatic relations with the major European powers and the United States in order to prevent any other power besides China from wielding too much sway over the kingdom. In 1885, China and Japan made a mutual agreement that they would not meddle in Korea's internal affairs. They also agreed to notify each other in advance if they were sending troops to Korea, and concurred that both countries had the right to station an equal number of troops to protect their interests in Korea. Thus, according to this agreement[11], when China sent its troops to Korea, at the request of the Joseon (or Chosŏn) dynasty, to assist in pacifying the Donghak Rebellion, the Japanese reciprocated by dispatching their troops. Japan saw an opportunity to settle the question of China's stewardship over Korea once and for all, and took it. In July 1894, the Japanese seized the Korean royal palace, and by the end of the month, China and Japan were practically at war.[12]

Among the first military actions between China and Japan was the controversial sinking of the British steamship Kowshing, which China had chartered for transporting troops to Korea. On 25 July, the Japanese cruiser Naniwa stopped the Kowshing and ordered the captain Thomas Ryder Galsworthy to follow Naniwa to a Japanese naval base. After the Chinese officers prevented the captain from obeying the orders, Naniwa attacked and sank the ship.[13] In a few days, the news of the incident started to trickle to *The New York Times*, first from British sources. On 31 July, the *NYT* reported about a "barbaric butchery" and "fiendish brutality" of the Japanese in opening machine gun fire against, and then torpedoing, a ship flying the British flag and under circumstances in which a formal declaration of war was wanting. According to the report, after the Kowshing sank, the Japanese fired at the crew and Chinese troops struggling in the water, leaving only 41 survivors.[14] *NYT* noted that the British

---

11   Known as the Tientsin Convention, or alternatively as the Li-Itō Protocol after the signatories Li Hongzhang (1823-1901) and Itō Hirobumi (1841-1909).

12   Kyung Moon Hwang, *A History of Korea* (Houndmills: Palgrave Macmillan, 2010), 129-130; Kane, "Each of Us," 24; Schencking, *Making Waves*, 80-81.

13   Douglas Howland, "Japan's Civilized War: International Law as Diplomacy in the Sino-Japanese War (1894-1895)," *Journal of the History of International Law* 9:2 (2007), 193–194; Douglas Howland, "The Sinking of the S. S. Kowshing: International Law, Diplomacy, and the Sino-Japanese War," *Modern Asian Studies* 42:4 (2008), 673, 680-681.

14   According to Douglas Howland, there had been approximately 1176 persons on board the Kowshing, of whom only around 205 survived. Howland, "Sinking," 683.

newspapers emphatically denounced the "outrage" as an unnecessary blood-shed, and demanded compensation from the Japanese. However, some of the newspapers remarked that so far the news largely rested on Chinese authority, and one should wait for official statements before jumping into conclusions in the matter.[15]

On the next day, *NYT* informed that the Japanese government had issued an official statement repudiating the claim that the Kowshing was under the British flag or that the Naniwa crew had been "brutal in their treatment of the Chinese sailors struggling in the water."[16] The Japanese government offered an apology to Great Britain, but insisted on their statement that the Japanese were unaware that the vessel was British.[17] The London sources, rely-ing on their Chinese correspondents, discounted the Japanese statement and asserted that the Japanese attack had been unprovoked, unjust, and that the Naniwa crew had not rescued a single Chinese soldier who had jumped over-board. Quite the contrary, they had made "strenuous attempts" to destroy all witnesses.[18] The Japanese authorities countered. Based on their interview of Captain Galsworthy and Chief Officer Tamplin of the Kowshing, they stated that the Chinese crew had taken control over the ship, thus effectively mak-ing it a Chinese ship, and that it had been the Chinese themselves who had shot the men in the water.[19] The Japanese Legation at Washington also stepped up, and shared with the *NYT* the official reports it had received from the gov-ernment at Tokyo concerning the incident.[20] While the speculation on what actually happened on that July morning – and who was to blame – was ongo-ing in the pages of the *NYT*, Japan officially declared war on 1 August, and the Chinese soon reciprocated.

In early August, the London correspondent of the *NYT* criticized the Japanese government for having done "little to remove the feeling" that the sinking of the Kowshing was "the most disgraceful and wanton piece of sav-agery of the century."[21] But in fact, as soon as the news of the Kowshing inci-dent spread to Europe and the United States, the Japanese did set to work on controlling the damage done to their international reputation. The Japanese

15   "Sinking of the Kow Shing," *The New York Times*, July 31, 1894, 5.

16   "Putting Blame on China," *The New York Times*, August 1, 1894, 5.

17   "Japan Makes Apology," *The New York Times*, August 2, 1894, 5.

18   "A Victory for the Chinese," *The New York Times*, August 22, 1894, 5; "Japan Makes Apology," 5; "Li Hung Chang in Command," *The New York Times*, August 7, 1894, 5; "Violated the Laws of Peace," *The New York Times*, August 13, 1894, 5; "What the London Papers Say," *The New York Times*, August 3, 1894, 4.

19   The British *Daily Chronicle* and *Daily Telegraph* appeared to share these Japanese views. ("What the London Papers Say," 4.)

20   "Sinking of the Transport," *The New York Times*, August 4, 1894, 5.

21   "Shining Specks on Mars," *The New York Times*, August 5, 1894, 1.

government issued official versions of the events and circulated them in their legations abroad, and the reports then made their way to publications such as the *NYT*. Soon, also prominent Japanese and British scholars of international law came to Japan's defense, studied the key disputes of the case, and absolved the Japanese from all blame with their findings.[22]

One of these scholars was Thomas E. Holland (1835-1926). Holland presented the viewpoint of international law in *The Times* of London, which was then quoted in the *NYT*. Supporting the Japanese side of the controversy, he argued that legally an actual state of war had existed even if not yet formally. The Kowshing was part of a hostile expedition, and since it refused to obey Japanese orders and Japan could not place a prize crew on board, it was perfectly justified for Japan to resort to force. Whether or not the Kowshing flew the British flag was wholly immaterial. The Japanese actions accorded with the international law, and there had been no violation of neutral rights, Holland concluded. Thus, Japan owed no apology or indemnity to Great Britain. Holland stayed silent on the question of the Japanese firing on the drowning men, and excused his silence by the lack of conclusive evidence and the irrelevance of the question as far as international law was concerned.[23] Indeed, the 1864 Geneva Convention, which stipulated that belligerents should provide assistance and medical care for the wounded and sick enemy combatants, did not extend to naval warfare.[24]

Following Holland's argumentation, one Japanese resident of the United States pointed out that "even if brutality was committed, Japan cannot be denounced for her barbarity," for it would be unfair "to condemn the Japanese in the case where international law does not condemn."[25] Holland exonerated the Japanese from the legal standpoint, but they still stood accused of barbarism, and the quote above did not even dispute the accusation. According to an article which was published in *The Naval & Military Record and Royal Dockyards Gazette*, and then quoted in the *NYT*, the Japanese could hardly be blamed for their conduct. Such acts as "to strike first and declare war afterward," and to summarily sink unarmed vessels, were lessons Japan had learned from "civilization," that is, from Europe.[26]

---

22   Howland, "Japan's Civilized War," 190-191, 193-194; Howland, "Sinking," 678-679, 682, 685.

23   "Li Hung Chang in Command," 5.

24   Howland, "Japan's Civilized War," 194.

25   "Dainties for Soldier Japs," *The New York Times*, August 13, 1894, 5.

26   "Violated the Laws of Peace," 5. Eventually, the British government officially concluded that Japan had acted according to international law and the matter was put to rest. Howland, "Sinking," 690.

Another question troubling the American spectators was: what were the grounds for the war, and were they legitimate? An article in the September 1894 issue of the *North American Review*, titled "China and Japan in Korea," delved into the question. The article presented the viewpoints of three authors: Augustine Heard Jr. (1827-1905), United States minister to Korea in 1890-1893; Durham White Stevens (1851-1908), honorary counsellor of the Japanese legation at Washington; and Howard Martin (1857-1926), former secretary of the United States legation at Beijing. Martin argued that the issue at hand in the war was the progress of "modern civilization in the 'Hermit Kingdom,'" meaning that Japan advocated governmental, social, and commercial reforms in Korea, and if successful in the war, Tokyo would press these reforms on Korea. The implication was that Japan was pursuing a civilizing mission: Europe and the U.S. had carried the torch of civilization to Japan, and now it was Japan's turn to pass it on around Asia. China, on the other hand, opposed reforms, and the success of China in the war would mean "the forcing back of the Koreans to Oriental sluggishness, superstition, ignorance, and anti-foreign sentiment and methods." For Martin, the war was a conflict between Japanese "modern civilization," upholding international law, and Chinese "barbarism," holding onto "its imperious ideas of vassal states."[27]

Stevens was on the same lines. China and Japan, "two civilizations which once had much in common," had gradually grown apart. They espoused very different views on world order and foreign affairs, and consequently, were inevitably headed towards a struggle for supremacy. Stevens noted that Korea was "a natural bulwark" to Japan. Hence, the stability and independence of Korea was vital for Japan's safety and interests in the region. China persisted in the "manifest absurdity" of claiming sovereignty over Korea, even though it was clearly unable to protect the country. China was also unwilling to urge the Korean court to adopt such reforms as would be needed to prevent disturbances like the Donghak Rebellion from emerging. Korea in Chinese hands was a menace to Japan's security, Stevens concluded, and thus the Japanese had just grounds for rooting out such a threat.[28]

Heard disagreed vehemently. The explicit object of his text was to put the readers on guard against the Japanese, who were clearly the American favorites. The Japanese were a progressive, ingenious, and courteous people, Heard admitted, but as far as Korea was concerned, their peaceful intentions were merely rhetorics. Plagued by internal unrest, wishing to divert the attention

---

27   Augustine Heard, Durham W. Stevens, and Howard Martin, "China and Japan in Korea," *The North American Review* 159:454 (1894), 316.

28   Heard et al., "China and Japan in Korea," 308-311, 313-315.

of quarreling politicians and divided people,[29] they had prepared for war. The Donghak movement was a pretext, perhaps even engineered by the Japanese. They forced China to make the first move in order to gain the sympathies of the world. They wanted to mask the fact that Japan was the real aggressor, resorting to force, not diplomatic persuasion in trying to protect its interests. Japan brought about this war with the aim to conquer Korea and subjugate the people, Heard opined.[30]

Martin granted that the Japanese, if successful, would take all the territory they could, while Stevens disavowed the claim and reminded that Japan was waging war for Korea's independence and progress.[31] In November, the Japanese minister at Washington, Kurino Shinichiro (1851-1937), responded by writing an article to the *NAR*. Kurino had studied law at Harvard College and worked in the Ministry of Foreign Affairs, so he was not only conversant in the English language, but well-versed in the niceties of international law, foreign relations, Korean issues, and conceivably, in the prevailing attitudes and opinions of the Americans. The *NYT* noted that the appointment of Kurino was perhaps too timely and fitting not to have a connection to the Sino-Japanese War.[32]

Kurino's expressed objective in writing the article was to appeal to "intelligent public opinion" and make the justness of Japanese cause clear and known to the Americans. Since the beginning of the war, Kurino observed, Japan had been accused of courting jingoism, of desiring territory, and of vain aspiration to become the leader of East Asia. None of these accusations hit the mark, Kurino maintained. Neither Japan nor China needed Korean territory; what they needed was a strong, independent, and friendly Korea. But China was weak, conservative, and stagnant. The Chinese refused to co-operate with Japan in reforming Korea; and instead, checked "every aspiration for improvement" and perpetuated "every ancient evil." The outcome of their policy would be that China would "surrender the poor victim, a sheep ready for the shearer, to the first comer strong enough to enforce his demands." Kurino emphasized

---

29   In their private discussions Japanese statesmen, such as the Foreign Minister Mutsu Munemitsu (1844-1897), had indeed contemplated on the idea of diverting the domestic attention from the unsettled political situation. The Japanese government was struggling with the recent political developments: elections, parliament, party politics, tug-of-war between the regional and central forces, and the growing demands of the army and navy. Subsequently, one of the aims of the war was indeed to unite the people behind the central government. Lone, *Japan's First*, 22, 24, 27.

30   Heard et al., "China and Japan in Korea," 300, 304-308.

31   Ibid., 310, 315, 320.

32   "Japan's Reasons for War," *The New York Times*, August 19, 1894, 5.

that war had been the last recourse for Japan, but because of Chinese obsti-nacy, it had become unavoidable since Japan's national security was on the line.[33] Some less authoritative Japanese voices were also quoted in the *NYT*, presenting the same arguments on Japan standing on the side of modern civi-lization and fighting a morally and legally just war for Korea's independence and self-defense.[34]

The discussion about the legitimacy of the war and the Kowshing incident gave a foretaste of the characteristics of American reporting on the war. First, there was the confusing and conflicting nature of the war reports. Whether the *NYT* reported about the casualties and damages of the war[35] or military engagements between China and Japan,[36] the facts and views were so widely contradictory that it was often impossible to fathom who was winning and who losing.

The *NYT* gathered news from a wide variety of sources: British newspapers with correspondents in, for example, Shanghai and Tianjin; news agencies such as Reuter and Central News; official reports from the Tokyo government and bulletins of the Japanese army commanders; private letters from American residents in East Asia; and interviews. Then there was the active – direct and indirect – Japanese participation in the discussion, especially by the Japanese legation at Washington, which was only accentuated by the silence of the Chinese voices in the media. The *NYT* remarked on the subject already in the early days of the war:

> The contrast between the Western tendencies of the Japanese and the retrograde policy of China is particularly noticeable in the freedom with which the representatives of the first-named Government communicate all the news they receive, and discuss the progress of events, and the ab-solute non-communicativeness of the Chinese representatives.[37]

---

33 Shinichiro Kurino, "The Oriental War," *The North American Review* 159:456 (1894), 529-534.
34 "Dainties for Soldier Japs," 5.
35 See e.g. "Japanese Ship of War Sunk," *The New York Times*, August 5, 1894, 5.
36 See e.g. "A Victory for the Chinese," 5; "Another Battle Reported," *The New York Times*, August 6, 1894, 5; "As a Japanese Tells It," *The New York Times*, November 27, 1894, 10; "Chinese Loss at Seikwan," *The New York Times*, August 9, 1894, 5; "Decisive Battle of the Yalu," *The New York Times*, September 21, 1894, 5; "The Battle at Song Hwan," *The New York Times*, August 19, 1894, 5; "Victories Claimed by China," *The New York Times*, August 30, 1894, 5.
37 "Japanese Ship of War Sunk," 5.

Trying to steer public opinion in Europe and the United States was a conscious strategy opted by the Japanese. They wished to reassert their sovereignty and to prevent foreign intervention in the war.[38] To achieve these objectives, Japan could not afford to alienate the sympathy of European powers and the United States, and hence the Japanese put all their diplomatic resources into use.

Use of war propaganda, especially carefully drafted and officially sanctioned reports, did not escape notice in the foreign press. Citing *The Times*, the *NYT* wrote that the news from the seat of war were either rumors or – mainly Japanese – official statements, "framed to suit official purposes" and "systematically misleading." Thus, it was concluded that majority of the war news were untrue and "the rest ridiculously exaggerated." Similarly, the London correspondent of the *NYT* called the authorities at Beijing and Tokyo as "purveyors of mendacity," who wrapped all war events in "an impenetrable cocoon of myth and fable."[39] The Japanese, for their part, made their distrust for the Chinese reports publicly known, and in February next year, also the *NYT* credited the Japanese official reports as "absolutely correct" in their "general tenor."[40]

A second characteristic of the press coverage was the profuse use of the two catchwords of the day: civilization and international law, and the ensuing prominence of legal scholars in the discussion. Both the concept of civilization and international law had their roots deep in the European history and were effectively European constructions. As the Europeans sought to extend their view of world order and international community on peoples outside Europe, the Christian values underlying international law were replaced with the vague principle of civilization. The standard of civilization was fashioned as the entry ticket to the international community of sovereign states. Yet, no one provided a clear-cut definition of what this standard exactly was. Certain prerequisites were formulated, such as a working legal system, guarantee of certain rights to citizens and foreign residents, participation in foreign relations and diplomacy, and adherence to international law and agreements. Japan fulfilled all the conditions, but was not guaranteed an automatic entrance to the 'family of civilized nations.' The so-called unequal treaties, with the foreign control of tariffs and extraterritoriality, still impinged on Japanese sovereignty in early 1894. Thus, in practice, international law was a flexible, pragmatic system, and

---

38   Chen, "Japan's Decision," 67; Iriye, *Japan*, 18; Lone, *Japan's First*, 30.
39   "China Will Eventually Win," *The New York Times*, October 28, 1894, 28; "Shining Specks on Mars," 1.
40   "Japan's Victorious Ships," *The New York Times*, February 17, 1895, 20; "The Japanese Moving North," *The New York Times*, September 2, 1894, 5; "The War Fever in Japan," *The New York Times*, August 28, 1894, 5.

all issues – including Japan's admittance as a sovereign nation on par with the 'civilized nations' – were negotiated case-by-case.[41]

When the Sino-Japanese war began, Japan had just concluded the renegotiations of the unequal treaties with Britain. Next, it had to convince the other powers of Japan's standard of civilization as well. Consequently, Japan made the war a showcase of their civilization in two ways. First, they framed the war as a struggle between Japanese civilization and Chinese barbarism, or as Kurino phrased: "a struggle between the forces of modern civilization" and "conservatism."[42] Eventually, this view was espoused also by some Americans and Europeans.[43] It has been argued that while the adoption of the civilization discourse in relation to the war was a publicity stunt, it also provided an ideological motivation and justification for the conflict, persuading the Japanese public to rally behind the war effort.[44]

Secondly, the Japanese sought to demonstrate that they were no strangers to the idea of civilized warfare. War and power politics were an integral part of nineteenth century conceptions of international law. A civilized nation waged a civilized war, that is, adhered to international rules and regulations, such as the Saint Petersburg Declaration of 1868, renouncing the use of small explosive projectiles; The Paris Declaration Respecting Maritime Law of 1856, regulating the relations between neutrals and belligerents in the seas and amending prize law; and the First Geneva Convention of 1864, guaranteeing care to prisoners of war and formalizing the International Red Cross. Japan was a signatory to the last two agreements, and the war provided a ground for testing Japanese observance of international law. Moreover, they could also manipulate the international law to their advantage: study the codes and precedents, and then prove that their actions were, indeed, legal and thus civilized.[45]

Legal advisors were assigned for the Japanese army and navy, and commanders instructed the troops on how to conduct a civilized warfare, and admonished them on tarnishing Japan's international reputation.[46] Japan's

41   Howland, "Japan's Civilized War," 182-183, 185; Lai, "Sovereignty," 284-287; Rune Svarverud, *International Law as World Order in Late Imperial China: Translation, Reception and Discourse, 1847-1911* (Boston: Brill, 2007), 21-22, 46-47.

42   Kurino, "The Oriental War," 536. See also "Dainties for Soldier Japs," 5.

43   David Scott, *China and the International System, 1840-1949: Power, Presence, and Perceptions in a Century of Humiliation* (Ithaca: SUNY Press, 2008), 122.

44   Lone, *Japan's First*, 58.

45   Howland, "Japan's Civilized War," 183-185, 189, 200; Kane, "Each of Us," 26; Lai, "Sovereignty," 294, 296-299.

46   Howland, "Japan's Civilized War," 181, 187; Lone, *Japan's First*, 144-147; S. C. M. Paine, *The Sino-Japanese War of 1894-1895: Perceptions, Power, and Primacy* (Cambridge: Cambridge University Press, 2003), 210.

strategy seemed successful. The *NYT* reported that the Japanese troops were disciplined and characterized by "kindness, magnanimity, and generosity," while the course of the Chinese troops was marked by "rapine and violence." The Chinese troops were reproached for "robbing the natives and committing horrible atrocities wherever they pass," having set a price on Japanese heads, and for firing upon Japanese Red Cross workers and patients.[47] The success proved short-lived, however. In late November 1894, first news of the fall of Port Arthur, today known by its Chinese name Lüshun, reached the *NYT*.[48] The Chinese fortress in the Liaodong Peninsula, one of the strongest and most modern of its day in Asia, surrendered to the Japanese in one day.[49] Within the next weeks, unsubstantiated rumors started to circulate in the American press of "frantic," "revengeful reprisals" the Japanese had committed upon the Chinese inhabitants of the city.[50]

The events at Port Arthur were eye-witnessed by British and American war correspondents and military attachés accompanying Japanese troops.[51] First of the American correspondents to take a stand on the rumor was James Creelman (1859-1915). Creelman's special dispatch was published in the *New York World* on 12 December, and six days later, a longer and more detailed sensational report followed. He portrayed a massacre lasting for several days, during which the Japanese soldiers summarily and brutally murdered and mutilated a large part of the civilian population of the city – including women and children.[52] The Japanese government hastened to counter the report. The Foreign Minister Mutsu instructed minister Kurino to denounce Creelman's version of events and present the official Japanese version, which the Japanese authorities have maintained since.[53] The *NYT* faithfully repeated the official

---

47   "Corean Light on the Far East," *The New York Times*, October 27, 1894, 12; "Flying Before the Japanese," *The New York Times*, November 7, 1894, 12; "Japan Pressing the Fight," *The New York Times*, August 20, 1894, 5; "Japan's Victorious Ships," 20.

48   "Capture of Port Arthur," *The New York Times*, November 26, 1894, 5; "Japan's Great Victory," *The New York Times*, December 9, 1894, 25.

49   Kane, "Each of Us," 23; Lone, *Japan's First*, 154.

50   "Victor not Implacable," *The New York Times*, December 9, 1894, 5.

51   Thomas Cowan of *The Times*; Frederick Villiers of the London *Standard* and *Black and White*; James Creelman of the *New York World*; A. B. (Amédée Baillot) de Guerville of *New York Herald* and *Leslie's Weekly*; Lieutenant Michael O'Brien; Captain Noel du Boulay; and Surgeon-Colonel W. Taylor. Kane, "Each of Us," 24; Henning, *Outposts*, 141; Lone, *Japan's First*, 155-156; Frederic Villiers, "The Truth About Port Arthur," *The North American Review* 160:460 (1895), 326.

52   Kane, "Each of Us," 29; Henning, *Outposts*, 141; Lone, *Japan's First*, 156.

53   Henning, *Outposts*, 141; Kane, "Each of Us," 29; Masahiro Yamamoto, *Rape of Nanking* (Westport: Greenwood Publishing 2000), 25. In addition, Foreign Minister Mutsu wrote an open letter to the *New York World*, in which he pleaded the American readers not to

explanation: majority of the civilians had quitted the town, and the remainders were armed and forced to attack the Japanese; Chinese soldiers were among the civilians under disguise; children and women were not killed; and the Japanese army temporarily lost its discipline as, on their entrance to the town, they saw "the fearfully mutilated bodies of the Japanese prisoners, some of whom had been burned alive and some crucified" and took revenge on the Chinese soldiers.[54] The same explanatory model was later utilized in debates on the event known as the Nanjing Massacre. In 1937, the Japanese troops occupied the city of Nanjing and committed a protracted series of atrocities. The Japanese press had been running stories about the cruelty of the Chinese soldiers for a long time. And when the news of the brutal conduct of the Japanese troops belatedly made it to the headlines, the blame for Japanese violence was shifted to the "aggressions" of the Chinese.[55]

From the Japanese point of view, the incident occurred at a very inconvenient time. On 22 November, during the first days of Japanese occupation of Port Arthur, Minister Kurino and American Secretary of State Walter Gresham (1832-1895) had signed a revised treaty and protocol, which abolished American consular jurisdiction in Japan. The *NYT* rejoiced that the treaty stood for a most complete recognition of Japan as a civilized power with a right to rule its own affairs.[56] When Creelman's report came out, the treaty had been handed over to the Senate for ratification. A massacre of Chinese civilians hardly accorded with the rules and regulations of civilized warfare. It could signal to the Americans that Japan fell short of the required standard of civilization, and obstruct the ratification of the treaty.[57] One writer in the *NYT* suspected that the charges of the Japanese "relapse" into "barbarism" were trumped up precisely for this purpose. The writer speculated that the allegations either came from British sources or, more probably, from the American opponents of the treaty.[58]

By the end of the month, the other American war correspondent, Amédée B. de Guerville (1869-1913), came to Japan's defense, using largely the same arguments as the official Japanese version submitted by Mutsu and Kurino. He also

---

make hasty judgments and promised that the incident would be thoroughly investigated. Lone, *Japan's First*, 161.

54   "Japan on its Behavior," *The New York Times*, December 18, 1894, 5.

55   Mark Eykholt, "Aggression, Victimization, and Chinese Historiography of the Nanjing Massacre," in *The Nanjing Massacre in History and Historiography*, ed. Joshua Fogel (Berkeley: University of California Press 2000), 11-12; Yamamoto, *Rape of Nanking*, 23, 27-28; Takashi Yoshida, *Making of the "Rape of Nanking"* (New York: Oxford University Press 2006), 12.

56   "Japan Gets Tariff Autonomy," *The New York Times*, November 25, 1894, 5.

57   Lai, "Sovereignty," 299; Lone, *Japan's First*, 157.

58   "Our New Treaty with Japan," *The New York Times*, December 17, 1894, 5.

conjectured that the accusation of Japan's barbarism had something to do with
the treaty ratification. He did not deny that the Japanese had committed ex-
cesses at Port Arthur, but he laid the blame for it on the Chinese, who mutilated
prisoners of war, used explosive bullets, and discarded their uniforms. In other
words, the Japanese may have sidestepped from the path of civilized warfare,
but the Chinese had never even entered it. De Guerville concluded his article
by stating that Japan had done nothing that could jeopardize its "right to enter
the great family of civilized nations," and that the war still remained a "battle
of civilization against barbarism."[59] At the break of the year 1895, the stance of
the Japanese and de Guerville continued to be supported in the *NYT*.[60]

In the *NAR* issue of March 1895, the British war artist and correspondent
Frederic Villiers (1851-1922) made one more attempt to prove that the Port
Arthur massacre took place on the scale and intensity described by Creelman.
According to Villiers, the "plain truth" about the massacre was that it had been
"a cold blooded butchery" of civilians lasting three days. Citizens had been
killed at their doorsteps in the act of kowtowing. What made the event more
startling, Villiers pointed out, was the previously immaculate discipline and
humane conduct of the Japanese troops. Considering this track record, then,
Villiers urged the Japanese government to own up, and apologize for, the "little
outburst of barbarism" of its military forces. But Japan, still "young in the ways
of civilization," had unblushingly lied and denied that a massacre took place.
In their "naughty childlike simplicity," Villiers continued, the Japanese had
managed to discredit even the eyewitness reports with the assistance of their
well-organized press system.[61] In the end, Port Arthur was declared as only
a human aberration, not a sign of Japan's lack of civilization. The U.S. Senate
gave its advice and consent to ratification of the treaty, and even before the
consent, articles in the *NYT* noted approvingly that "the report of cruelties
committed by the Japanese Army at Port Arthur" had "weighed a feather" and
made absolutely no impression upon the Senate.[62] On 15 February, the treaty
was ratified by the President of the United States.

---

59   "Japanese Accused Unjustly," *The New York Times*, December 30, 1894, 9.
60   See e.g. "Cruelty of the Chinese," *The New York Times*, January 1, 1895, 5; "The Japanese
      Danger," *The New York Times*, January 10, 1895, 4.
61   Villiers, "The Truth," 325-328. Afterwards, historical scholarship has largely confirmed that
      excesses took place at Port Arthur between November 21 and 25, and that women and
      children were among the incalculable victims. However, the claim that almost the whole
      civilian population of the city was wiped out, as Creelman initially suggested, is highly
      improbable. Kane, "Each of Us," 24, 29; Lone, *Japan's First*, 155-157.
62   "American Treaty with Japan," *The New York Times*, December 20, 1894, 5; "Japan Treaty
      Ratified," *The New York Times*, January 31, 1895, 2; "New Treaty with Japan," *The New York
      Times*, January 23, 1895, 9.

Menace in the Pacific

On 21 March 1895 ratifications for the new Treaty of Commerce and Navigation were exchanged at Washington. By that time, Japan had won a battle after battle in the war with China. The Chinese Beiyang fleet was in shambles, Japan had secured footholds in Manchuria, and Japanese forces kept Beijing under threat. China had few options but to send its peace negotiator Li Hongzhang to Japan. Japan, feeling confident in its military pressure and leverage, sat on the negotiation table.[63] For Foreign Minister Mutsu and Prime Minister Itō Hirobumi, equality with the so called civilized nations entailed not only the termination of unequal treaties, but making Japan a strong, colonial power. This was reflected in the conditions for peace. The problem for Mutsu and Itō was how to find a balance between extorting too much from China, which would undoubtedly lead to foreign intervention, and yet satisfying the clamors of the army, navy, and the Japanese public – all elated by the victory. Finally, China and Japan signed the peace treaty at Shimonoseki on 17 April 1895. The treaty contained the following terms: China had to acknowledge the independence of Korea; cession of Taiwan (Formosa), Penghu (Pescadores) islands, and Liaodong Peninsula; a huge indemnity; and a new commercial treaty granting extraterritorial privileges for Japan.[64] However, Japan had taken a risk in including the Liaodong Peninsula to the list of territories to be ceded, and in the end, the risk did not pay off. Immediately after the peace treaty was concluded, Russia, Germany, and France made a joint intervention "advising" Japan to give up its rights in Manchuria in exchange for an additional indemnity.[65]

Nevertheless, the war – in words of Benjamin Elman – became a culmination point for the perceived fall of China and rise of Japan. Or, it was the culmination of the story of Chinese failure at modernizing its society, army, and navy in contrast to Japanese success, and a significant contributor to the so called Chinese "century of humiliation."[66] In his article for *The Atlantic*

---

63   Chen, "Japan's Decision," 63–65, 69; Allen Fung, "Testing the Self-Strengthening: The Chinese Army in the Sino-Japanese War of 1894–1895," *Modern Asian Studies* 30:4 (1996), 1007; Schencking, *Making Waves*, 82-83.

64   Benson and Matsumura, *Japan*, 61; Chen, "Japan's Decision," 62, 64, 70-71; James Huffman, *Creating a Public: People and Press in Meiji Japan* (Honolulu: University of Hawaii Press, 1997), 215.

65   Iriye, *Japan*, 15; Iriye, *From Nationalism*, 119; Huffman, *Creating a Public*, 216; Paine, *Sino-Japanese War*, 248-249.

66   Dudden, *American Pacific*, 116; Benjamin Elman, "Naval Warfare and the Refraction of China's Self-Strengthening Reforms into Scientific and Technological Failure, 1865–1895," *Modern Asian Studies* 38:2 (2004, 285; Benjamin Elman, "The 'Rise' of Japan and the 'Fall' of China after 1895," in *The Chinese Chameleon Revisited: From the Jesuits to Zhang Yimou,*

Monthly, author Lafcadio Hearn (1850-1904) described how the war had exposed the Chinese "impotence" beneath the "military scarecrow of Western manufacture which China had purchased at so great a cost," and left China a hopeless wreck.[67] Japan, on the other hand, had "broken down the power of China, made a new Korea, enlarged her own territory, and changed the whole political face of the East." All this, Hearn claimed, Japan had achieved "without losing a single ship or a single battle."[68] The Japanese nation had regenerated itself through war and "obtained the recognition of her rights and of her place among nations."[69] U.S. Secretary of the Navy, Hilary A. Herbert (1834-1919), remarked that Japan had "leaped, almost at one bound, to a place among the great nations of the earth."[70]

First and foremost, Japan had proved to be a military success. It had taken its "just place among the peoples of the world" largely because it had distinguished itself in war.[71] This had been unexpected.[72] Initial assessments had run in China's favor. Article after article in the *NYT* confidently predicted that China would win by its sheer numbers. The war would be decided on land, and if prolonged, Japan stood no chance. China could "pour troops into Corea as a child would pour sand into a rathole – for amusement and as a pastime – without missing them" and "swarm the Japanese islands like locusts."[73] Still after Japan had "won every battle by land and sea with an ease shameful to the beaten party," it was thought that the information given on Japan's strength was misleading or that Japan was overstretching its powers and time was on the Chinese side.[74]

---

ed. Yangwen Zheng (Newcastle upon Tyne: Cambridge Scholars Pub., 2013), 146-147; Scott, *China,* 2; Yangwen Zheng, "Hunan: Laboratory of reform and land of revolution: Hunanese in the making of modern China," *Modern Asian Studies* 42:6 (2008), 1123.

67   Lafcadio Hearn, "China and the Western World," *The Atlantic Monthly* 77:462 (1896), 451.

68   Lafcadio Hearn, "The Genius of Japanese Civilization," *The Atlantic Monthly* 76:456 (1895), 449.

69   Lafcadio Hearn, "After the War," *The Atlantic Monthly* 76:457 (1895), 600; Hearn, "China," 451.

70   Hilary A. Herbert, "Military Lessons of the Chino-Japanese War," *The North American Review* 160:463 (1895), 685.

71   "Japan's Victorious Ships," 20.

72   Weipin Tsai, "The First Casualty: Truth, Lies and Commercial Opportunism in Chinese Newspapers during the First Sino-Japanese War," *Journal of the Royal Asiatic Society* 24:1 (2014), 148.

73   "Numbers Will Probably Win," *The New York Times,* August 2, 1894, 5; "The Two Countries' Chances," *The New York Times,* August 2, 1894, 5; "Thinks China Must Win," *The New York Times,* August 2, 1894, 5.

74   "China Will Eventually Win," 28; "The Japanese Danger," 4. One of the few things foretelling good for Japan in these estimates was that, after the Korean government had signed

The early war months witnessed very discrepant reviews of the Japanese Army in the American press. The Japanese Army was noted for being organized along first the French, and then the German model, and drilled by European officers. The officers and their troops were thought to be well trained, but their numbers were small when compared to China. Some commentators doubted the orderliness of the troops, while some emphasized precisely their good discipline. There were also contrasting opinions about the endurance and hardiness of the Japanese soldiers. Overall estimate was that, if well commanded, the Japanese Army was only slightly inferior to, or on par with, European troops.[75] In comparison, the Chinese Army was also lauded as thoroughly drilled, but unlike the Japanese, the Chinese lacked understanding of the military strategies and tactics of modern warfare.[76] Later on, however, views of the Chinese Army grew dimmer. In the *NYT*, the Chinese troops were declared inept and corrupt, and after the supposedly impregnable Port Arthur fell, the military prowess of China was characterized as "paper men, dummy guns, depleted stores, unignitable powder, undermanned ships, and an utter absence of all discipline and authority."[77] Once the war was over, there no longer seemed to be any doubt of the faultlessness of the preparations and conduct of the Japanese Army and the inferiority of the Chinese Army in comparison.[78]

As to the navy, the Chinese Beiyang fleet and Japanese fleet were believed to be quite equal in strength and resources. Both China and Japan had supplied themselves with modern, foreign-built battleships and cruisers, and both had been trained by European and American naval experts. But again in tactics, the Japanese were thought to outstrip the Chinese, and ultimately, this had

---

an agreement on August 26, declaring support for Japanese military actions in maintaining Korean independence, the Japanese were believed to have the firm backing of the Koreans. "China and Japan," 4; Huffman, *Creating a Public*, 207; "Japan's Treaty with Corea," *The New York Times*, September 12, 1894, 5.

75   Heard et al., "China and Japan in Korea," 317; "Military Reviews in Japan," *The New York Times*, August 27, 1894, 3; "The Army of Modern Japan," *The New York Times*, August 13, 1894, 5. The more pessimistic reviews accord with assessments made by historians insofar as the universal male conscription system of 1873, and the revised three-tier structure of active military service launched in 1883, were fraught with problems, such as discontentment and indiscipline, and also evading the draft was common. The Japanese forces were untried, undernourished, and the infantry was armed with outmoded single-shot rifles. Lone, *Japan's First*, 17-18, 28-29.

76   Heard et al., "China and Japan in Korea," 318-319; "Japan's Learned Soldiers," *The New York Times*, January 20, 1895, 14.

77   "Corean Light on the Far East," 12; "Japan's Victorious Ships," 20.

78   Herbert, "Military Lessons," 686-687.

decided the Japanese preponderance at sea.[79] The contemplation on the reasons for China's defeat has continued to the present day. In the "witch-hunt for the inadequacies of the Chinese army and navy," China has been criticized for its failure to industrialize, lack of financial resources, lack of military training, poor leadership, poor preparations, outmoded armaments, shortages of ammunition, being outnumbered in critical battles, and lack of a united, national fleet.[80]

But the contemporaries emphasized patriotism and martial spirit as the qualities that tipped the scales in Japan's favor. They asserted that, throughout their history, the Japanese had been distinguished in war and statecraft. The Japanese were "full of that esprit so essential to the soldier," while the Chinese were not. The Japanese were patriotic; the Chinese were not. And the Japanese nation was united and backing the war with enthusiasm, while the Chinese were "incapable of being aroused and united on any issue of foreign politics."[81] These assertions support Stewart Lone's claim that the stereotype of the Japanese Army and society as fantastically united, patriotic, and inclined to militarism, was established in the course of the Sino-Japanese War.[82] Minister to the U.S. Kurino, however, was intent on downplaying the militaristic image of Japan. Japan's success may have had something to do with the "warlike spirit" of its people, but mainly with patient and systematic planning of the Japanese military organization as an adjunct to national welfare and progress. Besides, the Japanese traditionally noted for their military mindset and accomplishments – the samurai – no longer existed as a class, Kurino reminded, and historically, they had formed only a small portion of the whole population. Japan had attracted the world's attention with its triumphs in war, but its real objective was to secure triumphs in peace, Kurino maintained.[83]

Nevertheless, the end of the Sino-Japanese War inaugurated a decade of further military – especially naval – build-up in Japan. One factor in this was

79   Heard et al., "China and Japan in Korea," 317; "Japan's Victorious Ships," 20; "The War in the East", *The New York Times*, August 1, 1894, 4. The Japanese fleet totaled 32 warships and 23 torpedo boats, built in Britain and France, and manned by 13,928 men. The ships were mainly fast, small protected cruisers. The Chinese navy was divided into the Beiyang, Nanyang, Fujian, and Guangdong fleets. The strongest of them, the Beiyang fleet, alone was roughly the size and strength of Japan's national fleet. Elman, "Naval Warfare," 295, 318-319; Lone, *Japan's First*, 29.

80   Elman, "Naval Warfare," 283, 319-320; Fung, "Testing," 1008, 1010, 1015-1016, 1022, 1026.

81   "China and Japan," *The New York Times*, August 23, 1894, 4; Heard et al., "China and Japan in Korea," 317; Hearn, "After the War," 600; Hearn, "Genius," 449, 457; "The Japanese Danger," 4.

82   Lone, *Japan's First*, 7-8, 69.

83   Shinichiro Kurino, "The Future of Japan," *The North American Review* 160:462 (1895), 622; Kurino, "The Oriental War," 532-533.

the humiliation of the Triple Intervention.[84] Russia, Germany, and France had deeply wounded the Japanese national pride, Lafcadio Hearn explained, and thus the Japanese Army, Navy, and public together clamored for revenge against the powers that snatched away their justly earned spoils of war. But the Japanese government knew that the national navy was yet no match against European navies, let alone a combination of three of them. Realizing that another costly war would be disastrous, the statesmen held the nation back. Instead, they decided to abide their time until they would be strong enough to attack, Hearn thought.[85] Also for the naval architect Charles H. Cramp (1828-1913), it was plain that the Japanese naval preparation was geared towards ensuring that next time Japan would be strong enough to defy any outside interference.[86]

In a series of articles published in the *NAR*, Cramp, together with other members of the American naval circles, urged their compatriots to watch the Japanese naval program very closely. Ships representing the "very latest and highest types of naval architecture in every respect of force, economy and efficiency" were constructed in British shipyards, and the strength of the Japanese Navy was growing in leaps and bounds. Cramp, Hilary A. Herbert, and Commodore George Wallace Melville (1841-1912) from the U.S. Navy warned that the Americans were falling behind Japan in the race for a strong and modern fleet; the American modern war-tonnage equaling to only "about 28 per cent that of Japan." All three authors pointed to Japan's prominence in the Pacific region. If the Americans were to maintain their proper status as a Pacific power, let alone defend themselves against Japan or any other potential menace, the United States could not afford to lose the naval race.[87]

The American Army, too, demanded their share of military expenditures on account of Japan's military strengthening. Japan, it was remarked in the *NYT*, was passing a transitional stage of complete reorganization of its land forces. The Japanese were casting aside all outdated arrangements, and had hugely increased their expenditures in order to create a fighting force ready to take on any opponent by 1902.[88] George B. Duncan (1861-1950), a military officer in the U.S. Army, argued in the *NAR* that the Americans needed to keep up with

---

84   Huffman, *Creating a Public*, 216-217; Lone, *Japan's First*, 45; Paine, *Sino-Japanese War*, 290.
85   Hearn, "After the War," 601-602.
86   Charles H. Cramp, "The Coming Sea-Power," *The North American Review* 165, 491 (1897), 448-449.
87   Cramp, "The Coming Sea-Power," 444, 446-449; Herbert, "Military Lessons," 688, 696, 698; George W. Melville, "Our Future on the Pacific: What We Have There to Hold and Win," *The North American Review* 166:496 (1898), 287, 291.
88   "Japanese Army of To-Day," *The New York Times*, July 2, 1898, 3.

the progress of transportation and science of warfare. They had to secure the latest and best armaments and equipment, and train their troops efficiently, because beyond the Atlantic were the armed camps of Europe, and beyond the Pacific Ocean, Japan had ascended to a first-class military and naval power. And Japan, Duncan claimed, was "ready to measure her strength with ours whenever occasion in conflicting interest presents itself."[89]

The American army and navy circles were more probably promoting their own interests, such as larger budgets, than genuinely alarmed of Japan's growing strength and presence in the Pacific region. But still, Lafcadio Hearn noted, the spectacle of power Japan had exhibited in the Sino-Japanese War had startled the world "like the discovery of a danger." It seemed evident that Japan could invade and subjugate the neighboring China with ease. Quoting the London newspaper, *St. James Gazette*, Hearn described how the Japanese would then civilize the Chinese people, drill the Chinese Army and Navy, arm them with the latest European weapons, and thus create an imposing military force. "If such a power chose to start on a career of conquest, what could resist? Nothing at present in Asia, not even Russia, could stand against it, and it might knock at the door of Europe," Hearn continued the quote. In the end, this "Japanned China" could assert the "supremacy of the yellow race" and rule the earth. Hearn thought that while the vision was indeed possible in theory, it was unrealistic in the sense that no European power would allow such an alliance to take form in the first place.[90]

Hearn did envision a coming struggle between the "white" and "yellow" races, but more on the line with Charles H. Pearson's (1830-1894) volume *National Life and Character* (1893). It would not be a military struggle, but a commercial and industrial contest, which would in the end lead to the demise of Occidental civilization and race. Coming under the influence of Western civilization, the Chinese, like the Japanese before them, would learn to master the tricks of trade and utilization of modern science in manufacture, and enter into keen competition with the Europeans. They would thrive and multiply, and facing the pressure of overpopulation, they would immigrate to other continents. Being adaptable, thrifty, industrious, and content to minimal living standards, they would challenge the Occidental race, accustomed to luxury and pleasure. In this struggle for living space and survival, the chances of the Occidentals looked dismal, Hearn concluded.[91] The low subsistence level of

---

89   George B. Duncan, "Reasons for Increasing the Regular Army," *The North American Review* 166:497 (1898), 452, 457-459.

90   Hearn, "China," 451-452.

91   Ibid., 453-460, 463-464.

the Chinese, and thus low wage claims, combined with their high fertility rates, were arguments that also formed the core of anti-Chinese agitation in the United States during the latter half of the nineteenth century. With the influx of cheap goods from Japan to the American market, the negative sentiments were extended also to the Japanese.[92]

But even though a Japanese and Chinese industrial and commercial threat seemed more plausible to many American observers than the military threat of a Sino-Japanese alliance, the latter idea persisted. For example, in January 1898, the *NYT* cited news from *The Spectator* that Itō Hirobumi had proposed an alliance to the Chinese in order to gain control over the Chinese soldiers and resources. Li Hongzhang was reportedly in favor of the proposal, and if the Chinese would accept it, the European peoples would be beaten, for they could not resist the "united yellow peoples."[93] Frederick Cunliffe-Owen took up the topic a couple of months later in the *Chicago Tribune*. Of all races of the Orient, Cunliffe-Owen announced, the Japanese were the ones capable of forming an alliance of the great Asian nations against those of the Occident. And this alliance, he explained, spelled the doom for the white race, and was the "yellow peril" that haunted Wilhelm II. The two nations together would form such a magnificent army that if this "vast horde" would decide to march westward – "which somehow or other is the trend of every Oriental race" – it would be a repetition of the Hun and Goth invasions of the ancient times.[94]

An alliance between China and Japan was indeed an idea that had been entertained in the Japanese Army before the Sino-Japanese War, but the idea had soon been dropped. After the war, the relations between the two empires grew warmer, as both had come to regard Russia as their mutual enemy. This was the beginning of the "golden decade of Sino-Japanese cooperation." But the Japanese, fully aware of the European and American suspicions and "yellow

---

92   Matthew Connelly, "To inherit the Earth. Imagining World Population, from the Yellow Peril to the Population Bomb," *Journal of Global History* 1 (2006), 300, 302; Iriye, *Japan*, 28; Marilyn Lake and Henry Reynolds, *Drawing the Global Colour Line: White Men's Countries and the International Challenge of Racial Equality* (Cambridge: Cambridge University Press, 2008), 18.

93   "The Policy of Japan," *The New York Times*, January 2, 1898, 19.

94   "No English Defeat," *The Chicago Tribune*, April 10, 1898, 31. A year later, Cunliffe-Owen declared that "the 'Yellow Peril' predicted by the Kaiser" had become "an accomplished fact and a grim reality." He claimed that China and Japan had concluded an agreement and effected an alliance between the two nations. He ventured to predict that the objective of this alliance was to drive off the foreigners from Asia, and perhaps even attack Europe, for both the Chinese and Japanese were "imbued with a bitter and mortal hatred of the white races." "Peril of Yellow Alliance" 1899, 28.

peril" discourse, made sure that these relations did not give an impression of a too close, friendly, and official relationship.[95]

In the 1890s, the fears of immigration and labor competition, and the idea of Japan as a military threat, merged in the *NYT* news reports about Hawaii. Emigration of Japanese contract laborers to Hawaii had started in 1868. Immigration was necessitated by the huge demand for labor in the sugar plantations, and the Japanese were favored as low-cost and reliable work force. The Japanese immigration was carefully regulated, and it was based on the Convention of 1886 negotiated between the Japanese and Hawaiian governments. By the end of the century, the Japanese made up a significant share of the immigrants, and around one quarter of the whole population in the islands. This demographic shift caused concern among the American population, who were intent on preserving their control over the government of Hawaii, and to have the islands annexed to the United States.[96] Some of them claimed that Hawaii should be made into a "white man's country," and the interests of working class whites should be protected from the competition of Asiatic labor.[97] To them, the Japanese laborers seemed like a threat, and they made these anxieties known through constant lobbying in the American press.

The annexationists had sympathizers and allies in the United States. Influential strategists, such as Alfred Thayer Mahan (1840-1914), argued that Hawaii was essential for American security, defense, and naval supremacy.[98] Arthur Curtiss James (1867-1941), wealthy businessman, voiced similar views. He listed reasons for annexation in the *NAR* and concluded that Hawaii was the key to the defense of the American Pacific coast in case a war with Japan should erupt.[99] It was a prevailing belief that if the Americans would not take the islands, some other power, such as Britain or Japan, certainly would. It was claimed that Japan definitely had designs on the islands, and if the United States would withdraw their protection from Hawaii, the Japanese would quickly move in. And as "the naval strength of that young giantess," Japan, grew

---

95   Iriye, *Japan*, 17; Lone, *Japan's First*, 25; Zachmann, *China and Japan*, 4-5, 59-60.

96   Monica Boyd, "Oriental Immigration: The Experience of the Chinese, Japanese, and Filipino Populations in the United States," *The International Migration Review* 5:1 (1971), 9; William Morgon, *Pacific Gibraltar: U.S.-Japanese Rivalry over the Annexation of Hawai'i, 1885-1898* (Annapolis: Naval Institute Press, 2011), 39, 41, 44, 197; William Nimmo, *Stars and Stripes Across the Pacific: The United States, Japan and the Asia/Pacific Region, 1895-1945* (Westport: Greenwood Publishing, 2001), 8-9.

97   "Willis seeks an answer," *The New York Times*, February 2, 1894, 4.

98   Dudden, *American Pacific*, 66; Morgon, *Pacific Gibraltar*, 2, 156, 172, 178, 202.

99   Arthur C. James, "Advantages of Hawaiian Annexation," *The North American Review* 165:493 (1897), 759.

fast, the Japanese would be in a very convenient position to attack the United States if they managed to obtain Hawaii.[100]

Whether Japan would carry out their plans of seizing Hawaii through a political or military coup, or a combination of them, was a matter of some debate. Some observers feared that if the Japanese were given a suffrage in Hawaii, they would "go far toward carrying the islands for their own country" with their large numbers[101]. To counteract this possibility, the (white) oligarchy set to task of creating a permanent government to replace the provisional government, a temporary caretaker of the country after the Hawaiian revolution of 1893. They convened a constitutional convention and established the Republic of Hawaii on 4 July 1894. The constitution they drafted settled the property and literacy qualifications for citizenship and voting rights so that these rights were practically denied from the Japanese.[102] Still, the issue surfaced in the *NYT* repeatedly, particularly during and after the Sino-Japanese War. It was feared that Japan, "flushed with its successes over the Chinese arms," would press on the issue of enfranchisement, and if the immigration would continue unhindered, this people with "great political ambition and martial qualities," was inclined to take over the Hawaiian government.[103] The Japanese Legation at Washington made several attempts to quell these allegations, maintaining that Japan was not an aggressor and did not have territorial ambitions in Hawaii, but apparently to little avail.[104]

The situation became even more strained after the Hawaiian authorities refused entrance from a shipload of Japanese immigrants to the islands in 1897. Japan sent their cruiser Naniwa to Hawaii, according to the Japanese authorities, for the purpose of investigating and settling the issue, and of providing protection for their citizens.[105] The Americans in Hawaii represented the story differently. For them, it was clear that the arrival of Naniwa was a prelude to Japan's seizure of the islands. Soon rumors started to spread in the *NYT* that the Japanese immigrants, "pouring into these islands under the guise of

---

100 "Greedy Eyes on Hawaii," *The New York Times*, March 29, 1893, 1; "Japan's Plans of Conquest," *The New York Times*, July 19, 1897, 5; Melville, "Our Future on the Pacific," 291.

101 "Greedy Eyes on Hawaii", 1.

102 Morgon, *Pacific Gibraltar*, 142, 144-145, 196.

103 "About Hawaiian Annexation," *The New York Times*, December 1, 1894, 3; "Hawaii Fears the Japanese," *The New York Times*, November 18, 1894, 1; "Hawaii Fears the Japanese: They Are Flooding the Islands and Asking for Votes," *The New York Times*, December 17, 1896, 2.

104 "'Japs' Answer Mr. Thurston," *The New York Times*, March 21, 1897, 17; "The New Japan," *The New York Times*, October 25, 1897, 6.

105 "Japan Not Seeking War," *The New York Times*, May 13, 1897, 4; "Japan Vexed At Hawaii," *The New York Times*, June 4, 1897, 4; "No Alarm At Washington," *The New York Times*, April 30, 1897, 3.

'students,'" were, in fact, trained soldiers, who had served in the Sino-Japanese War. "Suspicion of this fact was first aroused by their soldierly bearing and their military gait and movements," it was reported. Another piece of news informed that the Japanese passengers aboard the steamer City of Peking, although classed as laborers, were actually well-drilled soldiers sent to resist the possible American annexation of the islands. Again, this was evidenced by the "remarkably symmetrical movements" of the Japanese passengers. It was also claimed that Japan was about to send 1,500 men more to Hawaii, dressed up as "simple citizens, but drilled and ready for military duty at once," and these men would be transported by ships full of armaments, and followed by Japanese warships.[106]

In the end, these wild rumors died down after the U.S. Congress annexed Hawaii unilaterally on 6 July 1898. The Spanish-American War of 1898 had convinced the Americans of the strategic vitality of having Pearl Harbor as a naval base, and in the geostrategic discussions that preceded the annexation, also the emergence of Japan as a strong Pacific power was among the main considerations. Japan's military build-up and imperialistic foreign policies suggested that the Japanese were preparing for war, and consequently, the Americans should make their preparations, too.[107] Perhaps Japan was not an imminent threat, but it was a potential peril.

Conclusion

The Sino-Japanese War was a widely publicized and closely watched conflict. In a sense, it was a "war of the media," for press coverage had a huge impact on how the combatants were viewed, and thus also on the foreign relations of these nations.[108] The power of the press was not lost on the Japanese. While the Chinese either sought or received far less press exposure, the Japanese tried to influence the American public opinion actively and directly through publicizing official reports, using their diplomats as mouthpieces, feeding favorable images of the Japanese armed forces and their maneuvers to the public,

---

106 "Japanese in Hawaii," *The New York Times*, September 23, 1897, 5; "Hawaii Becomes Alarmed," *The New York Times*, April 18, 1897, 22; "Ready to Annex Hawaii," *The New York Times*, June 15, 1897, 4; "War Story from Japan," *The New York Times*, July 28, 1897, 7. According to William Morgon, it was more than probable that some of the Japanese laborers had indeed served in the army, considering the Japanese conscription laws. Morgon, *Pacific Gibraltar*, 113.

107 Dudden, *American Pacific*, 68; Morgon, *Pacific Gibraltar*, 5, 172-173.

108 Lone, *Japan's First*, 35; Paine, *Sino-Japanese War*, 4; Svarverud, *International Law*, 60; Tsai, "The First Casualty," 146, 159.

and marshalling legal experts to affirm their adherence to the laws of civilized warfare. There is also mounting evidence that the Japanese manipulated the foreign press more subtly. They controlled the access of foreign observers to the war front and telegraph; censored official dispatches; and forged close ties with the owner of the *Japan Weekly Mail*, who then forwarded the war news he received from the Japanese government to the British press and news agencies. The *NYT* obtained its war news from these sources, too. In addition, the Japanese attempted and succeeded in bribing certain European and American press organs.[109]

Initially, the Japanese propaganda machine was clearly successful in the United States. The Japanese military tactics were lauded. Towards the end of the war, the armed forces were extolled for their discipline and efficiency, despite of the few breaches of the Geneva Convention. Legal experts exonerated Japanese conduct in the Kowshing and Port Arthur incidents from the point of view of international law, and the perceived victory of Japanese 'civilization' over Chinese 'barbarism' ended the discussion on whether Japanese prosecution of the war had accorded with morality. But in the long-term, as Stewart Lone has suggested,[110] the Japanese victory, along with the Japanese diplomatic strategy, may have not been successes at all. Japan impressed the United States with its military strength, favorably at first, but the war also inaugurated the image of Japan as a military yellow peril, taking the forms of Sino-Japanese alliance and Japanese occupation of Hawaii in the United States press. Often the image was accentuated by racial and Orientalist discourses, and utilized for promoting the interests of various groups, ranging from the Americans residing in Hawaii to the U.S. Army and Navy circles.

We should heed the remark of Iriye Akira, that neither the Americans nor Europeans were hysterical about the Japanese yellow peril at the end of the nineteenth century. Because if they had been, they would have opposed, not assisted and celebrated, the Japanese military build-up and emergence as a great power.[111] Nevertheless, the image of Japan as a military threat proved lasting. The outcome of the Russo-Japanese War (1904–1905), coupled with fear of Japanese naval power, and alarm over Japanese immigration, ushered the yellow peril scenario back to the fore during the first decade of the twentieth century, and then again in the 1920s.[112] The image was also reflected in the joint U.S. naval and army strategy titled "War Plan Orange" – orange being the color

---

109   Kane, "Each of Us," 26-27; Barak Kushner, *The Thought War: Japanese Imperial Propaganda* (Honolulu: University of Hawaii Press, 2005), 14; Nimmo, *Stars and Stripes*, 19-20, 22.
110   Lone, *Japan's First*, 179-180.
111   Iriye, *Japan*, 20-21.
112   Sadao Asada, *Culture Shock and Japanese-American Relations* (Columbia: University of Missouri Press 2007), 38, 64.

code for Japan. The plan was first drafted in 1906, and then periodically updated and adapted to the changing circumstances up until the World War II. All versions of the plan identified Japan as the likely U.S. enemy, and maintained the importance of safeguarding American naval bases in the Pacific, especially Hawaii and the Philippines, from Japanese aggression.[113]

Works Cited

Asada, Sadao. *Culture Shock and Japanese-American Relations*. Columbia: University of Missouri Press, 2007.

Benson, John; and Takao Matsumura. *Japan, 1868-1945: From Isolation to Occupation*. Essex: Pearson Education, 2001.

Blue, Gregory. "Gobineau on China: Race Theory, the 'Yellow Peril,' and the Critique of Modernity." *Journal of World History* 10:1 (1999), 93-139.

Boyd, Monica. "Oriental Immigration: The Experience of the Chinese, Japanese, and Filipino Populations in the United States." *The International Migration Review* 5:1 (1971), 48-61.

Chen, Edward. "Japan's Decision to Annex Taiwan: A Study of Ito-Mutsu Diplomacy, 1894-95." *The Journal of Asian Studies* 37:1 (1977), 61-72.

Connelly, Matthew. "To Inherit the Earth. Imagining World Population, from the Yellow Peril to the Population Bomb." *Journal of Global History* 1 (2006), 299-319.

Dudden, Arthur. *The American Pacific: From the Old China Trade to the Present*. New York: Oxford University Press, 1992.

Elman, Benjamin. "Naval Warfare and the Refraction of China's Self-Strengthening Reforms into Scientific and Technological Failure, 1865–1895." *Modern Asian Studies* 38:2 (2004), 283-326.

Elman, Benjamin. "The 'Rise' of Japan and the 'Fall' of China after 1895." In *The Chinese Chameleon Revisited: From the Jesuits to Zhang Yimou*, edited by Yangwen Zheng, 143-171. Newcastle upon Tyne: Cambridge Scholars Publishing, 2013.

Eykholt, Mark. "Aggression, Victimization, and Chinese Historiography of the Nanjing Massacre." In *The Nanjing Massacre in History and Historiography*, edited by Joshua Fogel, 11-69. Berkeley: University of California Press, 2000.

Ford, Douglas. *The Elusive Enemy*. Annapolis: Naval Institute Press, 2011.

---

113   Asada, *Culture Shock*, 37–39, 65–67; Douglas Ford, *The Elusive Enemy* (Annapolis: Naval Institute Press 2011), 21-22; Louis Morton, "War Plan Orange: Evolution of a Strategy," *World Politics* 11:2 (1959), 222, 232, 234-235; David J. Ulbrich, "The Long Lost 'Tentative Manual for Defense of Advanced Bases' (1936)," *The Journal of Military History* 71:3 (2007), 890-891.

Fung, Allen. "Testing the Self-Strengthening: The Chinese Army in the Sino-Japanese War of 1894-1895." *Modern Asian Studies* 30:4 (1996), 1007-1031.

Henning, Joseph. *Outposts of Civilization: Race, Religion, and the Formative Years of American-Japanese Relations*. New York: New York University Press, 2000.

Howland, Douglas. "Japan's Civilized War: International Law as Diplomacy in the Sino-Japanese War (1894-1895)." *Journal of the History of International Law* 9:2 (2007), 179-202.

Howland, Douglas. "The Sinking of the S. S. Kowshing: International Law, Diplomacy, and the Sino-Japanese War." *Modern Asian Studies* 42:4 (2008), 673-703.

Huffman, James. *Creating a Public: People and Press in Meiji Japan*. Honolulu: University of Hawaii Press, 1997.

Hwang, Kyung Moon. *A History of Korea*. Houndmills: Palgrave Macmillan, 2010.

Iriye, Akira. *From Nationalism to Internationalism: US Foreign Policy to 1914*. London: Routledge, 1965.

Iriye, Akira. *Across the Pacific: An Inner History of American-East Asian Relations*. New York: Harcourt, Brace & World, 1967.

Iriye, Akira. *Japan and the Wider World: From the Mid-nineteenth Century to the Present*. London: Longman, 1997.

Kane, Daniel. "Each of Us in His Own Way: Factors Behind Conflicting Accounts of the Massacre at Port Arthur." *Journalism History* 31:1 (2005), 23-33.

Kowner, Rotem. "'Lighter than Yellow, but not Enough': Western Discourse on the Japanese 'Race', 1854-1904." *The Historical Journal* 43:1 (2000), 103-131.

Kushner Barak. *The Thought War: Japanese Imperial Propaganda*. Honolulu: University of Hawaii Press, 2005.

Lai, Junnan. "Sovereignty and 'Civilization': International Law and East Asia in the Nineteenth Century." *Modern China* 40:3 (2014), 282-314.

Lake, Marilyn and Henry Reynolds. *Drawing the Global Colour Line: White Men's Countries and the International Challenge of Racial Equality*. Cambridge: Cambridge University Press, 2008.

Lone, Stewart. *Japan's First Modern War: Army and Society in the Conflict with China, 1894-95*. New York: St. Martin's Press, 1994.

Metraux, Daniel. "First Introduction." In *E. Warren Clark's Life and Adventure in Japan*, edited by Daniel Metraux, and Jessica Puglisi, 3-22. San Jose: Writers Club Press, 2002.

Morgon, William. *Pacific Gibraltar: U.S.-Japanese Rivalry over the Annexation of Hawai'i, 1885-1898*. Annapolis: Naval Institute Press, 2011.

Morton, Louis. "War Plan Orange: Evolution of a Strategy." *World Politics* 11:2 (1959), 221-250.

Neumann, William. *America Encounters Japan: From Perry to MacArthur*. Baltimore: Johns Hopkins Press, 1963.

Nimmo, William. *Stars and Stripes Across the Pacific: The United States, Japan and the Asia/Pacific Region, 1895–1945*. Westport: Greenwood Publishing, 2001.

Paine, S.C.M. *The Sino-Japanese War of 1894-1895: Perceptions, Power, and Primacy*. Cambridge: Cambridge University Press, 2003.

Schencking, Charles. *Making Waves: Politics, Propaganda, and the Emergence of the Imperial Japanese Navy*, 1868-1922. Palo Alto: Stanford University Press, 2004.

Scott, David. *China and the International System, 1840-1949: Power, Presence, and Perceptions in a Century of Humiliation*. Ithaca: SUNY Press, 2008.

Svarverud, Rune. *International Law as World Order in Late Imperial China: Translation, Reception and Discourse, 1847-1911*. Boston: Brill, 2007.

Tsai, Weipin. "The First Casualty: Truth, Lies and Commercial Opportunism in Chinese Newspapers during the First Sino-Japanese War." *Journal of the Royal Asiatic Society* 24:1 (2014), 145-163.

Ulbrich, David J. "The Long Lost 'Tentative Manual for Defense of Advanced Bases' (1936)." *The Journal of Military History* 71:3 (2007), 889-901.

Yamamoto, Masahiro. *Rape of Nanking*. Westport: Greenwood Publishing, 2000.

Yoshida, Takashi. *Making of the "Rape of Nanking"*. New York: Oxford University Press, 2006.

Zachmann, Urs M. *China and Japan in the Late Meiji Period: China Policy and the Japanese Discourse on National Identity*, 1895-1904. New York: Routledge, 2009.

Zheng, Yangwen. "Hunan: Laboratory of Reform and Land of Revolution: Hunanese in the Making of Modern China." *Modern Asian Studies* 42:6 (2008), 1113-1136.

CHAPTER 4

Gallant Little Soldiers: The Boxer Uprising and the Development of a Martial Image of Japan

Joseph Fonseca

Introduction: a Grand Spectacle

On a sunny Saturday afternoon in early May, 1901, the Duke of Cambridge officially opened the Earl's-Court Military Exhibition in London.[1] Here, for the benefit of invalid soldiers and public opinion alike, civilians could marvel at all facets of British military life. Uniforms, paintings, souvenirs, and battlefield trophies were arrayed across many pavilions and halls for all to admire. If a visitor tired of wandering and wished to rest with a grand spectacle of recent military adventure and derring-do, they sought out the Empress Theatre. Travelling past a reception chamber constructed entirely from the detritus of war, past the Belgian artillery exhibit, up the novel "Reno Inclined Elevator," visitors confronted the beauty of the Central Hall, where they could purchase a ticket to witness Imre Kiralfy's (1845-1919) historical military spectacle "China" or "The Relief of the Legations."[2]

The spectacle, which played twice a day for the exhibition's duration, retold the story of the siege and relief of the Beijing legations, which had so recently ensnared the minds of the Western world as soldiers from eight nations fought to rescue civilians and diplomats trapped by the chaos of China's Boxer Uprising. The spectacle sought to convey the events surrounding the siege as accurately as possible, much to the dismay of some reviewers, who balked at the use of so recent an event.[3] Despite a grand set and expensive effects, the play was not well received. The use of a live pig in a scene, ostensibly for comic relief, instead drowned out the actors and elicited sympathy from the crowd. Though it never spread beyond the exhibition, "The Relief of the Legations" expressed many of the "truths" Westerners had come to hold about the Boxer Uprising. German Minister Baron Clemens von Ketteler (1853-1900), murdered

---

1 "Earl's-Court Military Exhibition," *The Times*, May 6, 1901, 8.
2 Imre Kiralfy, *Military Exhibition: 1901. Earl's Court, S.W.*, (London: J.J. Keliher & Co., 1901), 40-46.
3 Ibid., 8.

© VERLAG FERDINAND SCHÖNINGH, 2020 | DOI:10.30965/9783657702930_005

en route to discuss the Chinese government's reaction to the Boxers, was portrayed as a hero, saving local Christians from marauding Boxers with his bullwhip until he was eventually brought down. The heroic speech given by Captain Myers (1871-1952) of the United States Marines before he led a contingent to capture Qing Chinese guns threatening civilian positions also received a scene, though the Russians who accompanied the British and American troops were suspiciously absent. Finally, during a tense scene in which allied forces from the Eight Nation Army fought towards the capital, the Japanese were given centre stage, demonstrating their military prowess and unerring bravery by smartly setting up and firing cannon before urging the Americans and British to not tarry.[4]

While the play was confined to the Earl's-Court Military Exhibition, it offers an example, albeit grandiose, of how the Boxer Uprising was memorialized immediately after the event itself. By the summer of 1901, soldiers of the various involved armies remained in China with the final peace treaty, the Boxer Protocol, not yet signed. Yet for the nations of the West, especially Britain and America, the story of the Boxer Uprising ended with the relief of the Beijing legations on the 15 August 1900. The months and years that followed this relief saw many eyewitnesses, journalists, and military men publish accounts, dairies, newspaper articles, and narratives of their experiences besieged in Beijing or travelling with the relief forces. With so many Western nations involved, and the stark images of civilization and barbarism that encompassed discussion of the Boxers, the popularity of the Boxer Uprising in the West cannot be ignored. During the siege, newspapers constantly offered updates, sometimes completely unfounded, about conditions in Beijing or on the progress of the relief efforts. After the foreign legations in Beijing were freed, participants and eyewitnesses profited from this explosive popularity. These works will be collectively referred to as the Post-Boxer Publications. These publications offer many interpretations of the Boxer Uprising; yet important consistencies emerge among them.

This chapter will focus on one trend that appeared in many of these works. The portrayal of Japanese defenders of the foreign legations in the Chinese capital and Japanese members of the relieving force of the Eight Nation Allied Army was almost universal. The predominant image of the Japanese, which before this time consisted of a small, diminutive, "toy land" description, was supplemented in the Post-Boxer Publications by a civilizing, martial image. The sheer volume of these martial allusions and the appreciative and astounded tone with which Western authors described the Japanese helped to signal

---

4   Ibid., 40-46.

a definitive shift in the dominant Western image of the Japanese. The image of a valiant, modern, and martial nation would, from this point until 1904, be held alongside that of the previously dominant soft image. Kiralfy's play offered a visual representation of this phenomenon, with scene III's description reading, "With bugles playing a lively march, the gallant little Japanese arrive at the double with their three quick-firing guns, and they quickly demonstrate their smart artillery practice by sending a hail of bullets after the retreating Chinese. With equal alacrity they turn and prepare to attack the Upper Gate."[5] Demonstrating bravery and skill at arms, the Japanese were treated no differently in this stage play than the British or Americans.

Images of national characteristics are, by nature, complex and multifaceted. Multiple images often compete for dominance in the minds of observers, with several at play at once. Although these images overlap, generally one dominates. John Ferris's metaphor of a deck of cards, with several cards in motion and others at rest, conveys this complexity.[6] Images of a soft Japan, a barbarous Japan, or a martial Japan, all exist within the deck of cards, but only certain images are visible on the table. Less popular images remain hidden within the deck, potentially ready to play. Understanding when dominant images begin to lose ground or when other images become entrenched in the popular understanding, when cards are shuffled back into the deck or others are played on the table, to continue the metaphor, enables a fuller exploration of how images of national characteristics shape international diplomacy and military assessment.

Currently, the Russo-Japanese War of 1904/05 holds the spotlight as the moment a martial image of the Japanese supplanted the soft one and allowed Japan to take its place as an honorary civilized nation. Rotem Kowner suggests that, immediately before the Russo-Japanese War, some Westerners emphasized the soft image and viewed the Japanese military with contempt, sarcasm, and humour.[7] This assessment suggests that the soft image remained dominant during the period leading up to the Russo-Japanese War, but does not reveal the other images that lay alongside it on the table. The Post-Boxer Publications put a martial card in play alongside the soft one as early as late 1900. This newly played card, which had existed since the modern opening of Japan in 1853, did not replace the soft image. It merely joined it at the forefront of Western

---

5   Ibid., 45.

6   John Ferris, "Turning Japanese: British Observation of the Russo-Japanese War," in *Rethinking the Russo-Japanese War, 1904-5 Volume II: The Nichinan Papers*, ed. John Chapman and Inaba Chihiru (Folkstone: Global Oriental, 2007), 122.

7   Rotem Kowner, "Becoming an Honorary Civilized Nation: Remaking Japan's Military Image during the Russo-Japanese War, 1904-1905," *The Historian* 64:1 (2001), 19.

understanding. Only the grand scale of the Russo-Japanese War returned the soft image to the deck, but to ignore the martial image is to misconstrue how contemporary Westerners viewed Japan's place among the powers and the significance of the Boxer Uprising as a defining moment for Japan's Image.

Post-Boxer Publications conveyed so drastic a shift in the dominant image of Japan because of the uniquely international structure of the Boxer Uprising. The siege of the foreign legations in Beijing and the relief efforts that followed from the coast were organized multinational fighting forces. These forces fought cooperatively against a common Chinese enemy, and were always in close operational contact, with different nationalities fighting side by side. This created a unique situation wherein the cooperative struggle against the Boxers and regular Chinese units became an arena in which nationalities competed, often implicitly, but sometimes explicitly, against each other. The arena of the siege of Beijing and the arena of the Eight Nation Allied Army inform the structure of this chapter, as each provided a different set of circumstances that nevertheless contributed to a growing appreciation of Japanese martial skill in the Post-Boxer Publications. These arenas allowed the Japanese to demonstrate the modern military skill and the bravery that had led them to defeat China five years earlier and, more significantly, allowed them to match or even outperform Western nationals during the Boxer Uprising. The Boxer Uprising then becomes a watershed moment, where the martial image joins the soft image in the dominant collection on the table, beginning a process that continued until 1905 and their victory over Russia solidified that image as dominant. Instead of the defeat of a Western army in 1905, Japan's "defeat" of Westerners in the arenas of the Boxer Uprising provided the catalyst for change in perceptions.

Constructed Images: Understanding a Mysterious Japan

Constructed Western images of the Japanese had existed in Britain for some time before even the Sino-Japanese War (1894/95) caught attention there. As the American Commodore Matthew C. Perry (1794-1858) raced towards Japan on his mission to "open" the country in 1853, Western images were hurriedly thrown together with limited available knowledge. These images consisted of a mixture of established East Asian stereotypes and Japanese specific quirks gathered from the writings of early missionaries and sailors. Early British writing about the nature of Japan, especially that which predates Commodore Perry's expedition in 1853, introduced several important concepts.

First, Japan was unknown. Writers and scholars who wished to capitalize on Japan's sudden explosion in popularity had to use outdated sources. Toshio

Yokoyama notes in his work, *Japan in the Victorian Mind*, that Victorian writers assumed that Japan, as part of East Asia, would follow the societal and racial examples of China.[8] These assumptions generally went unquestioned by readers despite their dubious origins. Western images tended to view China as a great unchanging empire, and authors extended that assumption to Japan, influenced by the writings of sixteenth century explorers and missionaries that cast the Japanese in a diminutive role compared to China. Ultimately, a strange mixture of Chinese and outdated Japanese information created the bedrock of mid-nineteenth century perceptions of how the Japanese conducted themselves. The first British construction of a Japanese image therefore emphasized a small or "toy land" image, tempered by an unchanging medieval outlook that, despite its similarities to China, had the potential to become "civilized."

The small or "toy land" image reflected an idea that Japan was populated by dainty, effectively childlike, objects and people. The idea came to Europe not only through medieval writing, but also from the appearance of Japanese aesthetics, most obviously represented through what meagre quantities Europe received of Japanese art and architecture. In effect, the small image cast by Japanese art and architecture suggested a diminutive, feminine quality within Japanese themselves. This image was not monolithic. The small image meshed with the supposed "unchanging" and "medieval" aspects of the Western construction. Early writers blended these ideas together, reinforcing them with contemporary racial ideas to create a pervasive notion in the West of how the Japanese acted.

Western powers also saw a martial image in the highly visible samurai class. Their involvement in terrorism against Westerners produced images of barbarism and martial prowess. Beginning in 1859, samurai attacks on foreign sailors and merchants, including several murders, began to cause alarm. These and other high profile attacks, including the murder of Henry Heusken (1832-1861), the secretary to the American legation, were well documented. In light of this, Rutherford Alcock's (1809-1897) memoir portrayed the samurai as ruthless.[9] Writing from Alcock's dispatches, the *Edinburgh Review* echoed his sentiment in casting the samurai as bullies and a terror. This fear was epitomized by the bloody assault on Tōzenji, a Buddhist temple that housed the British legation. More than a dozen Samurai from Mito launched an attack that saw two killed

---

8 Toshio Yokoyama, *Japan in the Victorian Mind: A Study of Stereotyped Images of a Nation 1850-80* (London: MacMillan, 1987), 4.

9 Michael Auslin, "Terrorism and Treaty Port Relations: Western Images of the Samurai during Bakumatsu and early Meiji Japan," in *Images and Identity: Rethinking Japanese Cultural History*, eds. Jeffery E. Hanes and Hidetoshi Yamaji (Kobe: The Research Institute for Economics and Business Administration Kobe University, 2004), 151.

and at least ten wounded.[10] Similarly, when these attacks prompted British officials to push for an indemnity, and prepare a potential invasion to ensure payment, Admiral Küper, who planned the attack, expressed concern about the "... hundreds of thousands of armed and resolute men which it is in the power of Japan to produce at any point."[11] This martial image existed, but because of the scarcity of violence beyond these terrorist attacks, it remained firmly in the deck and away from any dominant position. The victories that Japan won in the arenas of the Boxer Uprising allowed the then dominant Western image of Japan as a nation of small, soft people to incorporate this dormant martial image.

Under Siege in Beijing: Japanese Military Grace Under Pressure

The siege of the Beijing legations was the most important arena of the Boxer Uprising. Marines, diplomats, and civilians of a dozen different nations occupied the tight space of the legation quarter as it came under fire, first from Boxers, and then regular Qing forces in the summer of 1900. Sir Claude M. MacDonald (1852-1912), the British Minister, quickly took control and organized the defences with input from the leadership of the other powers. Centring their defence on the British Legation and the closer, sturdier buildings, MacDonald and the others organized the approximately 400 marines and 100 volunteers to man different sections of the hastily constructed barricades. These different sections each came with their own set challenges and assumed level of danger. The United States and German forces on the Tartar wall, for example, were under near constant surveillance and harassing fire from without while the Japanese, who primarily made up the defense of the Su Wang Fu palace, endured regular assaults. Aside from the implicit connotations of nationally occupied defences, multinational sorties and nationals' actions during times of rest also played into the narratives. Almost all aspects of life during the siege were visible to the other besieged, and the abundance of academically inclined individuals among those trapped ensured that the arena was recorded along with all the biases one would expect of 1900.

Leadership roles played heavily into the narratives at Beijing beginning with MacDonald's appropriation of power at the outset of the troubles. The commander of the Austrian SMS Zenta, Eduard Thomann Edler von Montalmar

---

10   Ibid.

11   Hamish Ion, "Days of Seclusion," in *The History of Anglo-Japanese Relations, 1600-2000,* vol. 3: *The Military Dimension* (New York: Palgrave Macmillan, 2003), 7.

(d.1900), who was the senior ranking officer, was originally in command until a series of blunders, many of which endangered the entire legation quarter, saw him replaced by MacDonald. Thomann's replacement gave MacDonald a heroic disposition within the Post-Boxer Publications, creating a sense of fluidity to authority that supported the rise of skilled leadership.

This fluidity in particular affected Japan's role within siege leadership and eventually the Post-Boxer Publications. Colonel Shiba Gorō (1860-1945) was the Japanese military attaché in Beijing before the Boxer Uprising intensified. He played a major role as commander of the Japanese military and civilian volunteers throughout the duration of the siege.[12] Originally, Colonel Shiba's role was muted, and his quiet demeanour merely reinforced the contemporary dominant image of the Japanese as soft-spoken and small. Mary Hooker (1876-1918), an American, offered a sketch of the colonel in her diary:

> Apropos of Colonel Shiba, he is a splendid, small person. He has taken his position here by the strength of his intelligence, and good right arm, solely because the Ministers and the guard captains were not especially inclined at the first morning conference to listen to him – in fact, I don't know that he tried to talk, but it is all changed now.[13]

Hooker's account of Shiba demonstrates a continuation of accepted images, but also allowed the stark situation of the siege, his undeniable skill, and his bravery to color this interpretation. She continued, "He has done so splendidly in his active and continuous fighting in the Fu, and has proved himself such a general, that his opinion and help are asked by all the commanders."[14]

Shiba's excellent command of the Fu defences was critical to the achievement of this position of respect. The Fu was a large palace with a grand, once-beautiful garden at its centre. Colonel Shiba prepared a multilayered defense to allow for giving and retaking ground. The area was strategically significant, commanding a view of the last ditch, the British legation. Due to the strategic importance of the Fu, several nations contributed small contingents to its defence, but Shiba's Japanese were front and centre. Eugène Darcy, the commander of the French detachment at Beijing, normally very reserved in his account of the Siege, complemented Shiba's work calling the defenses at the

---

12   Claude A. MacDonald, "The Japanese Detachment During the Defense of the Peking Legations, 1900," in *Transactions and Proceedings of the Japan Society London*, ed. Henri L. Joly (Nendeln: Kraus Reprint, 1971), 2-5.

13   Mary Hooker, *Behind the Scenes in Peking: Being the Experiences During the Siege of the Legations* (London: John Murray, Albemarle Street, W. 1910), 95.

14   Ibid.

Fu "truly remarkable."[15] Mary Hooker was also pleasantly surprised by the Japanese soldiers at the Fu: "His men are all so patient and untiring in their long, long, hours behind the barricades, and are so game, in great contrast to the Italians who are with him defending the Fu. One can only hope for Italy's sake that her soldiers in [Beijing] are the worst she has."[16] Hooker's direct comparison reveals the importance of the arena. The Italian soldiers were occupying the same defences as the Japanese, but their relative performance was lacking, pushing the worth of the Japanese higher.

Not only was Colonel Shiba a brave commander, but he also had a cunning streak about him. With the Boxer and Qing forces continually pressing into the Fu and threatening to break the defences. Shiba approached Sir Claude MacDonald with an idea. MacDonald records in his official report that Colonel Shiba sent a messenger with a paper saying, "Dear Sir, They are nearing to break down the Fu's wall. I want to crush them when they come in. Will you please send some more reinforcements to me with the bearer?"[17] This MacDonald swiftly did. Shiba planned to position his meagre forces around the point of entry in such a way as to deny the attackers cover from any angle. When they broke through, they were met with a withering hail of fire that left twenty dead on the spot and put the rest to flight. News of the success quickly spread and was recorded in a number of journals. Roland Allen (1868-1947), a minister who often tended to the wounded defenders, wrote, "It was said that the Japanese, who defended that quarter, deliberately let the enemy in … It was said that a good many were killed, and it has further been argued that their failure to take advantage of mistakes made by some of the forces in retiring from their posts later on in the siege was due to the fear of being again caught in such a trap."[18] Lancelot Giles (1878-1934), a volunteer and son of the influential Sinologist Herbert A. Giles (1845-1935), stated that "Colonel Shiba wanted to let the Chinese force their way into the Fu, as they have been trying to do; and then slaughter them. This was considered too risky. He really is a splendid officer."[19]

15   Eugène Darcy, *La Défense de la Légation de France* (Paris: Augustin Challamel, Éditeur, Rue Jacob, 17, 1903), 151.

16   Hooker, *Behind the Scenes*, 95.

17   Sir Claude A. MacDonald, *The Siege of the Peking Legations: Sir Claude A. MacDonald's Report on the Boxer Rebellion*, ed. Tim Coates (London: The Stationary Office, 2000), 172.

18   Roland Allen, *The Siege of Peking 1900: Being the Diary of the Rev. Allen Roland Allen* (London: Smith Elder and Co, 1901), 162.

19   Lancelot Giles, *The Siege of the Peking Legations: A Diary by Lancelot Giles*, ed. L. R. Marchant (Nedlands: University of Western Australia Press, 1970), 131.

Many volunteers and civilians recorded their thoughts on the Fu and Colonel Shiba's role there. Giles often wrote in his siege diary about the skill of the various contingents around him. "[The Japanese Colonel Shiba] is considered the best officer up here, just as the Japanese are undoubtedly the best soldiers. Their pluck and daring is astounding, our marines are next to them in this respect; but I think the Japanese lead the way."[20] Giles account has less pleasant words for other contingents and officers as well, calling the French Minister a "poltroon" for his fear of a 3-pounder gun that lobbed shells into the compound.[21] Giles was also wary about the morality of some other contingents, and records hearing reports of overeager fire from Austrians and Russians which often resulted in civilian deaths.[22] William A. P. Martin (1827-1916), an American professor in Beijing and active defender, commended the Japanese in his memoir and grouped them with the Americans and Germans, who had a good deal of trouble defending the Tartar wall.[23] These reports all contain the same, almost surprised tone concerning the Japanese defence of the Fu. Pressed in an actual combat scenario, the Japanese were proving time and again to be more disciplined, better led, and martially skilled than most of the Europeans around them. The visible leadership of Colonel Shiba greatly compounded these arena successes. By treading the line between the stereotypical Japanese gentlemen of late Victorian imagination and the calm, resourceful, and brave commander he proved to be in the field, European observers were forced to acknowledge the martial side of Japan in their constructed images.

The legation quarter's makeshift hospital provides a second arena within the confines of the Siege of Beijing where the Japanese were compared against Europeans. Several civilians, both men and women, worked as doctors and nurses to treat and provide continued care to the wounded from the barricades. The hospital was cramped, with a persistent lack of supplies exaggerating the already dire situation facing many of its occupants. There was no separation of wounded along national lines, and doctors and nurses tended all regardless of linguistic difficulties.

Jessie Ransome (d. 1905), who served as a nurse, published her account of the siege under the name *The Story of the Siege Hospital in Peking* and dedicated space to the description of her patients. According to Ransome, the Japanese soldiers complained very little and she praises them for their stoicism. The

---

20   Ibid., 127.
21   Ibid.
22   Ibid., 118-119.
23   William A. P. Martin, *The Siege in Peking: China Against the World.* (London: Oliphant Anderson and Ferrier, 1900), 83, 99-100.

most she could get out of them were small inconsequential comments like "good" and "very little pain."[24] Against these contained individuals she ranked the quality of the Western nationalities under her care, with French and Italians being most hassle and British and Americans generally being much better.[25] Though these general levels held, she did acknowledge some diversity in her European patients, with a quiet Frenchman or arrogant American dotted amongst the crowd. The Japanese were reserved a special spot for their consistency, "the only nationality of whose conduct one could predict anything with almost absolute certainty was the Japanese. They invariably were brave and cheery, and made as light as possible of their pains."[26] The hospital arena created stark, easily visible contrasts for Ransome and again demonstrated martial qualities within the diminutive Japanese. Treating these "small" individuals against the Westerners created an image of the Japanese that reinforced martial ideas and began to marginalize the dominant soft image, and justify one that incorporated both soft and martial qualities

Roland Allen, the minister quoted above, also recorded his thoughts of the Japanese patients, his major contribution being a short anecdote that would occasionally resurface in later tales of the siege. Allen's story, which appears in his memoir, contains several allusions to the mixture of soft and martial images of the Japanese.

> When I went into the ward I found that Kuchiki, the Japanese with the shattered knee, had moved his pillows to the other end of his bed, and had swung himself round, so that his feet were in the place where his head had been. I asked the reason, and was told that the sun shone on his head, and he found it hot. I asked who had moved him and he explained that no one had moved him, he had moved himself. I point out with some vigour that he had run great risk in screwing himself about whilst his knee was in that critical condition, and generally tried to impress upon him that he had played the fool. Alas! I only succeeded in making him understand that I was annoyed at his moving, and when I returned in ten minutes' time he had changed round again, and received me with a smile of conscious virtue. I was vain to upbraid, one could only laugh.

---

24   Jessie Ransome, *The Story of The Siege Hospital in Peking: And Diary of the Events from May to August, 1900*. (London: Society for Promoting Christian Knowledge, 1901), 20.

25   Ibid.

26   Ibid.

> But what European afflicted with even a simple fracture would have attempted such a thing?[27]

Allen's story presents a soldier that both exhibits supreme physical strength and also a childish naivety that easily demonstrates the combined images. As with most of these stories, Kuchiki's actions are contrasted against that of the Europeans, who would never have attempted something so foolhardy. Europeans who read these works were able to more easily slot a martial image of the Japanese, which emphasized such bravery into their perceptions while maintaining the integrity of the small image.

As with other areas of the siege, the hospital's arena allowed observers to judge the relative ability and character of a variety of nations. Though it was not always clear how Ransome actually ranked the Europeans, it is clear that the Japanese composed themselves well where many Europeans did not, allowing for the reassessment of images to continue in this arena and to place Japan as a more martially inclined nation than several of the other present Europeans.

Putting aside individual stories of bravery and the highly visible Colonel Shiba, most post-boxer narratives include general praise for the effort that the Japanese volunteers and marines exerted in the defence. The Japanese soldiers were exposed to a seemingly greater deal of danger, and their collective heroism was clearly visible to those who depended on them to keep the British Legation safe. Therefore, it became common in diaries and reports to comment on the martial prowess of the Japanese soldiers and volunteers as a group. Nigel Oliphant recounts a scene after the siege was lifted where the Japanese defenders were separated and given a rousing cheer for their efforts.[28] Other reports make it clear that the Westerners were especially thankful of the Japanese effort throughout the siege. After several weeks of constant vigilance, Colonel Shiba asked Claude MacDonald to relieve his soldiers. MacDonald reported:

> The men were exhausted; they had been up on duty night and day since the commencement of the siege, and had none of them even changed their clothes since the 20th June nor had they had more than three or four hours of consecutive sleep during that time; he begged that, if possible, half might be taken off duty for a clear twenty-four hours, and

---

27   Allen, *Siege of Peking*, 199-200.
28   Nigel Oliphant, *A Diary of the Siege of the Legations in Peking During the Summer of 1900* (New York: Longmans, Green, and Co., 1901), 75, 181.

replaced by British marines and volunteers, after which the second half might be relieved in a similar manner ... It was arranged that, although our people were in the same plight, an effort should be made to carry out Colonel Shiba's wishes. The marines and volunteers responded with alacrity to this call made upon them, for they knew what splendid work the Japanese had done and were doing.[29]

MacDonald's report suggested that it was common knowledge that the Japanese contingent had been pulling more than its weight in the defence of the legations, and the enthusiastic response from the British volunteers and marines makes it clear that they were well respected for their martial qualities as little as a few weeks into the siege proper.

Relieving the Legations: the Japanese Contingent on Campaign

Though the siege proved to be a critical space for the development of the British perception of the Japanese image, the organized relief of Beijing provided a similar opportunity on a larger scale. The specifics of these relief campaigns also created a unique situation that generally benefitted the construction of a more martial Japanese image. The difficulty in rapidly deploying soldiers to China in response to the Boxer crisis forced European governments to call upon Japan to provide the bulk of the force. By the time the Eight Nation Allied Army set out for Beijing the Japanese made up fully half of the contingent. Their predominance gave them certain advantages in manoeuvre that could have affected image construction. For example, a general rule that the Japanese forces insisted on was the right to position themselves at the head of the column, and therefore be first to move and first to action. British observer George Lynch (1868-1928), noted that this positioning, along with their desire to keep their supplies close at hand, meant that British and American forces were obliged to do most of their marching under the midday sun.[30] Yet despite these potentially advantageous positions, the Japanese force was regarded well by its fellows, and often exceeded their expectations.

The Relief Arena gave many opportunities for the stark contrast between Japanese and European action. Arnold Henry Savage Landor (1865-1924)

---

29   MacDonald, *Report*, 235.
30   George Lynch, *The War of the Civilisations: Being the Record of a "Foreign Devil's" Experiences with the Allies in China* (London: Longmans, Green, and co., 1901), 27.

dedicated a portion of his 1901 work *China and the Allies* to a "study of the looters."[31] Landor reinforces the arena-like qualities of the internationalism of the Boxer Uprising. Examining the looters of various contingents, "brought out the characteristics of each nationality and of each individual in a most extraordinary manner."[32] Landor's brief description of the Japanese forces in this section reinforced the softer image that had previously dominated Western views of Japan, but alluded to a firmer, more martial character underneath:

> The Japanese soldier in many respects resembled the British, but was more reserved, and less anxious to be everybody's friend. The innocent and frank simplicity of the Briton was replaced in the Oriental by a more graceful, yet a stolid and dignified demeanour. But at heart both were alike, both dare-devils, yet gentle enough if treated the right way. The point where a marked difference lay between the two was in the true and keen artistic sense of the beautiful inborn in the sons of the Mikado's Empire, and altogether absent in the British Tommy.[33]

Landor's description gives the Japanese a sense of European civility, but recognized underlying martial currents. He goes on to describe the unique qualities of the Japanese looter, which suggested another merging of the predominant Western images of a soft Japan and the rising tide of martial quality.

> The Japanese – I am talking of the common soldiers, not of the officers – were the only soldiers in the field who showed any natural and thorough appreciation of art and of things artistic. They – like everybody else, of course, looted, but they did it in a quiet, silent, and graceful way, with no throwing about of things, no smashing, no confusion, no undue vandalism. They helped themselves to what they fancied, but it was done so nicely that it did not seem like looting at all – at least, not like looting as understood by people at home.[34]

Landor is giving the Japanese a civilized veneer, similar to that ascribed to Colonel Shiba during the siege. Views like Landor's ensured that the soft image was not completely overwritten by the martial one.

---

31 Arnold Henry Savage Landor, *China and the Allies*. (London: W. Heinemann, 1901), 191.
32 Ibid.
33 Ibid., 196.
34 Ibid., 199.

The French novelist Pierre Loti (1850-1923), who accompanied the relief expeditions held the Japanese in similar high regard. He referred to their "... surprisingly good military bearing in their new European uniforms ..."[35] when it came to first describe them in his work *Les Dernier Jours de Pékin*. Loti, like Landor, also offers descriptions of the looting that occurred as the army moved towards Beijing.

> Then the Japanese – heroic little soldiers of whom I do not wish to speak ill, but who destroy and kill as barbarian armies were wont to do. Still less do I wish to speak ill of our friends, the Russians; but they have sent here their Cossack neighbors from Tartary, and half-Mongolian Siberians, all admirable under fire, but looking at war in the Asiatic fashion. Then there are the cruel cavalrymen of India sent by Great Britain. America has let loose her soldiers. And when, in the first desire for vengeance for Chinese cruelties, the Italians, the Germans, the Austrians, and the French arrived, nothing was left intact.[36]

Loti takes a generally unfavourable outlook when it came to the looting he saw, but he made two important qualifications; one for the Japanese, in respect to their martial skill, and one for the Russians, France's current major ally. Loti's description exemplifies the special position the Japanese forces occupied. Surprised by their military skill, Western observers often offered the Japanese a special place in their writing, one that reinforced the "toy land" image but also made way for the growing militaristic image.

The preservation of the softer elements of the Japanese image aside, the actions of the Japanese forces throughout the campaign to relieve Tianjin and Beijing allowed for many accounts to take note of the individual bravery and military competence of the Japanese soldier. The battle of Beicang allowed the Japanese to exhibit their skill in a relatively open engagement. Japanese, British and American soldiers had planned to attack a well-entrenched position. The fighting was fierce, but the Japanese forces carried the day. Landor recorded, "The battle of Beicang was a great battle, well fought on both sides, and will always remain a fine page in the history of Japan, for the Japanese alone did practically all the work, and won the victory for the Allies."[37] James Martin Miller (1859-1939) described the Japanese assault, which did not wait

---

35   Myrta L. Jones, *The Last Days of Pekin: Translated from the French of Pierre Loti*. (Boston: Little, Brown, and Company, 1902), 10.

36   Ibid., 47.

37   Landor, 351.

for Americans and British reinforcements to arrive, and focused on the determination and coordination of the Japanese soldiers.

> In a beautiful line and in magnificent order the little fellows went to their work, the white caps showing through the cornfields like the bullseyes of a thousand targets ... the Japanese kept on steadily, and when the Chinese stopped their guns Fukushima's men only pressed the harder ...[38]

Japanese organization and determination played a central role in this description, as Miller followed his description with an account of the Japanese forces overtaking the positions intended for the British and Americans. Their key role in winning the battle was underlined in Miller's account by the toll it took. The Japanese lost 300 wounded or killed.[39]

Large battles like these allowed the Japanese forces, eager in their own way to prove their martial ability, the opportunity to demonstrate their skill and bravery. The Battle of Beicang was one of several encounters in which Japanese forces played highly visible and important roles. The taking of the Dagu forts, which occurred earlier on June 17, saw many nations landing marines to take control of the forts and gain access to the Hai River to move troops inland. The forts provided a very real prize to be won, and a very real competition broke out to be the first over the walls. George Crowe, in *The Commission of the H.M.S. Terrible*, recounts the specific case of the north-western fort, in which both Japanese and British soldiers assaulted the walls:

> When about 300 yards off, the "advance at the double" was sounded. The gallant Japanese then doubled up from the nearest flank, and vied with the British as to which nation should gain the honour of first entering the fort. Both scaled the parapet together, the brave Japanese commander being killed at the moment of victory. The Chinese garrison then fled, declining further resistance to such an irrepressible assault.[40]

Direct comparisons like the Battle of the Dagu forts or the Battle of Beicang in which Japanese forces demonstrated their ability in direct competition with

---

38 Martin J. Miller, *China, The Yellow Peril at War with the World* (Chicago: Monarch Book Co., 1900), 372.
39 Ibid.
40 George Crowe, *The Commission of H.M.S. 'Terrible' 1898-1902* (London: George Newnes Limited, 1903), 238.

Western forces offered the most easily identifiable impetus behind a more
martial image for Japanese soldiers in Western writing.

Early actions, and the initial composure of the various forces arranged to
push onto Tianjin and Beijing also played a role in informing national images.
Richard Steel's (1874-1928) account, *Through Peking's Sewer Gate*, offers an
interesting comparison of the images he was greeted with when he arrived
in China. When talking with a Major Johnstone of the Royal Marine Light
Infantry, Steel heard, "He and all others eulogized Japanese bravery and splendid medical and other arrangements. The Russians, they said were very slow
and had done a good deal of wanton damage and slaughter."[41] Steel, and others
like him coming in with the major bulk of the relief forces would have been
exposed to the early stereotypes that emerged with early contact. As time
progressed, Steel reinforces these stereotypes, noting in a letter to his brother
several days later that, "The Japs are splendid little chaps. Their arrangements
are wonderful, and they are as keen as can be. Of course it is fearfully difficult
to get concerted action between all the Powers. The Japs, Americans, and we
ourselves are in perfect accord, and I think the Russians mean to play up."[42]
Steel had never lost the thread of the soft image of the Japanese, but the tone
that greeted his arrival and that was reinforced through time spent with the
Japanese on the march created a justification for a more martial image. This
was encouraged by the arena-like confines of the campaign, and in Steel's case,
the incompetence of the second most visible group, the Russians, who had
contributed the second largest detachment behind Japan.

Members of most of the European armies in China composed themselves
well, and it is this fact that contributed so heavily to the creation of a more
martial image of the Japanese. The American forces were highly regarded during the relief expedition, a position that is supported by many accounts of
the campaign. Yet instances occur, like this anecdote from Frederick Brown's
(b. 1860) 1902 memoir, *From Tientsin to Peking with the Allied Forces*, which
showed the Japanese maintaining cohesion when others faltered. When
fighting was particularly intense during the march, a devastating barrage of
fire threatened to put the Americans to flight. They had been forced back to
low positions as a result of sustained fire, and were wavering when their commander was killed.[43]

---

41   Richard A. Steel *Through Peking's Sewer Gate: Relief of the Boxer Siege, 1900-1901*, ed.
      George W. Carrington (New York: Vantage Press, 1985), 3.
42   Ibid., 9.
43   Frederick Brown, *From Tientsin to Peking with the Allied Forces* (London: Charles H. Kelly,
      1902), 37.

> The soldiers went almost wild when they knew their commanding officer had been killed, but they were taken over by the second in command, and made a charge by the side of the Japanese. The way these Japanese fought was a revelation. A regiment acted like one man. The Chinese might shoot them down by the dozen, but those left did not even waver. They were resolved on victory all through.[44]

The Japanese forces, though taking high casualties, were seen as impervious to the death and destruction around them, providing an anchor of morale that impacted their predominant image.

The Relief Arena was not as concentrated as the Siege Arena, but similar developments occurred in the writing that followed each campaign. Japanese soldiers in the Eight Nation Allied Army were still treated as small and soft. They never lost that image during the Boxer Uprising. Yet, just as in the Siege Arena, Japanese composure and civility, especially in a less than civil capacity like looting, allowed for a more gentlemanly quality to be applied to the general Japanese soldier. Their conduct in battle, though aided by circumstance and their sheer numbers created several opportunities for the Japanese forces to outshine their European comrades, much to the surprise of observers and those inclined to write about the campaign. Japanese military competence and bravery under fire allowed for a distinctly martial tone, often coupled with admiration, to develop in the writing that emerged from the Relief Arena.

Conclusion: Solidification of the Martial Image during the Russo-Japanese War

If the Boxer Uprising made the martial image a reality, the Russo-Japanese War ensured it would surpass the "toyland" image as dominant. This solidification of the Japanese martial identity was done by war correspondents and military attachés who found themselves observing the Japanese military in Manchuria. When these men sought to record Japanese military virtue, they recalled an already established image, the one brought forward during the Boxer Uprising. In these terms, the Russo-Japanese War did not dramatically change the way the world viewed Japan. Instead, it reinforced the martial images that had been present since the inundation of post-boxer narratives that began in the last months of 1900, at the expense of the waning soft image. Early observations by British military attachés released assessments that called back to earlier Japanese successes. Captain B. Vincent of the Royal Artillery, for example,

---

44   Ibid., 38.

observing the landing of Japanese soldiers at the front, noted that, "Their cavalry is also very weak, so they will have to depend almost entirely on their infantry which has the reputation of being very good."[45] Similarly, Ian Hamilton (1853-1947), the lead British military attaché was positively certain about Japanese martial quality before he had even seen them at the front:

> [The Japanese] were surely Gurhkas; better educated, more civilized: on the other hand, not quite so powerful or hardy. The majority of the company, perhaps two thirds of it, conformed to the type of the Muggurs of Nepaul[sic]; squat and square: bullet-headed and pudding-faced. The remaining third were different; more slightly built; with a keen, grave, aquiline cast of countenance, they gave me the impression that they also would prove to be forward in the fight.[46]

Though emphasizing racial qualities, Ian Hamilton is here adhering to the Boxer War images of the Japanese military. The soldiers before him were small and soft, but with a deep and dominant martial character. As the war progressed, and the Japanese forces defeated those of the Russian Empire, their general acceptance as a great power was complete, yet it should not be understated that the popular image of the Japanese as a martial people was already well developed before this great conflict erupted. A 1909 work by the Italian Enrico Cocchia about the rise of Japan, still saw fit to recall their exceptional action during the Boxer Uprising saying the Japanese "gave everyone the example of the greatest moderation and composure; the officers ... amaze[d] their allied forces with their profound competence."[47] The Japanese had fought the same enemy, not across a no man's land, but side by side in the arenas of the Boxer Uprising.

Recognizing the importance of the Boxer Uprising enables a rather subtle appreciation for the nuanced importance of image. Kowner argues that by 1900, the Japanese government was actively attempting to promote a positive image of itself in the West.[48] The Boxer Uprising provided the perfect opportunity for

---

45   Captain B. Vincent, "Notes," in *The Russo-Japanese War: Reports from British Officers Attached to the Japanese and Russian Forces in the Field* (London: Eyre and Spottiswoode, 1908), vol. 1, 9.

46   Ian Hamilton, *A Staff Officer's Scrapbook During the Russo-Japanese War* (London: Edward Arnold, 1905), vol. 1, 10.

47   Enrico Cocchia, *Il Giappopone Vittorioso: Ovvero La Roma Dell'Estremo Oriente: A Rapida Evoluzione Dello Spirito Giapponese Sue Cause Storiche E Sue Conseguenze Politiche E Social* (Milan: Ulrico Hoepli, 1909), 279.

48   Kowner, "Becoming an Honorary Civilized Nation," 21.

such a campaign, and foreigners independently promoted a positive, civilized, martial image of Japan. The martial card lay alongside the soft on the table. Aside from greasing the wheels for Western observers commenting on the Russo-Japanese War, the growth of a martial image downplayed other, more negative images. Japanese forces exhibited such civility and alacrity during the Boxer Uprising and so actively suppressed a "Yellow Peril," as manifested in the Boxers, that they evaded putting themselves in that place. "Yellow Peril" images had a shadow existence in the metaphorical deck of cards.

Japan's conduct during the Boxer Uprising also influenced the Anglo-Japanese alliance, with key figures from the siege of Beijing pushing for closer ties with Japan. Sir Claude M. MacDonald was a fervent supporter of the Anglo-Japanese Alliance, and scholars generally acknowledge the importance of positive images in garnering support for the alliance. Ian Nish argues that,

> the end result of the Boxer campaign was that Japan won widespread respect in Britain. The large force the Japanese sent confirmed their reputation for bravery and endurance and their decision to pull out the main force certainly enhanced their image in Britain ... All in all, Japan's behaviour helped in steering British Opinion towards recognizing Japan as a useful ally against Russia in Asia.[49]

Anthony Best also suggests that Japanese conduct played a role, with supporters of the alliance arguing that Japan had, "elevated itself from the mire of barbarism and had adopted the laws and values of Western civilizations."[50] The Boxer Uprising, and especially the Post-Boxer Publications, played a significant role in the development of Western images of Japan that would continue to inform Western interaction with that country until 1904. The period from 1900-1904 can therefore be seen first as the origin of the combined soft and martial images of Japan, and second as a period of gradual transformation, in which the dominant image of Japan incorporated soft and martial qualities that would eventually lead to wide-ranging social, military, and diplomatic repercussions.

The very same public who filled the Empress Theatre twice daily in the summer of 1901 to watch smartly ordered Japanese soldiers and their European

---

49   Ian Nish, "Origins of the Anglo-Japanese Alliance: In the Shadow of the Dreibund," in *The Anglo-Japanese Alliance, 1902-1922*, ed. Phillips Payson O'Brien (New York: Routledge, 2004), 17.

50   Anthony Best, "Race, Monarchy, and the Anglo-Japanese Alliance," in *Social Sciences Japan Journal* 9:2 (2006), 174.

and American allies fight to relieve Beijing were the ones who yearned for popular works to fill the shelves in the autumn of 1900. The sheer volume of different narratives that arrived before Western audiences in that year and afterwards connected the public with the tragic and mystifying events that had engulfed China and put Western nationals in mortal danger. Though not all these works address the Japanese, the occurrences are significant enough not to be ignored. Popular narratives and memoirs, while occasionally suspect in their factual content, undoubtedly contribute to the creation of wide spread images and stereotypes, and in the case of the Boxer Uprising, the surprising military efficiency and bravery of the Japanese was a recurring theme. The Boxer Uprising, and more importantly, the barrage of literature that followed it, played a significant role in diffusing a martial image of the Japanese into the West. This image cooperated with the already dominant soft image to portray the Japanese military as gentlemanly, yet brave and efficient. The image of the Japanese military in the West would be forever altered after this period, only to be reinforced by the ferocity of the Russo-Japanese War. The stage play is now long forgotten, and the effect of the Boxer War as a defining moment for the Japanese military is less accepted than it was in 1901. Yet the importance of this event in the development of Japanese martial images should not be ignored.

Works Cited

Allen, Roland. *The Siege of Peking 1900: Being the Diary of the Rev. Allen Roland Allen.* London: Smith Elder and Co, 1901.

Auslin, Michael. "Terrorism and Treaty Port Relations: Western Images of the Samurai during Bakumatsu and early Meiji Japan." In *Images and Identity: Rethinking Japanese Cultural History*, eds. Jeffery E. Hanes, and Hidetoshi Yamaji. Kobe: The Research Institute for Economics and Business Administration Kobe University, 2004.

Best, Anthony. "Race, Monarchy, and the Anglo-Japanese Alliance," in *Social Sciences Japan Journal* 9:2 (2006), 171-186.

Brown, Frederick. *From Tientsin to Peking with the Allied Forces.* London: Charles H. Kelly, 1902.

Cocchia, Enrico. *Il Giappopone Vittorioso: Ovvero La Roma Dell'Estremo Oriente: A Rapida Evoluzione Dello Spirito Giapponese Sue Cause Storiche E Sue Conseguenze Politiche E Social.* Milan: Ulrico Hoepli, 1909

Crowe, George. *The Commission of the H.M.S. 'Terrible' 1898-1902.* London: George Newnes Limited, 1903.

Darcy, Eugène. *La Défense de la Légation de France.* Paris: Augustin Challamel, Éditeur, Rue Jacob, 17, 1903.

"Earl's-Court Military Exhibition." *The Times*, May 06, 1901, London, England, 8.

Ferris, John. "Turning Japanese: British Observation of the Russo-Japanese War," in *Rethinking the Russo-Japanese War, 1904-5* Volume II: The Nichinan Papers, eds. John Chapman and Inaba Chihiru. Folkstone: Global Oriental, 2007.

Giles, Lancelot. *The Siege of the Peking Legations: A Diary by Lancelot Giles*, ed. L.R. Marchant Nedlands: University of Western Australia Press, 1970.

Hamilton, Ian. *A Staff Officer's Scrapbook During the Russo-Japanese War, Volume I*. London: Edward Arnold, 1905.

Hooker, Mary. *Behind the Scenes in Peking: Being the Experiences During the Siege of the Legations*. London: John Murray, Albemarle Street, W. 1910.

Ion, Hamish. "Days of Seclusion" in *The History of Anglo-Japanese Relations, 1600-2000. Vol. III, The Military Dimension*. New York: Palgrave Macmillan, 2003.

Jones, Myrta L. *The Last Days of Pekin: Translated from the French of Pierre Loti*. Boston: Little, Brown, and Company, 1902.

Kiralfy, Imre. *Military Exhibition: 1901. Earl's Court, S.W.*, London: J.J. Keliher & Co., 1901.

Kowner, Rotem. "Becoming an Honorary Civilized Nation: Remaking Japan's Military Image during the Russo-Japanese War, 1904-1905." *The Historian* 64:1 (2001)19-38.

Landor, Arnold Henry Savage. *China and the Allies*. London: W. Heinemann, 1901.

Lynch, *The War of the Civilizations, Being the Record of a "Foreign Devil's" Experiences with the Allies in China*. London: Longmans, Green, and co., 1901.

MacDonald, Claude A. "The Japanese Detachment During the Defense of the Peking Legations, 1900," in *Transactions and Proceedings of the Japan Society London*, eds. Henri L. Joly. Nendeln: Kraus Reprint, 1971.

Martin, William A.P. *The Siege in Peking: China Against the World*. London: Oliphant Anderson and Ferrier, 1900.

Miller, Martin J. *China, The Yellow Peril at War with the World*. Chicago: Monarch Book Co., 1900.

Nish, Ian. "Origins of the Anglo-Japanese Alliance: In the Shadow of the Dreibund." In *The Anglo-Japanese Alliance, 1902-1922*, ed. Philips Payson O'Brien. New York: Routledge, 2004.

Oliphant, Nigel. *A Diary of the Siege of the Legations in Peking During the Summer of 1900*. New York: Longmans, Green, and Co., 1901.

Ransome, Jessie. *The Siege Hospital in Peking*. London: Society for Promoting Christian Knowledge, 1901.

Steel, Richard A. *Though Peking's Sewer: Relief of the Boxer Siege, 1900-1901*, ed. George W. Carrington. New York: Vantage Press, 1985.

Vincent, B. "Notes" in *The Russo-Japanese War: Reports from British Officers Attached to the Japanese and Russian Forces in the Field. Volume I*. (London: Eyre and Spottiswoode, 1908.

Yokoyama, Toshio. *Japan in the Victorian Mind: A Study of Stereotyped Images of a Nation 1850-80*. London: MacMillan, 1987.

CHAPTER 5

The Russo-Japanese War and the Perception of the Japanese Army in Imperial Germany

Frank Jacob

The Russo-Japanese War (1904/5) between Czarist Russia and Imperial Japan was an expansionist war for influence in Korea. It was also the first war between industrialized powers in the 20th century and should, with all its new technologies and the increased level of destruction, have pointed towards the First World War a decade later. Contemporaries like Rosa Luxemburg (1871-1919) realized that the Russo-Japanese War highlighted the interrelations between events far away from Europe and the great power politics in the capitals of the latter continent.[1] The war was, after all, a historical watershed of global importance.[2] In Japan, this war was even more important than the Great War, as it marked the end of Japan's successful modernization process and international acceptance of a great power of equal rank to the Western ones.[3] The role of the Japanese Empire during the war was also often perceived as that of a defender of democratic ideas against an autocratic and backward Czarist Empire, an image as depicted, for example, in the writings of famous US travel writer and "Russia expert" George Kennan the Elder (1845-1924).[4] This image was also

---

1   Rosa Luxemburg, "In the Storm," (1904). Accessed June 27, 2015. http://www.marxists.org/archive/luxemburg/1904/05/01.htm.

2   For a detailed analysis of this global impact see: Frank Jacob, *The Russo-Japanese War and Its Shaping of the Twentieth Century* (London: Routledge, 2018).

3   The importance of the war in Japan is also resembled in many publications related to its centennial in 2004/5. Some of them are *Nichi-Ro Sensō to Higashi Ajia sekai* (The Russo-Japanese War and the East Asian World), ed. Higashi Ajia Kindaishi Gakkai (The Academic Society for the Modern History of East Asia) (Tokyo: Yumani Shobō, 2008); Numata Takazō, *Nichi-Ro rikusen shinshi* (A New History of the Land Battles of the Russo-Japanese War) (Tokyo: Fuyō Shobō, 2004); Tsuchiya Yoshifuru, *Teikoku no tasogare, mikan no kokumin: Nichi-Ro Sensō, Daiichiji kakumei to roshia no shakai* (The Twilight of the Empire, the Unfinished Nation: The Russo-Japanese War, the First Revolution and Russian Society) (Tokyo: Seibunsha, 2012); Yomiura Shinbun Shuzaihan, *Kenshō Nichi-Ro Sensō* (Analysis of the Russo-Japanese War) (Tokyo: Chūō Kōron Shinsha, 2005). Despite these rather recent publications, which are just a few examples, there are also very good earlier studies, like Shimomura Fujio, *Nichi-Ro Sensō* (The Russo-Japanese War) (Tokyo: Jinbutsu Ōraisha, 1966), to name just one example.

4   Kennan published more than 20 articles on the war, e.g. George Kennan, "War by Prearrangement," *Outlook* 77 (August 13, 1904), 977-983 and George Kennan, "A Japanese Naval School," *Outlook* 77 (August 27, 1904), 890-896.

© VERLAG FERDINAND SCHÖNINGH, 2020 | DOI:10.30965/9783657702930_006

shared by British news reports, and the military correspondent of *The Times* highlights the importance of the Japanese victories over the Russian armies in Manchuria for international observers:

> No great campaign fought out within the memory of this generation of-
> fers such a vast and fruitful field for study by men of the British race as
> the Russo-Japanese War of 1904-5. For the first time for nearly a hundred
> years we have seen an island Empire at grips with a first-rate continen-
> tal Power. For the first time the new machinery with which science and
> modern invention have endowed the navies of the world has been put to
> the practical test of serious war. For the first time, almost in the history
> of the world, we have seen naval and military forces, directed by mas-
> ter hands, co-operating in close and cordial fashion to impose, by their
> united efforts, the national will upon the enemy.[5]

The present chapter, however, will focus on the perception of the war and the Japanese soldiers by the German military, whose representatives were quite interested in the events of the Far East. The government in Berlin and Kaiser Wilhelm II (1859-1941) had hoped to bind Russia closer to Germany during the conflict, but failed to gain a full reciprocal alliance with the Czarist Empire, although the Emperor and the Czar had drafted such an agreement during the war.[6] More important, however, was the impact of the war, when it came to German military planning in the aftermath. It was the perception of Japanese strength and Russian weakness that would define Germany's future military goals and chances alike, which will be discussed in more detail in the second part of the present chapter.

The German Observation of the War

In the beginning, German military and naval officers were sceptics when the chance of a Japanese victory in a war against Russia was considered. Like many others, the German military observers did not believe that the tiny island

---

5   Military Correspondent of *The Times, The War in the Far East 1904-1905* (New York: E. P. Dutton and Company , 1905), 1.

6   Nicholas II to Wilhelm II, Peterhof, October, 7, 1905 in *Die Große Politik der europäischen Kabinette, 1871-1914: Sammlung der diplomatischen Akten des Auswärtigen Amtes*, eds. Johannes Lepsius et al., 40 vols. (Berlin: Deutsche Verlagsgesellschaft für Politik und Geschichte, 1922-1927) (henceforth GP), No. 6247. I will identify the specific documents by their No. All the relevant documents can be found in vol. 19.1 and 19.2.

nation would stand a chance against the Russian "steam roller" everyone had been fearing in a war scenario on the European continent.[7] Naval officers, however, were keen to know more about the actual performance of modern ships and especially naval artillery, which is why the observation of the events by German officers was specifically requested.[8] Wilhelm II, i.e. "Admiral Berlin", consequently sent naval officers to the Far East to observe the war and ordered them

a) To gather experience of the impact of modern armory against modern targets.

b) To form an opinion about the tactics and use of modern squadrons, ships and torpedo boats at day and night.

c) To gather experience of the execution of larger troop transports and landing operations, on the necessary and suitable food supplies and facilities, and on the method of joint ventures between army and naval administration.

d) To closely study the material and personnel capabilities of the participating naval force.[9]

In contrast to other observing nations, Germany had access to the Russian perspective of the war and Wilhelm could send his officers to Port Arthur, from where they would send their reports about the war effort of the Czarist Empire. The reports highlighted the bad situation of the Russian fleet, especially considering the low morale of its sailors. The German military experts had clearly overrated the potential of the Czarist Navy.[10] The victories of the Japanese Navy, commanded by Admiral Tōgō Heihachirō (1848-1934), highlighted that better ships – in this case built in Britain – as well as better training and morale were important for Japan's success. One of the reports from August 1904 emphasizes the results of accurate Japanese artillery bombardments for the Russian cruiser *Gromoboi* at Ulsan and draws the following conclusion from the first naval battles of the war: "Now, armored protection, protection and again protection is necessary. This battle answered many questions."[11]

---

7   Philip Towle, "The Russo-Japanese War and the Defence of India," *Military Affairs* 44:3 (1980), 113.

8   Commander of the Naval Station of the North Sea to the Chief of the Admiral Staff of the Navy, Wilhelmshaven, February 28, 1904, Federal Archives, Military Archive Freiburg i. Brsg., Germany (henceforth BArch MArch), RM 5/5777.

9   Wilhelm II, Order for the Naval Officers Sent to the Russian or Japanese Forces, Berlin, February 13, 1904, BArch MArch, RM 5/5772.

10   Report of Bonsart von Schellendorf, Major in the General Staff, Schettnienen, July 14, 1905, BArch MArch, RM 5/5773.

11   Battle Report of Captain Finograzky, Commander of the Cruiser Gromoboi, Wladiwostok, August 14, 1904, BArch MArch RM 5/5773. On the battle of the Gromoboi at Ulsan

These early observations were further proved by the Battle of Tsushima in May 1905, in which the Japanese fleet was eventually able to destroy the menace of Russian ships in the region and force the Czar and his government in St. Petersburg to accept the necessity for peace talks.[12] While submarines had also been active during the war, they had not yet played an important role.[13] More effective were torpedo boats, which would launch torpedoes against the Russian fleet during the surprise attack on the Russian fleet at Port Arthur in early February 1904, especially since the torpedo nets that were supposed to protect the ships were practically useless.[14]

However, the Japanese soldiers were not only successful on sea, but also on land – the Russian troops stood no chance against the Asian enemy. The so-called "Prussians of Asia" – as they were called due to the initial training of the Japanese General Staff by Prussian officers, like Jacob Meckel (1842-1905), who had served as a military advisor to the Japanese Army in the years after the Meiji Restoration of 1868, namely in the early to mid-1880s – gained battle after battle and the German newspapers joined the international laudation of Japan's military apparatus.[15] The first land battle at the Yalu River, which marked the border between Korea and Manchuria, was the first Japanese victory against a Western nation, and was a real surprise.

General Kuroki Tamemoto (1844-1923) had to cross the river with his 42,000 men, while 19,000 Russians defended the positions on the antagonists' side.[16] The Japanese were able to cross the river very quickly and defeated the Czarist army without much resistance. This was a pattern that would characterize the initial period of the war, when General Alexei Kuropatkin (1848-1925), the supreme commander of the Russian Army during the Russo-Japanese War and

on 14 August 1904, see Peter Brook, *Armoured Cruiser vs. Armoured Cruiser: Ulsan 14 August 1904* (London: Conway Maritime Press, 2000).

12 On the Battle of Tsushima see: Frank Jacob, *Tsushima 1905: Ostasiens Trafalgar* (Paderborn: Schöningh, 2017).

13 Naval Attaché for the Nordic Empires, Paul von Hintze, to the State Secretary of the German Imperial Naval Office, Berlin, St. Petersburg, November 17, 1904, BArch MArch, RM 5/5769.

14 Secret Report of the Imperial Dockyard Kiel, Scheibe, to the State Secretary of the German Imperial Naval Office in Berlin, Kiel, June 28, 1906, BArch MArch RM 5/5771, 4-5.

15 "Der Japanismus im Schwinden," *Hamburger Nachrichten* 710 (October 8, 1904), Federal Archives Berlin (henceforth BArch), R 8034-II/8170.

16 John W. Steinberg, "The Operational Overview," in *The Russo-Japanese War in Global Perspective: World War Zero*, vol.1, eds. John W. Steinberg et al. (Leiden/Boston: Brill, 2005), 111. Freiherr Eberhard von Tettau, *Achtzehn Monate beim Heere Russlands* (Berlin: Mittler und Sohn, 1907), vol. 1, 89, however, speaks of 5,600 Russians and 36,000 Japanese. For a detailed account of the battle, see: Ibid., 85-106.

War Minister, was eager to avoid a direct confrontation and the possible annihilation of his troops in the region until the Trans-Siberian Railway had transported sufficient additional troops to the war zone from European Russia. For
him, like for most observers after the Japanese success at the Yalu, it was obvious that the present war was everything but a little colonial war, as the Western
powers had known from the previous centuries.[17] The Japanese crossed the
river in only one night, before launching a large scale attack on the positions
of Russian commander Mikhail Zasulich (1843-1910) on 1 May 1904, who could
only eventually withdraw his troops to Liaoyang.

Eberhard von Tettau (1857-1922), who accompanied the Russian army as a
military observer for the German Empire, later highlighted the importance of
heavy guns: "120 Japanese guns fired at the same time ... The few Russian guns
tried to return fire, but were immediately silenced."[18] The Czarist Army also
had problems with coordination during the battle, and friendly fire caused
quite a lot of casualties. The better training of the Japanese soldiers was obvious and the amount of munitions and shells used that day already highlighted
the fact that a new age of warfare had begun.[19] This was also visible with regard
to the high number of casualties, counting 2,000 men on the Russian side and
900 on the Japanese side.[20] While many international observers realized the
Japanese superiority on the battlefield and argued it to be related to better
planning and preparation, as well as better equipment and the higher morale
of the troops from the island nation, Tettau instead highlighted the Russian
incompetence, especially when describing the role of the Czarist officers in
the defeats and steady retreats that followed the Battle of the Yalu. According
to him, it was not the Russian soldiers that had failed, as the typical man in the
Czar's troops was "[l]oyal, self-denying, totally trusting his officer, the Russian
soldier provides solid material in the hand of good capable leaders, which is
almost incomparable among other armies of the world... . The fact that this

---

17   See, for example, the comparative evaluation in: "Buren- und japanische Taktik," *Der Tag*
     445, September 22, 1904, BArch R 8034-II/8170.
18   Tettau, *Achtzehn Monate*, 90.
19   A. L. Haldane, "Fourth Japanese Army: Operations from the Date of its Disembarkation
     in Manchuria to the 31st July 1904," in *The Russo-Japanese War. Reports from British
     Officers Attached to the Japanese and Russian Forces in the Field*, vol. 1 (London: Eyre
     and Spottiswoode, 1908), 129; C. V. Hume, "First Japanese Army: The Battle of the Ya-Lu;
     lecture given by a Japanese General Staff Officer, with remarks by Lieut.-General Sir
     Ian Hamilton," in *The Russo-Japanese War. Reports from British Officers Attached to the
     Japanese and Russian Forces in the Field*, vol. 1 (London: Eyre and Spottiswoode, 1908),
     15-18.
20   *Der Russisch-Japanische Krieg*, Beihefte zur *Marine-Rundschau* (Berlin: Mittler und Sohn,
     1904), 100.

excellent material failed anyway had multiple reasons; they were due to the way of preparation and the use of the material."[21] It is clear that the German observer pointed the finger towards his officer colleagues in the Russian Army, while at the same time arguing that, with better leadership, the Czarist soldiers could easily be superior. In some way, it was obvious what impact education, in the case of the Japanese Army a Prussian military education, could have. The war consequently did not only prove Japan's capability to hold its own in a military contest with Russia, it indirectly also proved the superiority of the German military education over the one that had produced the weak military leadership within the Czarist forces.

The German press, however, also emphasized racist arguments for Russia's defeat, as the Eastern European empire could not be considered truly Western, but rather had to be seen as a "half-Asia[n]"[22] power. In military circles, however, there was also an expression of understanding for Kuropatkin's tactics, who did not want to lose his army in the region, leaving it totally undefended against the Japanese, while he was waiting for reinforcements from Europe.[23] Yet the worth of such a long period of inactivity that caused countless casualties and gave the Japanese all the time necessary to take over important strategic positions was also discussed.[24] One important aspect that probably clouded the German view of Russia's military potential in the following years was the problems the Czarist Empire faced with regard to the mobilization and transport of troops to East Asia.[25] At the same time, the Russian soldier was neither well trained, nor well treated, sometimes even provided with food that could no longer be eaten.[26] The bad morale of Russian officers in Manchuria was probably also related to the region, where there was a "poor rations and munitions supply and a command expectation of reinforcements, which explained the inactivity that had such a debilitating effect on morale."[27] All in all, the loyalty of the Russian soldiers and officers was not very strong, and military order could collapse in the first moment of pressure. A report by the German General Consulate in China also reported that the Russian sailors whose ship

---

21   Tettau, *Achtzehn Monate*, IV.

22   "Die gelbe Gefahr," *Deutsche Tageszeitung* 115, May 28, 1904, BArch R 8034-II/8169.

23   *Der Russisch-Japanische Krieg*, Beihefte zur *Marine-Rundschau*, 94.

24   Ibid., 95.

25   *Berliner Lokal Anzeiger* 400, August 26, 1904, BArch R 8034-II/8170.

26   "Das Aussehen des russischen Soldaten," *Hamburger Courier* 500, November 4, 1904, BArch R 8034-II/8170.; "Russische Konserven," *Schlesische Zeitung* 813, November 18, 1904, BArch R 8034-II/8170.

27   Oleg R. Airapetov, "The Russian Army's Fatal Flaws," in *The Russo-Japanese War in Global Perspective: World War Zero* vol.1, eds. John W. Steinberg et al. (Leiden/Boston: Brill, 2005), 163.

was interned in Shanghai in December 1904 seemed to be only interested in amusement, instead of getting back to Russia to fight the enemy again.[28]

All in all, the war evoked a rather negative image of the Russian Army in Germany.[29] This, at the same time, stimulated a positive perception of the performance of the Japanese soldiers, but also provoked, and not only in Germany, an increase of fears of a "yellow peril." It was nevertheless obvious for any military observer that the two armies technically had nothing in common: "The Russian soldiers are masterly in retreat, whilst the Japanese are very unskilled in it."[30] Kuropatkin, who after the war was personally blamed for the Russian defeats, also emphasized the inequality of his troops and the Japanese soldiers when it came to capability, due to training and equipment.[31] The Russian war plan, however, was not an offensive one and the first defeats rather seemed to be a calculation, as the Naval Attaché for the Nordic Empires, Paul von Hintze (1864-1941), had reported from Russia in April 1904: "The Russians, with regard to their own announcements, were totally bargained for their check back after 9 February and for being driven back beyond Manchuria and losing control of the sea."[32] One has to highlight here as well that although the Russian Army never won a battle during the Russo-Japanese War, it remained a dangerous factor for Japan, whose military leaders realized the threat of the existence of an enemy force which could still be strengthened by further troop transports, while their own manpower seemed to be almost overstretched after extremely high casualties, as caused, for example, by the siege of Port Arthur during the previous months.

Regardless of their heavy losses, the Japanese never stopped the attacks, something that caused a lot of admiration,[33] but also misconceptions about

---

28   Imperial German General Consulate in China, Dr. Knappe, to Chancellor Count von Bülow, Shanghai, December 17, 1904, BArch MArch, RM 5/5775.

29   "Die Zustände in der russischen Armee," *Vossische Zeitung* 248, 27 May 1905, BArch R 8034-II/8170.

30   Sakurai Tadayoshi, *Human Bullets: A Soldier's Story of Port Arthur* (Boston/New York: Houghton, Mifflin and Company, 1907), 48.

31   Alexei Kuropatkin, *The Russian Army and the Japanese War* (New York: Dutton, 1909), vol.1, 241. For a detailed analysis of Kuropatkin's war diary, see: Hirono Yoshihiko "Kuropatokin Nihon Nikki ni tsuite (Thoughts on Kuropatkin's Japan Diary)," in *Nichiro Sensō Kenkyū no shin-shiten* (New Research Perspectives on the Russo-Japanese War), ed. Nichiro Sensō Kenkyūkai (Yokohama: Seibunsha, 2005), 31-45.

32   Naval Attaché for the Nordic Empires, Paul von Hintze, to the State Secretary of the German Imperial Naval Office, Berlin, St. Petersburg, April 1, 1904, BArch MArch, RM 5/5766, 4.

33   Naval Attaché at the Japanese Embassy, Trummler, to His Majesty Emperor and King Wilhelm II, Tokyo, December 29, 1904, BArch MArch RM 5/5769.

the role of spirit for the success of an assault attack that would mislead so many military decision makers during the First World War – that they could overcome well defended positions just by better mental conditions. While piles of corpses and rivers of blood could be seen on the battlefield during the siege of Port Arthur and beyond, the German observers were cheering about the indestructible Japanese spirit: "Both officer and ordinary man knew what he was fighting for and invested his highest ambition to lose his life for his godlike ruler and 'Dai Nippon' on the battlefield."[34] The military lessons were obviously poisoned by a wish to believe that a frontal assault could still decide the war.

In his article "Attack and Defense," published in the *Vierteljahrshefte für Truppenführung und Heereskunde* (Quarterly Journal of Troop Leadership and Military Art), General Ludwig Freiherr von Falkenhausen (1844-1936) was convinced that the Japanese success had proved, according to the German interpretation of the war, that military commanders should rather take the initiative and seek to decide a battle by attacking the enemy with full forces.[35] It was obvious that the infantry and artillery needed to cooperate better, while the role of the cavalry was reduced to an observing or pursuing force.[36] The Russians, argued Falkenhausen, only lost due to a failure in strategy, i.e. Kuropatkin's decisions to retreat instead of a more aggressive attack being undertaken by the Czarist Army against the Japanese positions. The overall lesson seemed simple: "In my opinion the Russo-Japanese War provides us after a longer break with another example to conclude that attack is the stronger form – or better expressed – the more effective means of warfare, something one however must well know and be capable of."[37] But it was false lessons that had been learned from the Russo-Japanese War, and when the soldiers of the First World War were sent into no man's land, wave after wave, it was to die while being shot multiple times by machine guns, bleeding out in barbed wire or being physically destroyed while their bodies were torn apart by artillery shells.[38] The "Japanese spirit" (*Yamato-damashii*) was deemed superior than the morale of the Russian soldier and the question of success was no longer

34   Military Report No. 18/06 of the Military Attaché in Tokyo, Major v. Etzel, to the Royal Prussian Ministry of War, Berlin, Tokyo, February 25, 1906, BArch MArch, RM 5/5771.

35   General der Infanterie z.D. Frhr. v. Falkenhausen, "Angriff und Verteidigung," *Vierteljahrshefte für Truppenführung und Heereskunde* 3, no. 2 (1906): 390.

36   Ibid., 398 and 403.

37   Ibid., 411-413, quote from 413.

38   Gary P. Cox, "Of Aphorisms, Lessons, and Paradigms: Comparing the British and German Official Histories of the Russo-Japanese War," *The Journal of Military History* 56:3 (1992), 392.

solely related to leadership and equipment, to strategy and tactics, it was a question related to the mind. It was a doctrine that many military leaders would refer to when looking for answers to the stalemate of the trench war of the Western front of the Great War.[39]

At the same time, the official German history of the Russo-Japanese War is steadily repeating the argument that a lack of professional military leadership, i.e. Prusso-German military leadership, was responsible for Russia's defeat and therefore for the success of the Japanese soldiers. It was Russian indecisiveness that determined the outcome of the war.[40] The aggressive war plans in the years leading from the Russo-Japanese War to the First World War[41] must consequently be considered a response to Japan's victory, which was considered more of a Russian failure than a Japanese success in the end.

The Military Impact of the War in Germany

The interest in the Russo-Japanese War in Germany was definitely existent, considering that there were quite a few publications dealing with the events in the Far East.[42] Especially after the Battle of Tsushima, the naval performance of the Russian sailors, who were said, in strong contrast to the sailors of the Japanese navy, to be incapable of maneuvering a ship and accurately firing its guns, was harshly criticized in German navy circles.[43] Some German observers

---

39   On the cultural history of this Japanese concept see: Saitō Shōji, *"Yamatodamashii" no bunkashi* (A Cultural History of the "Japanese Spirit") (Tokyo: Kōdansha, 1973). For a detailed study on offensive military doctrines before the First World War see: Jack K. Snyder, *The Ideology of the Offensive: Military Decision Making and the Disasters of 1914* (Ithaca, NY: Cornell University Press, 1984).

40   Cox, "Aphorisms," 396-397.

41   M. Christian Ortner, "Die Kriegs- und Aufmarschpläne Österreich-Ungarns, Deutschlands, Frankreichs und Russlands im Juli 1914," in *Erster Weltkrieg: Globaler Konflikt – Lokale Folgen – Neue Perspektiven*, ed. Stefan Karner and Philipp Lesiak (Innsbruck/Wien/Bozen: StudienVerlag, 2014), 45-61.

42   A. Janson, *Das Zusammenwirken von Heer und Flotte im russisch-japanischen Kriege 1904/5* (Berlin: Eisenschmidt, 1905); Hauptmann Lothes, "Befestigte Flottenstützpunkte am Beispiel der Kwantung-Halbinsel (Port Arthur 1898-1904)," *Vierteljahreshefte für Truppenführung und Heereskunde* 7 (1905), 556-577; H. Polmann, *Der Küstenkrieg und das strategische Zusammenwirken von Heer und Flotte im russisch-japanischen Kriege 1904/05* (Berlin: Mittler, 1912); E. Reventlow, *Der russisch-japanische Krieg: Armeeausgabe* (Berlin: C.A. Weller, 1906). Those who had observed the war also later published their experiences: Albert Hopman, *Das Logbuch eines deutschen Seeoffiziers* (Berlin: August Scheel, 1924).

43   German Embassy in China, von Mumm, to Chancellor Count von Bülow, Peiteiho, August 20, 1905, BArch MArch, RM 5/5768.

went so far as to claim that "Russia ... would never be a great seapower."[44]
Russian Admiral Fyodor Avelan (1839-1916), in a private talk with Paul von
Hintze in July 1905, confessed the following facts about the Russian naval force:

a) We knew that personnel reforms were needed. But the war prevented
    us from starting them. However we did not guess that the revolution-
    ary movement would win so much ground within a year, as was shown
    by the riots in the navy. Propaganda was introduced to the ranks by the
    reservists.

b) The recuperation of the material losses will be the next step in personnel
    reforms; new orders will only be issued when they are necessary to keep
    the Russian dockyards busy. This will only happen to provide the workers
    with tasks. Ships will be ordered later, as soon as the personnel question
    is solved.

c) The navy would prefer to hold off on internal orders until the experiences
    of the Battle of Tsushima have been processed. However, this informa-
    tion is not available yet, because the Japanese do not allow captured Rus-
    sian officers to send messages other than about their condition.[45]

For the officers of the German navy, it was obvious that Russia would not be
able to pose a threat against Germany's Imperial Fleet in the near future. The
naval military planners therefore could omit the Russian navy from their war
plans for several years to come. However, the war would not only cause such
considerations among German naval officers, as the success of Japan's soldiers
also played an important role with regard to the plans for a future war in the
heart of Europe,.

The chief of the German general staff, Alfred von Schlieffen (1833-1913),
was well informed about the war in East Asia.[46] While Schlieffen, as well as
many others like him, might have initially believed in a final Russian victory, he
changed his mind about Russia's military strength as a consequence of the war
and Japan's steady successes on all Manchurian battlefields.[47] When the chief

---

44 "Der Kampf um die Seeherrschaft," Special Print from *Marine-Rundschau*, First Issue,
    1906, BArch MArch, RM 5/5771, 513.

45 Naval Attaché for the Nordic Empires, Paul von Hintze, to the State Secretary of the
    German Imperial Naval Office, Berlin, St. Petersburg, July 14, 1905, BArch MArch, RM
    5/5769.

46 Chief of the General Staff of the Army, Alfred von Schlieffen, to the Imperial Vice Admiral
    and Chief of the Admiral Staff of the Navy, Wilhelm von Büchsel, Berlin, January 28, 1904,
    BArch MArch, RM 5/5777.

47 Notes of the Reporting Secretary in the Foreign Office, Count von Lichnowsky, Berlin
    19 April 1904, GP No. 6031. It must be highlighted here, that French military thinkers and
    planers, due to the alliance with Russia, also observed the events in the Far East and had
    to begin to incorporate them into their strategy for a future war. For a detailed analysis of

of the general staff was asked for his opinion about Russia and its role in a possible war in Europe by Chancellor Bernhard von Bülow (1849-1929), Schlieffen
gave an answer that highlights his conclusions being related to the experiences
of the Russo-Japanese War, and therefore should be quoted at length here:

> Russia will, as soon as it signs peace with Japan, withdraw its army corps
> and divisions from East Asia. After around six months there will probably
> be the same number of troops in European Russia as there were at the
> beginning of 1904. It will be a bit longer before weapon and munition
> supplies are recovered and the artillery material is renewed. After a while
> the old army could be externally recovered. Internally, however, there will
> be many differences. We have known for a long time that the Russian
> army has no important leaders, and it was known that the majority of
> officers had little worth, and that the training of the troops could only be
> described as insufficient. In contrast, the Russian soldier was regarded as
> one of the best in the world. His unasked for loyalty, his patient persever-
> ance, his calm defiance of death were recognized as invaluable qualities.
> Now the faith in these qualities has been badly shaken. The loyalty was
> not always truly blind. Many cases have been reported in which the offi-
> cers did not order, but beg, persuade, or negotiate. ... Troops rarely fought
> to their last [during the Manchurian campaigns]. ... Most notably, the
> Russian soldier is not trained. He does not know how to shoot or to ma-
> neuver in battle. ... The perfection of the armory now demands very care-
> ful training. Since the Russians did not receive it, they are no match for
> another army, and not useful in any attack. The East Asian war has shown
> that the Russian army was even worse than estimated by common sense,
> and the war did not improve it but made it worse. ... It is doubtful there
> will be an improvement, since self-awareness is lacking. The Russians do
> not seek the reason for their defeat in their own general incapabilities,
> but in the superior numbers of their enemy and the inability of indi-
> vidual leaders... . It will therefore just match the natural development of
> things when the Russian army does not get better but worse.[48]

Schlieffen eventually took the lessons of the Russo-Japanese War and incorporated them into his thoughts about a German two-front war against Russia

---

the French side: Olivier Cosson, *Préparer la Grande Guerre – L'armée française et la guerre
russo-japonaise (1899-1914)* (Paris: Les Indes savantes, 2013), especially chapters 3-6.

48   Chief of the General Staff, Alfred von Schlieffen, to Chancellor Count von Bülow, Berlin,
      June 10, 1905, GP, No. 6195.

in France, which he named *Denkschrift für einen Krieg gegen Frankreich* (*Memorandum for a War against France*, written during the winter of 1905/06), and which was later called and is usually referred to as the Schlieffen Plan.[49] Some elements of this plan would eventually be the basis for Germany's early operations in the First World War,[50] although one has to be careful not to conclude that the ideas of the plan remained fully uncontested or unchanged between 1905 and 1914.[51]

Due to the Russo-Japanese War, the military success of Japan, and the weak performance of the Russian officers and soldiers, Schlieffen could, as a consequence of his observations

> design a much more aggressive plan, which would be directed towards France during this particular window of opportunity of Russian absence. His *Memorandum* must consequently be read as a war plan for a limited time span, when the weakness of the Czarist Empire could be used to fight a war against the isolated French enemy. The plan was based on the idea that Germany would have a free hand against the Western "arch enemy" and be victorious in a fast war of four to six weeks. After the victory on the Western front, all troops would then turn towards the East to fight against the Russian steamroller.[52]

Regardless of its bad performance, the idea of the "Russian steamroller" was still alive and Schlieffen did not change his considerations about the task with regard to a possible two-front war. For Germany, France seemed to be the easier enemy and Russian weaknesses would just provide an easy start to the war, if these weaknesses, especially with regard to the mobilization of the Czarist Army, could be exploited to fight a fast war of annihilation against the French troops, before attacking the more dangerous enemy in the East later.

---

49   Alfred Graf von Schlieffen, "Denkschrift: Krieg gegen Frankreich" [Schlieffen-Plan], December 1905. Accessed January 5, 2017. http://www.1000dokumente.de/pdf/dok_0097_spl_de.pdf.

50   Hans Ehlert, Michael Epkenhans, and Gerhard P. Gross, "Introduction: The Historiography of Schlieffen and the Schlieffen Plan," in *The Schlieffen Plan: International Perspectives on the German Strategy for World War I*, eds. Hans Ehlert, Michael Epkenhans, and Gerhard P. Gross (Lexington: Kentucky University Press, 2014), 1.

51   See in more detail the analysis of Annika Mombauer, "The Moltke Plan: A Modified Schlieffen Plan with Identical Aims?" in *The Schlieffen Plan: International Perspectives on the German Strategy for World War I*, ed. Hans Ehlert, Michael Epkenhans, and Gerhard P. Gross (Lexington: Kentucky University Press, 2014), 43-65.

52   Jacob, *Russo-Japanese War*, ch. 6. A more detailed discussion of the war plan and its relation to the Russo-Japanese War is provided in the same chapter.

It was Erich Ludendorff (1865-1937) who for a short time span considered a reversal of the Schlieffen idea, i.e. a victory against weak Russian troops in the East first before sending all forces against France, but as soon as Ludendorff was in full command and needed to find a solution to the military dilemma of the Western front, he also began to increase his focus on the war efforts against France and Britain, leaving Russia aside while profiting from the bad Russian performance and the eventual revolutions in 1917.[53] However, Japan's victory had changed not only the power relations in East Asia, but also the military thinking, especially with regard to the image of Russia's military might, for the years to come.

Conclusion

The Japanese attack on the Russian fleet at Port Arthur in the night of 8/9 February 1904 was probably only a real surprise for the Czar and his military advisors. What was a surprise for the whole world were Japan's uninterrupted victories on land and sea. British and American newspapers cheered about these victories, as a defeat for Russia also resembled a defeat for an autocratic regime and an imperial contestant in East Asia, especially in China. The Japanese became known as "Asia's Prussians," gallant soldiers who treated their enemies and POWs even better than the latter were usually treated by their own officers and governments.[54] Japan's soldiers – regardless of a growing fear related to the idea of a "yellow peril" – were perceived as well trained, well equipped, and extremely loyal to the Japanese Emperor and state. Without question they were sacrificing themselves when wave after wave of human bullets (*nikudan kōgeki*) surged against the fortress walls at Port Arthur, creating mountains of bodies and rivers of blood. Eventually, their behavior would lead to the military misconception that soldiers' spirit could decide their military fate, an idea that would be disproved by the actual experiences of the First World War a decade later.

---

53   On Ludendorffs military ideas and concepts see the forthcoming chapter Frank Jacob, "General der Infanterie Erich Ludendorff," in *Des Kaisers militärische Elite*, ed. Lukas Grawe (Darmstadt: WBG, 2019).

54   Kita Yoshito, "Nichi-Ro Sensō to jindōshugi: Matsuyama furyo shūyōjo ni okeru Roshia shōbyōsha kyūgo no kentō" (The Russo-Japanese War and Humanitarianism: A Study of the Measures for Relief for Russian Wounded and Sick in the Matsuyama POW Camp), *Nihon Hōgaku* 80:2 (2014), 591-627; Mōri Yoshihiko, "'Roshiajin horyu shashin korekushon' ni miru 'hakuai no kokoro' shozai" (The Existence of 'Philanthropy' as Seen in the 'Photograph Collection of Russian POWs'), *Yūrashia Kenkyū* 49 (2013), 24-30.

In the case of Germany, the Japanese victories were considered indirect German victories, since the Japanese officer corps had been trained by Prussian soldiers during the Asian country's Westernization process. The sailors, soldiers, and officers in Japan's navy and army were in addition only considered successful due to Russian incapabilities. If the Russian Army had been led by German officers, as the usual narrative highlighted, its performance might have been much better. In contrast to many other military observers, the German officers and observers were in a way determined by racist views and a non-acceptance of Japan as a real great power. While the Japanese Empire eventually proved to be an equal member of the concert of powers in East Asia, in Germany, the military weakness of Russia in the aftermath of the war was of much more interest than Japan's military strength. War planners, like Alfred von Schlieffen, had to deal with new facts and answered them by a reconfiguration of war plans for the case for a two-front war.

All in all, the cultural arrogance of some of the observers and military personnel in Germany led to a misperception of the war. The actual strength of the Japanese was only considered possible due to Russian weakness, and this caused extreme strategic misconceptions for the future. If the interest in Japan's success had been more intense, one might have realized that a defensive position was much better for a war that was increasingly determined by modern technology than human spirit. Eventually, there was no glory in dying for a military cause, neither in the Russo-Japanese War, nor in the First World War.

Works Cited

Archival Material

Federal Archives Berlin, Germany
R 8034-II/8169
R 8034-II/8170

Federal Archives, Military Archive Freiburg i. Brsg., Germany (BArch MArch)
RM 5/5768
RM 5/5769
RM 5/5771
RM 5/5772
RM 5/5773
RM 5/5775
RM 5/5777

Cited Secondary Literature and Published Sources

Airapetov, Oleg R. "The Russian Army's Fatal Flaws." In *The Russo-Japanese War in Global Perspective: World War Zero* vol.1, eds. John W. Steinberg et al., 157-177. Leiden/ Boston: Brill, 2005.

Brook, Peter. *Armoured Cruiser vs. Armoured Cruiser: Ulsan 14 August 1904*. London: Conway Maritime Press, 2000.

Cosson, Olivier. *Préparer la Grande Guerre - L'armée française et la guerre russo-japonaise (1899-1914)*. Paris: Les Indes savantes, 2013.

Cox, Gary P. "Of Aphorisms, Lessons, and Paradigms: Comparing the British and German Official Histories of the Russo-Japanese War." *The Journal of Military History* 56:3 (1992), 389-402.

Der Russisch-Japanische Krieg, Beihefte zur *Marine-Rundschau*. Berlin: Mittler und Sohn, 1904.

Ehlert, Hans, Michael Epkenhans, and Gerhard P. Gross, "Introduction: The Historiography of Schlieffen and the Schlieffen Plan," in *The Schlieffen Plan: International Perspectives on the German Strategy for World War I*, eds. Hans Ehlert, Michael Epkenhans, and Gerhard P. Gross, 1-16. Lexington: Kentucky University Press, 2014.

Falkenhausen, General der Infanterie z.D. Frhr. v. "Angriff und Verteidigung." *Vierteljahrshefte für Truppenführung und Heereskunde* 3:2 (1906), 383-414.

Haldane, A.L. "Fourth Japanese Army. Operations from the Date of its Disembarkation in Manchuria to the 31st July 1904." In *The Russo-Japanese War. Reports from British Officers Attached to the Japanese and Russian Forces in the Field*, vol. 1., 106-134. London: Eyre and Spottiswoode, 1908.

Higashi Ajia Kindaishi Gakkai (The Academic Society for the Modern History of East Asia), ed. *Nichi-Ro Sensō to Higashi Ajia sekai* (The Russo-Japanese War and he East Asian World). Tokyo: Yumani Shobō, 2008.

Hopman, Albert. *Das Logbuch eines deutschen Seeoffiziers*. Berlin: August Scheel, 1924.

Hume, C.V. "First Japanese Army: The Battle of the Ya-Lu; lecture given by a Japanese General Staff Officer, with remarks by Lieut.-General Sir Ian Hamilton." In *The Russo-Japanese War. Reports from British Officers Attached to the Japanese and Russian Forces in the Field*, vol. 1., 15-22. London: Eyre and Spottiswoode, 1908.

Jacob, Frank. "General der Infanterie Erich Ludendorff." In *Des Kaisers militärische Elite*, ed. Lukas Grawe. Darmstadt: WBG, 2019 (forthcoming).

Jacob, Frank. *The Russo-Japanese War and Its Shaping of the Twentieth Century*. London: Routledge, 2018.

Jacob, Frank. *Tsushima 1905: Ostasiens Trafalgar*. Paderborn: Schöningh, 2017.

Janson, A. *Das Zusammenwirken von Heer und Flotte im russisch-japanischen Kriege 1904/5*. Berlin: Eisenschmidt, 1905.

Kennan, George. "War by Prearrangement." *Outlook* 77 (August 13, 1904), 890-896.

Kennan, George. "A Japanese Naval School." *Outlook* 77 (August 27, 1904), 977-983.

Kita Yoshito, "Nichi-Ro Sensō to jindōshugi: Matsuyama furyo shūyōjo ni okeru Roshia shōbyōsha kyūgo no kentō" (The Russo-Japanese War and Humanitarianism: A Study of the Measures for Relief for Russian Wounded and Sick in the Matsuyama POW Camp). *Nihon Hōgaku* 80:2 (2014), 591-627.

Lepsius, Johannes et al. *Die Große Politik der europäischen Kabinette, 1871-1914. Sammlung der diplomatischen Akten des Auswärtigen Amtes*, 40 vols. Berlin: Deutsche Verlagsgesellschaft für Politik und Geschichte, 1922-1927.

Lothes, Hauptmann. "Befestigte Flottenstützpunkte am Beispiel der Kwantung-Halbinsel (Port Arthur 1898-1904)." *Vierteljahreshefte für Truppenführung und Heereskunde* 7 (1905), 556-577

Luxemburg, Rosa. "In the Storm." (1904). Accessed June 27, 2015. http://www.marxists. org/archive/luxemburg/1904/05/01.htm.

Military Correspondent of *The Times. The War in the Far East 1904-1905*. New York: E. P. Dutton and Company, 1905.

Mombauer, Annika. "The Moltke Plan: A Modified Schlieffen Plan with Identical Aims?" In: *The Schlieffen Plan: International Perspectives on the German Strategy for World War I*, eds. Hans Ehlert, Michael Epkenhans, and Gerhard P. Gross, 43-65. Lexington: Kentucky University Press, 2014.

Mōri Yoshihiko. "'Roshiajin horyu shashin korekushon' ni miru 'hakuai no kokoro' shozai" (The Existence of 'Philantropy' as Seen in the 'Photograph Collection of Russian POWs'). *Yūrashia Kenkyū* 49 (2013), 24-30.

Numata Takazō. *Nichi-Ro rikusen shinshi* (A New History of the Land Battles of the Russo-Japanese War). Tokyo: Fuyō Shobō, 2004.

Ortner, M. Christian. "Die Kriegs- und Aufmarschpläne Österreich-Ungarns, Deutschlands, Frankreichs und Russlands im Juli 1914." In *Erster Weltkrieg: Globaler Konflikt – Lokale Folgen – Neue Perspektiven*, ed. Stefan Karner and Philipp Lesiak, 45-61. Innsbruck/Wien/Bozen: StudienVerlag, 2014.

Polmann, H. *Der Küstenkrieg und das strategische Zusammenwirken von Heer und Flotte im russisch-japanischen Kriege 1904/05*. Berlin: Mittler, 1912.

Reventlow, E. *Der russisch-japanische Krieg: Armeeausgabe*. Berlin: C.A. Weller, 1906.

Saitō Shōji. *"Yamatodamashii" no bunkashi*. (A Cultural History of the "Japanese Spirit") Tokyo: Kōdansha, 1973.

Sakurai Tadayoshi. *Human Bullets: A Soldier's Story of Port Arthur*. Boston/New York: Houghton, Mifflin and Company, 1907.

Schlieffen, Alfred Graf von. "Denkschrift: Krieg gegen Frankreich" [Schlieffen-Plan]. December 1905. Accessed January 5, 2017. http://www.1000dokumente.de/pdf/ dok_0097_spl_de.pdf.

Shimomura Fujio. *Nichi-Ro Sensō* (The Russo-Japanese War). Tokyo: Jinbutsu Ōraisha, 1966.

Snyder, Jack K. *The Ideology of the Offensive: Military Decision Making and the Disasters of 1914*. Ithaca, NY: Cornell University Press, 1984.

Steinberg, JohnW. "The Operational Overview." In: *The Russo-Japanese War in Global Perspective: World War Zero*, Vol.1, eds. John W. Steinberg et al., 105-128. Leiden/ Boston: Brill, 2005.

Towle, Philip. "The Russo-Japanese War and the Defence of India." *Military Affairs* 44:3 (1980), 111-117.

Tettau, Freiherr Eberhard von. *Achtzehn Monate beim Heere Russlands*, vol. 1. Berlin: Mittler und Sohn, 1907.

Tsuchiya Yoshifuru. *Teikoku no tasogare, mikan no kokumin: Nichi-Ro Sensō, Daiichiji kakumei to roshia no shakai* (The Twilight of the Empire, the Unfinished Nation: The Russo-Japanese War, the First Revolution and Russian Society). Tokyo: Seibunsha, 2012.

Yomiura Shinbun Shuzaihan. *Kenshō Nichi-Ro Sensō* (Analysis of the Russo-Japanese War). Tokyo: Chūō Kōron Shinsha, 2005.

CHAPTER 6

The Japanese Soldier in American Popular Songs: A Comparison of Songs from the Russo-Japanese War (1904-05) and from the Pacific War (1941-1945)

Sepp Linhart

It is probably no longer part of the collective memory of present-day US citizens that there ever was a war between Japan and Russia, which lasted factually from 8 February 1904 until 28 May 1905 when the naval battle near Tsushima ended with a Japanese victory,[1] or officially until 5 September 1905, when through the services of the American President Theodore Roosevelt a peace agreement was concluded between the two warfaring states in Pourtsmouth, Maine. And it is certainly even less known that during that war quite a number of popular songs were composed and published as sheet music in the United States which dealt with this war.

It is probably better known or can at least be easily imagined that during the Pacific War between 8 December 1941 and 15 August 1945 again many songs were composed and recorded about the Japanese although probably not even one of these songs is known by the average American today.

In this short essay I would like to give an overview about the Japan-related American popular songs during these two wars, based on the published sheet music and the music left on records, after which I will try to analyze and compare them with a special focus of how the image of the Japanese army changed in these two groups of songs.

Songs from the Russo-Japanese War

I'll start with a list of songs about the Russo-Japanese War from the years 1904 and 1905, which I could identify, in strict alphabetical order:

---

1 On the Battle of Tsushima see Frank Jacob, *Tsushima 1905: Ostasiens Trafalgar* (Paderborn: Schöningh, 2017).

© VERLAG FERDINAND SCHÖNINGH, 2020 | DOI:10.30965/9783657702930_007

RJo1 *Battle Hymn written by the Mikado of Japan* and sung by the Japanese Armies on the Battlefields. Christmas Music Supplement of the *Chicago Sunday American*, Sunday, Dec. 4, 1904.[2]

RJo2 *For the Flag of Old Japan*. Patriotic March Song. Words by Lewis A. Browne, Music by Thos. S. Allen. Boston: Walter Jacobs, 1904.

RJo3 *Happy Jappy Soldier Man*. Japanese War Song. Sung with great success by Eleanor Falk. Words by Paul West, Music by John W. Bratton. New York etc: M. Wittmark & Sons, 1904.

RJo4 *Little Fighting Soldier Man*. Words and Music by Lillian Coffin. Music Supplement Hearst's Boston Sunday, May 14, 1905. Published by Permission of the American Advance Music Co., N.Y.

RJo5 *Little Japan*. Words and Music by T. J. Rider. New York: Theatrical Music Supply 1904.

RJo6 *One Little Soldier Man*. Words by Edward Madden, Music by Neil Moret. New York: Shapiro Remick and Co. 1904.

RJo7 *Prince Fushimi's Song "A Soldier of Old Japan".* Words and Music by Richard C. Dillmore. Music Supplement *New York American and Journal*, Sunday Feb. 5, 1905. Published by Permission of Blasius and Sons, Philadelphia.

RJo8 *The Little Brown Man of Japan*. Words by George Totten Smith, Music by William H. Penn. New York and Chicago: Sol Bloom 1904

RJo9 *The Little Jap*. Characteristic Two-Step. Words and Music by Percy Wenrich. Chicago & New York: McKinley Music Co 1905.

Apart from these nine songs I found several instrumental pieces of a martial character without words:

RJ10 *Charge of the Japs*. March and Two Step. Composed by Harry Louis Hayes. Springfield, Ohio: L. C. Gorsuch 1904.

RJ11 (To the Yankees of the Far East) *Japan's Triumphal March*. Two Step. Composed by C. M. Vandersloot. Williamsport, Pennsylvania: Vandersloot Music 1904.

RJ12 *The Japanese Patrol*. Composed by Fred Hylands. New York: Fred Hylands 1904.

---

2   For clarity's sake I numbered the Russo-Japanese War songs with RJ and a current number, and the Pacific War songs with PW and a current number.

> RJ13 *The Jap Behind the Gun*. March & Two Step. Composed by
> A.E. Wade. Hoquiam, Washington: The Wade Music Co. 1904.[3]

Presently, I am convinced that there exist a few more, but not many more popular American songs and musical pieces about the Russo-Japanese War, but I
was quite surprised when I discovered the first piece of this kind. This is in contrast to other popular media such as e.g. postcards. The war and the Japanese
soldiers were subject of many European postcards, but hardly of any American
ones.[4] The US was not directly involved in this war, but indirectly. Both warfaring nations had to rely heavily on foreign loans to finance the war.[5] Russia
got the biggest loan from its ally France, and a smaller one from Germany,
while Japan got loans from the US, Canada, the UK and again Germany. Most
important for Japan was the loan mediated through the services of Jacob Schiff
(1847-1920), an American banker of German-Jewish origin who hated the
Russians. Even so, it is probably not this loan given to Japan which created the
American interest in the war. Rather, the fact that two "neighbors" of America
fought a war for hegemony in East Asia might have aroused the public interest
to such an extend that even a number of songs were composed about this war,
the Japanese and the Japanese Army.

All the above songs are about the Japanese (army), while I did not find a
single song about the Russians. Starting with a visual analysis, it is interesting
to note, that out of the nine songs, six depict modern Japanese soldiers on
their title pages which as eye catchers were very important. On two title pages,
Battle Hymn of the Mikado and *Prince Fushimi's Song*, samurai in ancient armor
are shown, while *The Little Brown Man of Japan* is the only piece which from
the outside is not at once recognizable as a song with militaristic contents. Out
of the four pieces of instrumental music, three again show modern Japanese
soldiers, while the title page of *Japan's Triumphal March* consists of a map of
East Asia. Without doubt we can interpret this as a proof that the modernity
of the Japanese Army at the beginning of the 20th century was generally acknowledged in the US. The samurai figures are only drawn on the two pieces

---

3 Some of this sheet music is contained in Joanne Bernardi's interesting website
   ReEnvisioningJapan. Japan as Destination in 20th Century Visual and Material Culture.
   Accessed December 6, 2016. http://humanities.lib.rochester.edu/rej/, on which the songs are
   newly recorded. All songs about the Russo-Japanese War are owned by the author.

4 Compare Sepp Linhart, *"Dainty Japanese" or Yellow Peril? Western War Postcards 1900-1945*
   (Vienna: LIT, 2005).

5 For Japan see Edward S. Miller, "Japan's other Victory: Overseas Financing of the Russo-
   Japanese War," in *The Russo-Japanese War in Global Perspective. World War Zero*, vol. 1, ed.
   John W. Steinberg et al., History of Warfare, vol. 29 (Leiden/Boston: Brill, 2005), 465-483.

Fig. 6.1   RJ01 *Battle Hymn written by the Mikado of Japan* and sung by the Japanese Armies on the Battlefields. Christmas Music Supplement of the *Chicago Sunday American*, Sunday, Dec. 4, 1904. Author's collection

connected to the *tennō* (Mikado) and Prince Fushimi,[6] probably meaning that such old institutions as the *tennō* and the Japanese aristocracy need to be honored with pictures of Japan's traditional military upper class, which at the time of the Russo-Japanese War had been abolished for more than thirty years, and thus in Japan itself was already rather obsolete.

As for the title words, in seven songs Japan is indicated directly through its correct name or the attribute Japanese, while in four cases the abbreviations Jap (RJ09, RJ10, RJ13) or Jappy (RJ03) are used. As will be seen later, Jap or Jappy at that time were not pejorative terms, but rather used as a pet name, which expressed sympathy for the Japanese. Two more titles (RJ04, RJ06) speak only of "soldier" without mentioning Japan explicitly, but from certain pictorial codes like Mount Fuji or a "geisha" it becomes immediately clear that Japan is meant.

As next step I will take a closer look at the contents of the nine songs identified. The *Battle Hymn written by the Mikado of Japan* and sung by the Japanese Armies on the Battlefields is a rather strange piece since the Japanese Emperor Meiji, in the West often called Mutsuhito, is not known to have written a battle hymn for his army. The Japanese characters in the middle of the English title on page 2 of the sheet music say *kokka*, national anthem, *Kimigayo*, the name of the national anthem, and *tenchō-setsu*, birthday of the *tennō*, one of the four great Japanese holidays since 1873, which occurred on November 3. The words of this "hymn" are quite different from the national anthem *Kimigayo*, which was not written by the *tennō*. It is a song in praise of Japan, and says, that like the heroes of the past, who had gladly died for their country the heroes of today are also happily dying for the country and the emperor, and thus are securing the emperor's ruling over Japan for the next thousand years. For our theme it seems important, that the Japanese soldiers are called heroes, as were their ancestors, who are happily sacrificing themselves for their country, Nippon, as well as for the emperor.

The composer of the song *For the Flag of Old Japan. Patriotic March Song* was Thomas S. Allen (1876-1919), an early Tin Pan Alley and vaudeville composer,[7] but about the writer of the lyrics, Lewis A. Browne, I could not find anything. The song consists of two verses and a chorus, and tells the sad story of a young

---

6   The remark on page 2 of this song's sheet music edition, "The beautiful march song that delighted Prince Fushimi during his visit to the United States," as well as the photograph on the title page make it clear that Prince Fushimi Sadanaru (1858-1923) is meant, who during the Russo-Japanese War visited the US as a general on a diplomatic mission. The song is not referring to his son Fushimi Hiroyasu (1875-1946), who participated in the War as lieutenant commander of the Japanese navy.

7   Uncle Dave Lewis, "Biography of Thomas S. Allen," All Music. Accessed January 5, 2017. http://www.allmusic.com/artist/thomas-s-allen-mn0002162312/biography.

Japanese couple which has to part, because the man has been called to fight "for the flag of old Japan." When he did not return, the woman volunteered to become a Red Cross nurse and arrived at the battlefield just in time to see him die "for the flag of old Japan." The main theme, the selfless sacrifice for the country and the emperor, is obviously symbolized through the flag itself.

Happy Jappy Soldier Man, called a Japanese War Song, bears on its title page the words "Sung with great success by Eleanor Falk" as well as a photograph of the singer with a fan. Falk sang also songs like *You are the only one* (1899) by George Totten Smith and Robert A. Keiser[8] or *Cecelia and Amelia* by Oscar Hammerstein (1901)[9], always with her photograph on the titlepage of the sheet music. Thus, she seems to have been quite a star around the turn of the 19th to the 20th century. The song's words are by Paul West, the music is by John W. Bratton (1867-1947).[10] Whereas I could not find anything about Paul West, John W. Bratton was a famous Tin Pan Alley composer and representative of the so-called gay nineties. Paul West seems to be his long time collaborator as text writer, but also composed music by himself.[11] The lyrics do not tell us much about the army. A geisha declined to a guest to sing for him, because her "happy Jappy soldier man" had to go to fight the big Russians. After some years the same geisha was merry and happy, because her lover had come back as a general of Japan. Even though these lyrics are not very enlightening about the state of the Japanese Army, the sympathies of the song are clearly with the little geisha and her "Jappy soldier."

Little Fighting Soldier Man was published as Music Supplement to Hearst's Boston Sunday, 14 May 1905[12] and written and composed by Lilian Coffin whose photograph again adorns the title page. The narrative tells us about a "Jappy soldierman," who went to fight the Russians "with heart and sword in hand to save the honor of old Japan," while his "fair maid of Japan" was "singing

8   Music Division, The New York Public Library. "You're the Only One," *The New York Public Library Digital Collections*. 1899-1899. Accessed February 13, 2017. http://digitalcollections. nypl.org/items/510d47df-ef5b-a3d9-e040-e00a18064a99.

9   Music Division, The New York Public Library. "Cecelia and Amelia," *The New York Public Library Digital Collections*. Accessed February 13, 2017. http://digitalcollections.nypl.org/ items/8da39ecb-f039-380c-e040-e00a180654ab.

10   "John W. Bratton," All Music. Accessed January 5, 2017. http://www.allmusic.com/artist/ john-w-bratton-mn0001921435.

11   Music Division, The New York Public Library. "I Want dem Presents Back," *The New York Public Library Digital Collections*. 1896-1896. Accessed February 13, 2017. http://digitalcol lections.nypl.org/items/510d47e3-fc9e-a3d9-e040-e00a18064a99.

12   A recording of *Little Fighting Soldier Man* can be found among the songs included in the exhibition Japan-In-America held at Indiana University in 2005. Accessed January 5, 2017. http://www.indiana.edu/~jia1915/music.html

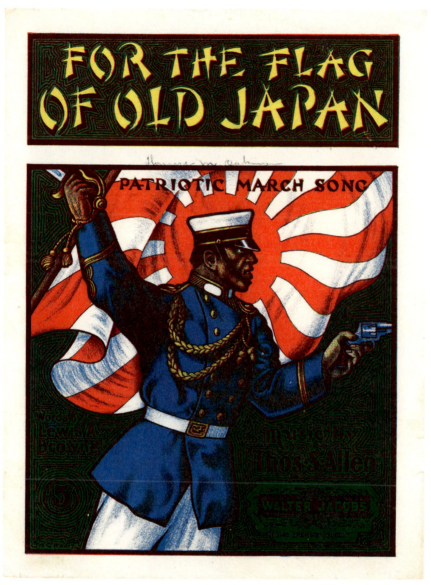

Fig. 6.2   RJ02 *For the Flag of Old Japan*. Patriotic March Song. Words by Lewis A. Browne, Music by Thos. S. Allen. Boston: Walter Jacobs, 1904. Author's collection

softly all the day." The Japanese soldiers were "marching tho shot and shell," "over soldier boys who fell," "like the mighty samurai," "with victory their joyous cry, Banzai." Finally, "the little fighting soldierman" gained "victory for his gracious Emperor" and returned to Japan. Lillian Coffin seems to have been an actress, who in 1903 and 1904 performed even on the Broadway in the New York Theatre and the Lyric Theatre.[13]

Little Japan with words and music by T. J. Rider was published by the Theatrical Music Supply Company in New York in 1904, which might mean that it was written for a play performed in the first year of the war, but I have no confirmation for this. Whereas the three afore mentioned songs are ballads which tell a story, *Little Japan* is quite different. It describes the Japanese and their army. The Japanese people are "loyal, brave, and true, as ever were born under the skies," always "ready to suffer and dare," and therefore God is with brave little Japan. Since "honor and justice commands" the Japanese, Russia "never can muster the force to whip Little Japan." Summed up, the song contains only praise for the Japanese and their army, and contempt for the Russians.

One Little Soldier Man was sung by Della Fox (1870-1913)[14] who was quite a famous singer at the turn of the century, and the songwriter, Edward Madden (1878-1952). The composer, Neil Moret (pseudonym for Charles N. Daniels, 1878-1943), and the publishing house Shapiro, Remick and Company were also famous in their respective fields. Thus we might speculate that this song was perhaps more influential than the other ones. This is a sad ballad again of the love of a geisha girl and a soldier, who does not return from the battlefield. It, however, does not make much contribution to our theme, because no characteristics of the Japanese army or soldiers are mentioned.

Prince Fushimi's Song "A Soldier of Old Japan" is not a composition by Prince Fushimi, but a song that he was said to have appreciated very much when he visited the US. Words and music are by Richard C. Dillmore, who was known for his song *The American Soldier*, march song and chorus, from the year 1904. The sheet music for this song also carries a photograph of Dillmore on the title

---

13   She appeared in 40 performances of *Dorothy Vernon of Haddon Hall*, a Broadway melodrama that opened in December 1903 and ended in January 1904 at the New York Theatre, and again in December 1904 at the Majestic Theatre. Accessed February 13, 2017. https://www.ibdb.com/broadway-production/dorothy-vernon-of-haddon-hall-5800.

14   Another edition of this sheet music has a photograph of the Castle Square Quartette, two women and two men, on its title page. On Della May Fox see Lewis Clinton Strang, *Famous Prima Donnas* (New York: L.C. Page & Co., 1906), 192-207, on Edward Madden see "Edward Madden." Accessed January 6, 2017. *http://songwritershalloffame.org/exhibits/C254*, and on Neil Moret see "Charles N. Daiel (music). Accessed January 6, 2017. *http://www.songwritershalloffame.org/exhibits/C281*. On Shapiro, Remick and Company see "Jerome H. Remick." Accessed January 6, 2017. http://imslp.org/wiki/Jerome_H._Remick.

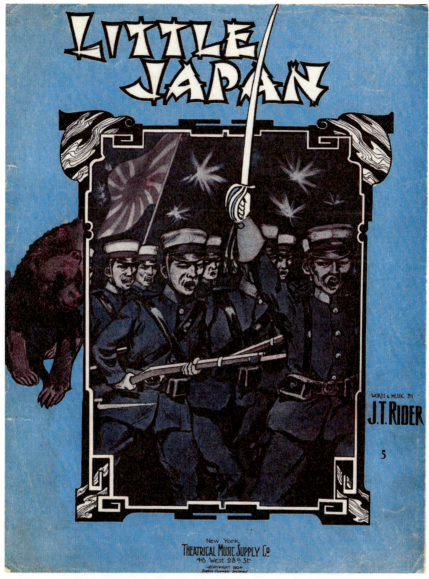

Fig. 6.3   RJ05 *Little Japan*. Words and Music by T. J. Rider. New York: Theatrical Music
            Supply 1904. Author's collection

page as the song's singer. *A Soldier of Old Japan* is again a sad ballad about a brave soldier and his little maid, who weeps for him when she realizes that he will never come back to her. In this song the soldier is called "brave" and a "hero," but otherwise nothing is said of the characteristics of the Japanese and their army.

George Totten Smith (1871-1918), Broadway director, composer, writer, and lyricist wrote the words for *The Little Brown Man of Japan*, while the music is by William H. Penn. The song consists of two strophes, a refrain, and is also a ballad. The story of the relations between Russia and Japan is told as story of a hungry bear, who wants to seize the land of a little brown man who peacefully cultivates rice fields and tea. After the bear had invaded the little brown man's island, a lion, probably Great Britain, and an eagle, the US, tell him to better get away, because the little brown man "has proved he can fight, when he thinks he is right." The little brown man can be the best friend, as long as one is peaceful, but he can also be "the bitterest foe." Interesting in this song is the mentioning of the Japanese's skin color, brown and not yellow, as it will be common later.

If the composer of *The Little Jap*, Percy Wenrich, is identical with the famous ragtime composer and composer of popular music Percy Wenrich (1887-1952),[15] he was only 18 years old, when he composed this song. Lyrics are only added to the trio, and they are as short as one can think of: "My little Japan, you are a warrior, Just like a hero brave, Keep on a fighting for your country, the flag you'll surely save." Short as the words are, they contain laudatory remarks about the Japanese soldiers.

Summing up these nine songs, six are ballads about Japanese couples, who have to part because the men are summoned to the arms, and in five of them the soldiers never return but sacrifice themselves for the country and the emperor. The remaining three songs are songs in praise of Japan or the Japanese soldiers.

Thomas S. Allen, John W. Bratton, Richard C. Dillmore, Edward Madden, Neil Moret, William H. Penn, George Totten Smith, and Percy Wenrich were all relatively well known Tin Pan Alley composers and lyricists, and Lilian Coffin, Eleanor Falk and Della Fox, especially the last one, were outstanding performers of popular music. *The Chicago American, The New York American,* and *The Boston American* (*Hearst's Boston Sunday*) in which one song appeared each, were in 1904/05 all owned by the famous newspaper publisher William Randolph Hearst (1863-1951), while all the other songs seem to have been

---

15   On Percy Wenrich see "Percy Wenrich 'The Joplin Kid'," *The Parlor Songs Academy,* September 2001. Accessed January 6, 2017. http://parlorsongs.com/bios/pwenrich/pwenrich.php.

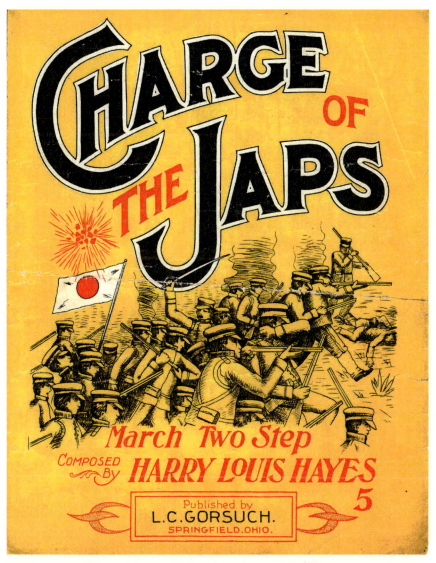

Fig. 6.4   RJ10 *Charge of the Japs*. March and Two Step. Composed by Harry Louis Hayes. Springfield, Ohio: L.C. Gorsuch 1904. Author's collection

published by well established sheet music publishers. I mention this, just to clarify, that these songs seem to have represented mainstream America at the time of the Russo-Japanese War, but there is possibly one exception: the West Coast. The nine pieces of sheet music mention 13 publishing places: New York (seven times), Chicago (three times), Boston (two times), and Philadelphia (once). This is a high concentration of publishers on the East Coast and shows an absolute absence of publishers from the West Coast. If we consider that Californians already tried to exclude Japanese children from common schools in 1893, that there was much talk about a "Yellow Peril" there, and that in 1905 the Asiatic Exclusion League had been organized in San Francisco, we can assume that American opinion was divided into the pro-Japanese East Coast and the anti- (or at least not pro-) Japanese California.

The four instrumental popular music pieces in my sample were published in Springfield (Ohio), Williamsport (Pennsylvania), New York, Chicago, and Hoquiam (Washington). Whereas of the six song pieces, which did not appear in newspapers five carry a lot of advertisments for other songs, of the four instrumental pieces three have no advertisments at all. I tend to interpret this as an indication that the songs catered to a larger audience, being written by better known composers and lyricists, while the instrumental pieces were more likely "hobby" compositions. What leads to this assumption is the fact that out of the four pieces three were published by publishing companies owned by the composers. If they are non-professional compositions, they can of course appear everywhere, where people are sympathetic to the Japanese case, even in a small lumbering town like Hoquiam (Washington), or in Springfield (Ohio). The only composer among the four composers of instrumental pieces known by several titles is Fred Hylands (1872-1913).

While I am not in a position to judge the quality of the instrumental pieces and what they wanted to express about Japan and her army, I will try to sum up the lyrics of the nine songs. Firstly, they all show a positive attitude towards the Japanese, who in almost all songs are called "little," thus invoking something like a people of nice children. As if "little" were not enough, the Japanese are regularly abbreviated to become child-like "Japs" or "Jappies," and it appears almost as a major crime that a creature like the big Russian Bear attacks these peaceful, "happy little Japs." But even if the "brown men" on their islands in the Eastern Sea are little, they know how to fight, because their ancestors were samurai heroes. Thus with this ancestral background they are naturally "brave" and committed to fight for their Emperor, for their country, for their flag, and they face death without hesitation for these great goals. Of course the women of the soldiers that died are very sad, but they understand that their men had to sacrifice themselves for Japan.

Perhaps one should conclude this chapter with a 1905 song with lyrics by Paul West and music by John W. Bratton, "sung with success by Inga Orner"[16]: *When America is Captured by the Japs*, a song published again by M. Witmark & Sons, like *Happy Jappy Soldier Man*, which was produced by the same men a year earlier. It starts with an outlook that Japan after defeating Russia might go on to fight and win over Prussia, England and finally the United States. Of course, this is a funny song, but at the same time it expresses considerable respect for the strength of the Japanese Army:

> Ev'ry day you read in papers of the Japanesy capers,
> They have chloroformed the Russians and jujitsued all their foes,
> They have taught us all a lesson, they've got ev'rybody guessin',
> Now they've caught the fussing fever, where they'll stopp nobody knows.
> When they've finished up with Russia, they may take a whack with
>   Prussia,
> Take the king of England pris'ner, and the other potentates,
> Then with cries of battle frantic, sail across the broad Atlantic,
> And before we see them coming, grab the big United States.[17]

The lyrics are almost like a warning of what was to happen in December 1941 with the attack on Pearl Harbor and Japanese aggression in East and South East Asia.

The Intermezzo-Years (1905-1941)

The time after the end of the Russo-Japanese War was a period with many tensions between Japan and the US, and many people thought that a war between Japan and America was inevitable. An illustration from the French *Petite Journal* at the end of 1906 shows the vision of a war between Japan and the USA in the coming year 1907. When in December 1907 the American war flottila, the Great White Fleet, started a tour around the world, many commentators expected that this was only a camouflage for an attack against Japan, but the visit to Japan in October 1908 to the contrary of expectations proceeded quite harmoniously.

---

16   Inga Orner or Örner (1876-1963) was a Norwegian Opera singer, who spent many years in the US and sang also Tin Pan Alley songs.

17   The sheet music is contained in John Hopkins University Library, Levy Sheet Music Collection, Box 150a, Item 020, and can be accessed at https://jscholarship.library.jhu.edu/handle/1774.2/22106?show=full. Accessed October 6, 2016.

Fig. 6.5   *When America is Captured by the Japs*. Words by Paul West, Music by
John W. Bratton. New York etc: M. Wittmark & Sons, 1905. Courtesy of John
Hopkins University, Levy Collection, Box 150a, Item 020

American popular music concerning Japan had been initially published during the last two decades of the 19th century, of course very much under the influence of two British music theatrical works, the comic opera *The Mikado or The Town of Titipu* (1885) and the operetta *The Geisha: A Story of a Tea House* (1896), several songs of which became immediate hits. With the beginning of the 20th century more and more songs about Japan appeared as individual sheet music editions and formed an important part of the so called Oriental Songs of the Tin Pan Alley songs' repertoire.[18] I tried to find as many American "Japanese songs" as possible and arrived at a figure of 124 songs published between 1901 and 1940. If one takes a look at how many songs were published per year, one notices that the distribution is fairly uneven. The peak of Japan related songs' production was between 1917 and 1921, when in every year at least five songs were published with the peak years 1917 with 16 songs and 1919 with 14 songs. The small output between 1906 and 1913 can probably be explained with the worsening of the relations between the two countries after the Russo-Japanese War, but when Japan fought Germany at Tsingtao in 1914 sympathy for the Japanese seems to have been on the rise again. From 1925 onwards popular music producers seem to have lost interest in Japanese songs, and in the 1930s this category of popular music obviously disappeared (Table 6.1).

Table 6.1   US popular songs about Japan, 1901-1940.

Period	Number of songs	Average number of songs per year
1901-05	27	5,4
1906-10	7	1,4
1911-15	12	2,4
1916-20	47	9,4
1921-25	21	4,2
1926-30	9	1,8
1931-35	1	0,2
1936-40	0	0,0
Sum	124	3,01

Computed according to number of songs identified by the autor.

---

18   The Parlor Song Academy which has an interesting website about Tin Pan Alley songs, in 2003 published two articles about "Far Away Places with Strange Sounding Names. Tin Pan Alley Goes to Asia," and "Music About Asian Places, Page 2." Accessed October 30, 2016. http://parlorsongs.com/issues/2003-1/thismonth/featurea.php. It contains several pieces about Japan.

Most of these songs are sentimental love songs, as becomes already clear from their titles like *My Japanee* (1904), *Fair Flower of Japan* (1909), *My Little Jap-O-Baby* (1910), *Be My Little Fan-Tan-Girl* (1915), *My Yokohama Girl* (1917), or *When it's Moonlight in Tokio* (1917), to name just a few. The most popular song, though, was not a love song, but a kind of lullaby: *The Japanese Sandman* (1920), by one of America's greatest popular music composers, Richard A. Whiting (1891-1939), with lyrics by Raymond B. Egan (1890-1952). First sung by Nora Bayes, it became an evergreen and a Jazz standard.[19]

Another conspicuous exception is a song published in the 23 July 1916 edition of one of Hearst's newspapers, *The New York American*, called *Look Out! California – Beware! A Warning in Song Against the Menace of Japan*. Words and lyrics are from Edith Maida Lessing, whose best known songs were *Oh! You Circus Day*, and a song about the Titanic tragedy, *Just as the Ship Went Down*, both from 1912, but about whom otherwise is little known. Only eleven years after the Russo-Japanese War and at a time when – if one takes the number of songs published as indicator – the interest in and the sympathy for the Japanese seemed to have been risen again this song is filled with negative stereotypes about the Japanese, who are "waiting just to steal our California!" The Japanese immigrants can't be trusted, because they are all hidden soldiers, while they are smiling and working all the time. There is nothing which they won't dare, and they can never be trusted. The word "Japs" in this song is clearly a pejorative one, and the Japanese are no longer belittled as "little Japs." The Chorus is enough to understand the character of this song:

> They lurk upon thy shores, California!
> They watch behind thy doors, California!
> They're a hundred thousand strong,
> And they won't be hiding long;
> There's nothing that the bastards would not dare!
> They are soldiers to a man,
> With the schemes of old JAPAN!
> Look out! California! Beware!

I could not find anything about the reception of this song, but the fact that it was published in a mainstream newspaper in New York at a time when Japan was an ally of the US during World War I is remarkable. The song's character resembles the songs which were published after the Japanese attack on Pearl Harbor 25 years later.

---

19   Several songs can be seen and heard on Joanne Bernardi's website mentioned above.

Fig. 6.6   *Look Out! California – Beware! A Warning in Song Against the Menace of Japan.*
Words and lyrics by Edith Maida. *The New York American* July 23, 1916. Author's
collection

Songs after Pearl Harbor

Nobody will be surprised to hear that during World War II quite a number of popular songs against Japan appeared in the US. Again I would like to list up what I found in strict alphabetical order:

PW01 *All You Japs Look Alike to Me.* Written by Leon A. Cofield, Hollywood, Calif.: Nordyke, 1945[20].

PW02 *Banzi You-All.* Written by Charles Dunlavy and Bob Carleton. Hollywood, Calif.: Cine-Mart Music Publishing, 1946[21].

PW03 *Bomb Tokyo***. Written by Amherst Turner and Jim Syracuse. Recorded by Music Operator Band, circa 1942.[22]

PW04 *Come on and Fight!* Written by E. E. Birks. Hollywood, Calif.: Nordyke, 1945[23].

PW05 *Come On, Jap**. Words and music by Ida Holquist. Chicago: United Music 1944.[24] TP[25]

PW06 *Cowards over Pearl Harbor***. Words and music by Fred Rose 1942. Recorded by Denver Darling, February 22, 1942.

PW07 *From Broadway to Tokyo**. Words and music by Harey Frohlichstein. Featured by Bea Wain. St. Louis, Mo.: Shattinger 1943. TP

PW08 *Fud-g-ama: get this straight Mister Jap, Jap, Jap: a united marching song for all opposed the Sneak-up-onese lie-gression*[26]. Words and Music by Ernest F. Thulin. Cicago, Ill: Niluth Publishers [1942]. TP JAP

PW09 *Get Your Gun And Come Along (We're Fixin' To Kill A Skunk)**, **. Written and performed by Carson J. Robison. Recorded December 1941, Bluebird Record No. B-11415. New York: Robbins Music Corporation 1942. TP

---

20   Mentioned in Krystyn R. Moon, "'There's No Yellow in the Red, White, and Blue': The Creation of Anti-Japanese Music during World War II," *Pacific Historical Review* 72:3 (2003), 342.

21   Mentioned in ibid., 344.

22   Songs marked with a double asterix are introduced on the website The Authentic History Center (AHC). Primary Sources from American Popular Culture. World War II in American Music. Accessed November 21, 2016. http://www.authentichistory.com/1939-1945/3-music/index.html.

23   Mentioned in Moon, "No Yellow," 340.

24   Sheet music of the songs marked with one asterix is owned by the author.

25   TP indicates that I have a picture of the title page of the sheet music, JAP indicates that the title page contains a picture of a Japanese.

26   Sheet music cover only found in the internet. Accessed December 12, 2016. http://maurice.bgsu.edu/search/o=243597049.

PW10 *Good-bye Jappys*. Written by Margaret J. Green and Ortha Green: Hollywood, Calif.: Nordyke Publishing, 1945[27].

PW11 *Goodbye Mama (I'm Off to Yokohama)**. Words and music by J. Fred Coots. New York: Chappell 1941. TP

PW12 *Hallelujah Fo' De U.S.A.* Gilbert Lee and Mae Cook. No publisher, 1943[28].

PW13 *Here I Go to Tokio (Said Barnacle Bill, The Sailor)**. Words and music by Carson J. Robison and Frank Luther. New York: Southern Music Publishuing Company 1941. TP

PW14 *Here's to You, MacArthur* * TP.Words by Nat Burton, music by Walter Kent. New York; Shapiro, Bernstein & Co. 1942. TP

PW15 *It's a K.O. For Tokyo**. Words by Le Roy Redman, music by Will Livernash. New York: Art Music Company 1942. TP

PW16 *It's Taps for the Japs**. Words and music by Rev. James R. Cox. Pittsburgh, PA: Rev. James R. Cox 1942. TP JAP

PW17 *I've Got Them all Wool-Gathered Because I never Chatter*. Written by Emilio O'Brien Motta and Simon Emilio O'Brien Motta and Simon Peter Haley: New Orleans: Haley Music, 1944[29].

PW18 *Japan and Uncle Sam*. Written by John A. Alms. Hollywood: Nordyke Music Publications, 1945[30]. TP

PW19 *Johnny Zero**, **. Words by Mack David, music by Vee Lawnhurst. New York: Santly-Joy 1943. TP

PW20 *Keep your Mouth Shut and Listen*. Written by Charles P. Bieber. Akron, Ohio: Moose Arcade Music Publisher, 1942[31].

PW21 *Let's Take a Rap at the Japs****[32], ****[33].

PW22 *MacArthur's Here Again**, **. Words and music by Ralph F. Bragg. Milo, Maine: Ralph F. Bragg 1945. TP

PW23 *Modern Cannon Ball***. By A.P. Carter, Bill Boyd and Earl Nunn. New York: Peer International Corporation 1942. Recorded by Denver Darling, July 14, 1942. TP

---

27   Mentioned in Moon, "No Yellow," 338.

28   Ibid.

29   Mentioned in ibid., 340.

30   Bernardi, *ReEnvisioningJapan*.

31   Mentioned in Moon, "No Yellow," 339.

32   Songs marked with a triple asterix are mentioned on the AHC website World War II in American Music, but neither the sheet music cover nor the record/music or other details are presented.

33   Songs marked with a quatruple asterix are mentioned in John W. Dower, War Without Mercy: Race and Power in the Pacific (New York: Pantheon Books 1986), 81 or 162, but no further information is given there.

PW24 *1945 Mother Goose Rhymes.*** Written and performed by Carson Robison. Recorded 1945

PW25 *Mow the Japs Down!****. Arranged by John Royce. Chicago: Hall & McCreary Company, c1942. https://www.esm.rochester.edu/sibley/specialcollections/findingaids/wwii-sheet-music/#V2

PW26 *Nimitz and Halsey and Me!* Written by Gordon Beecher and Ralph Bardhart: New York: Robbins Music, 1945[34].

PW27 *Oh, You Little Son of an Oriental****.

PW28 *Pearl Harbor Blues***. Written by Joe Clayton. Recorded by Doctor Clayton, March 25, 1942.

PW29 *Remember Pearl Harbor*, ***. Words by Don Reid, music by Don Reid and Sammy Kaye. New York: Republic Music Corporation 1941. TP

PW30 *Remember Pearl Harbor***. Words and music by Frank Luther. 1941. Recorded by Carson Robison, December 1941.

PW31 *Remember Pearl Harbor***. Words and music by Johnny Noble. New York: Miller Music, Inc.1942. TP

PW32 *Salt Water Cowboy (A United States Marine)*, ***. Lyrics and music by Redd Evans. New York: Jefferson Music Co. 1944. TP

PW33 *Satan's Angels from the Rising Sun.* Written by Anna Adams Beste: Wilmington, Del.: Anna Adams Beste Publishers, 1942[35].

PW34 *Sing, Mister Roosevelt, Sing* Written by Reginald Wilcox and Aaron A. Clark. No publisher, 1942[36].

PW35: *So we go to Tokio!** Words and music by Ivan Martin. Arranged by Geo.Beals. Title design by Murray Wado. No place ind. Ivan Martin 1944.TP JAP

PW36 *Spanking the Jap!* Written by O. J. Jenkins and O. T. Feagin. No publisher, 1942[37].

PW37 *Stars and Stripes on Iwo Jima*, ***. Words and music by Bob Wills and Cliff Johnsen (Cactus Jack). Hollywood, Cal.: Hilla and Range Songs, Inc. 1945. TP

PW38 *Taps For The Japs***. Written by Bud Averill and Rome Seemon. Recorded by Freddie Fisher, August 28, 1944.

PW39 *Tell Them all in Tokio We're Coming*.* Words and music by Daniel F. Fogarty. New York: Charles Coleman 1942. TP

---

34   Mentioned in Moon, "No Yellow," 340.

35   Mentioned in ibid., 338.

36   Mentioned in ibid., 340.

37   Mentioned in ibid., 339.

PW40 *The Cranky Old Yank (in a Clanky Old Tank)**. Words and music by Hoagy Carmichael. Beverly Hills, Calif: Carmichael Music Publications 1942. TP JAP

PW41 *The Cocky Jap.* Old English Tune. Words by C. H. White. C. H, White, San Francisco, 1942. TP JAP

PW42 *The Dirty Jap.* Written by Albert Granger. No publisher, 1944[38].

PW43 *The Japs Haven't Got a Chinaman's Chance* (renamed *"The Japs Haven't Got a Ghost of a Chance"*)***.[39]

PW44 *The Remember Pearl Harbor March*****.[40]

PW45 *The Rising Sun has Gone Down for all Time**. Words and music by Jimmy Lawson. No place indicated: Lawson Publications, no year indicated. TP

PW46 *The Sun Will Soon Be Setting (For The Land of The Rising Sun)***. Written by Sam Lerner. Recorded by Frankie Masters, December 15, 1941. New York: Berlin, Inc., 1942.

PW47 *There'll Be A Little Smokio In Tokio***. Written by Pat Kellogg and Jim Rice. Recorded by Don Baker with the Polka Dots, circa 1942.

PW48 *There 'll be no Adolph Hitler nor Yellow Japs to Fear.* Written by William C. Freeland and George D. Barnard: Lomax, Ill.: Barnard Music Publishers, 1943[41]. TP JAP

PW49 *There's no Yellow in the Red, White, and Blue.* Written by Bert Salter, Lou Shelly, and Bette Cannon: New York: Murray Singer Music Publishing, 1942[42].

PW50 *They're Gonna Be Playing Taps on the Japs*****.

PW51 *To Be Specific, It's Our Pacific*****.

PW52 *Tokyo, Beware!* Written by Betty De Frank: Philadelphia: Tioga Lodge, 1944[43].

PW53 *Uncle Sam's The Japanese Sandman**. Words and music by Ronald F. McElroy. Littleton, Co: R. F. McElroy 1945. TP

PW54 *Wasn't That An Awful Time at Pearl Harbor***. Recorded by Selah Jubilee Singers, May 1942.

---

38   Mentioned in ibid., 340-341.

39   Songs marked with a triple asterix are mentioned on the AHC website World War II in American Music, but neither the sheet music cover nor the record/music or other details are presented.

40   Songs marked with a quatruple asterix are mentioned in John W. Dower, *War Without Mercy: Race and Power in the Pacific* (New York: Pantheon Books 1986), 81 or 162, but no further information is given there.

41   Mentioned in Moon, "No Yellow," 339.

42   Ibid.

43   Ibid.

PW55 *We Did it Before and We Can Do It Again**, **. Words and music by Cliff Friend and Charlie Tobias. New York: M. Witmark and Sons 1941. TP

PW56 *We'll Have a Rodeo in Tokyo and a Roundup in Old Berlin**, **. Words and Music by Forest 'Trees' Johnson and Ozie Waters. New York: Joe McDaniel Music Co. 1943. TP

PW57 *We'll Knock The Japs Right Into The Laps of The Nazis***. Lyric by Ned Washington, music by Lew Pollack. New York: Mills Music 1942. TP

PW58 *We'll Smash the Japanee!* Written by Charles E. Burns and Larry Besson: No publisher, 1942[44].

PW59 *We're Going to Find a Fellow Who Is Yellow and Beat Him Red, White and Blue****

PW60 *We're Going to Lick those Dirty Japs.* Written by Roger Crombie. Cincinnati: Acme Music Service Printers, 1942[45].

PW61 *We're Gonna Have to Slap, the Dirty Little Jap and Uncle Sam's the Guy who Can Do It**, **. Words and music by Bob Miller. New York: Bob Miller, Inc. 1941. TP JAP

PW62 *We're Gonna Stop Your Yappin Mister Jap.* Written by Floyd Wilkins, Russ Hull, and Hal Kent: Chicago: Country Music, 1942[46].

PW63 *We're on our Way to Tokyo, Rome and Berlin**. Lyrics by Chester Gemmell. Music by Esthel Benner. Salem, Oregon: Benner & Gemmell 1942. TP

PW64 *We're Picking the Japs from the Lap of Yokohama**. Words and music by May Weyer McKague. Hollywood: Norman Edwards Music Publisher 1943. TP JAP

PW65 *We 're Setting the Rising Sun.* Written by Frank J. Daley. No publisher, 1944[47].

PW66 *We've Got to Do a Job on the Jap's, Baby**, **. Words and music by Edgar Leslie, Abel Baer and George W. Meyer. NewYork: Bregman, Vocco and Conn, Inc. 1942. TP

PW67 *When The Atom Bomb Fell***. Written by Davis and Taylor. Recorded by Karl and Harty, December 1945.

PW68 *When Those Little Yellow Bellies Meet the Cohens and the Kellys****

PW69 *When We Set that Rising Sun**. Written by Cliff Japhet and Sgt. Benny Doss. New York: Joe Mc- Daniel Music, 1945. TP

---

44   Mentioned in ibid., 340.
45   Mentioned in ibid., 338.
46   Mentioned in ibid., 340.
47   Mentioned in ibid., 339.

PW70 *Who Do You Think We Are?* Lyrics by Mark Minkus, music by Henry Kane. New York: Patriotic Music Publishing Co 1943[48]. TP JAP; https://thea.com/Military-Historical-Ww-II-Sheet-Music/

PW71 *Win The War Blues***. Written and performed by Sonny Boy Williamson. Recorded December 14, 1944

PW72 *You Can't Win This War Through Love**, **. Lyrics by Mark Minkus and music by Henry Kane. New York: Patriotic Music Publishing Co 1943. TP JAP

PW73 *You're a Sap, Mister Jap**, **. Words and music by James Cavanaugh, John Redmond and Nat Simon. New York: Mills Music 1941. TP JAP

I would like to start with a visual analysis of the title pages of the sheet music. Out of the 73 war songs related to Japan I could get 35 title pages, but of these only eleven, a third, depict a Japanese soldier. It is remarkable that always only one Japanese soldier is drawn, never a group of soldiers, as was the case in the Russo-Japanese War songs. This soldier has three features: he is small, he is yellow and he screams out of fear or pain, because he is attacked by a strong American soldier or by Uncle Sam himself. Only one cover is different, and this one was drawn by the rather famous designer Arthur Szyk (1894-1951), a Polish Jew who lived in the US since December 1940. Szyk became famous for his many caricatures of the Axis leaders Hitler, Mussolini and Hirohito. After the Japanese attack on Pearl Harbor, he drew a picture of "Japan's aggressor: Admiral Yamamoto" on the *TIME Magazine*'s cover of 22 December 1941, which can be clearly interpreted as his version of the "Yellow Peril."[49] Szyk's cover of Hoagy Carmichael's song *The Cranky Old Yank (in a Clanky Old Tank)* shows an ugly elderly Japanese soldier with spectacles, very big ears, a moustache, a chrysanthemum concorde on his cap, a swastika on his shoulder and the inscription "Honorary Arian" on his collar. Since he bears three stars on his shoulder he is probably meant to be a Japanese three-star-general, one of the Japanese military leaders, who were thought to be responsible for waging the war against the United States. But the same picture was used three years later for a US army pamphlet[50] in 1945, after the end of the war in Europe. It bears the inscription "Two down and one to go," showing Hitler and Mussolini

---

48   https://thea.com/Military-Historical-Ww-II-Sheet-Music/ . Accessed August 12, 2019.

49   On Szyk see: Katja Widmann and Johannes Zechner, eds. *Arthur Szyk: Bilder gegen den Nationalsozialismus und Terror /Drawing Against National Socialism and Terror* (Munich/ Berlin: Deutscher Kunstverlag, 2008).

50   War Department Pamphlet, 21-31.

crossed out with red ink and a not yet crossed out Japanese, who thus has to be Hirohito, the nominal commander of the Japanese Army. Therefore, the Japanese general on the title page of *The Cranky Old Yank* is surely the Japanese Emperor Hirohito.[51] However, and regardless of the fact that Hoagy Carmichael (1899-1981) was one of the most successful American composers and performers of popular music in the 20th century, it seems that this song did not become a really popular one.

On the yellow cover of *We're Picking the Japs from the Lap of Yokohama* Mussolini, Hitler and a Japanese are shown speared on bayonets. The Japanese is supposed to be Tōjō Hideki (1884-1948) or Emperor Hirohito, but from the drawing it is not clear who is meant. Since the text of the song mentions "Mister Hirohito," he is probably the one on top of the three. He wears military boots, has the Japanese navy flag with the sun stripes on his cap and a dagger in his hand, an indication that Japan in the attack on Pearl Harbor proved that it is a back stabber.[52] Another feature of the Japanese in this and many other drawings is the open mouth with enormous front teeth and his closed slant eyes. A Japanese with even two daggers, one in his mouth and one in his right hand, together with a German soldier with a handgun and decorated with a swastika is drawn on the title page of *You Can't Win This War Through Love*. To make the Japanese more animal-like he is represented with claws on his hand instead of finger-nails. Although the Japanese is a frightening appearance he is confronted by a mighty American fist, against wich he probably cannot succeed.

The cover of *We're Gonna Have to Slap, the Dirty Little Jap and Uncle Sam's the Guy who Can Do It* is signed Barbelle and thus was probably made by Albert Wilfred Barbelle (1887-1957), a sheet music cover artist of Tin Pan Alley songs.[53] This impressive propaganda work shows something like a prototype of America's reaction to the Pearl Harbor attack. An all yellow Japanese soldier with two pistols in his hands – the "dirty little Jap" – is beaten by a mighty white hand, that of Uncle Sam, so that he looses one pistol and cries in anger and desparation. This picture and the one of *You're a Sap, Mister Jap* on which

---

51   In Japan people out of respect never call the emperor by his name, but only by his posthumous name. In Japanese practice, thus, Emperor Shōwa would be the appropriate denomination, but in the West and especially during the Pacific War the Japanese Emperor was always called Hirohito, a name which rhymed on Benito (Mussolini). The axes were most often represented in Western propaganda as "Hitler, Mussolini and Hirohito." Prime Minister Tōjō Hideki was seldom used in the allied propaganda.

52   Already during World War I, Japan was presented in this form on German propaganda postcards and cartoons, after it had attacked the German colony Tsingtao.

53   On Albert Wilfred Barbelle see Bernard S. Parker, *World War I Sheet Music* (Jefferson, NC: McFarland), vol. 1, 17.

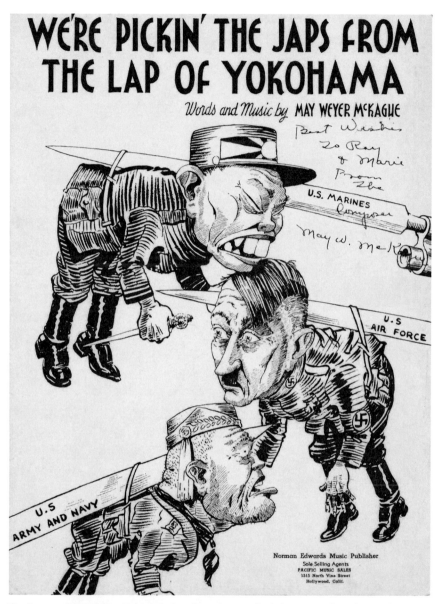

Fig. 6.7   PW64 *We're Picking the Japs from the Lap of Yokohama*. Words and music by May
              Weyer McKague. Hollywood: Norman Edwards Music Publisher 1943. Author's
              collection

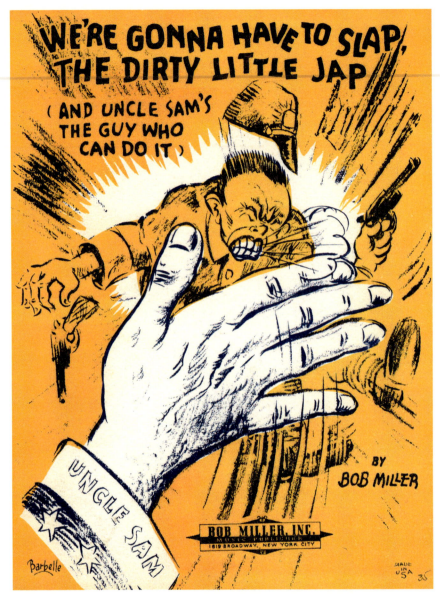

Fig. 6.8   PW61 *We're Gonna Have to Slap, the Dirty Little Jap and Uncle Sam's the Guy who Can Do It*. Words and music by Bob Miller. New York: Bob Miller, Inc. 1941. Author's collection

a big Uncle Sam holds a small Japanese soldier on his knee and beats him up, so that he looses his military cap and his spectacles (signed IM-HO[54]), both published already in 1941, seem to represent the general popular American opinion about the Japanese and their army in the Pacific War. Japan is seen like a naughty child which has to be beaten up in order to make her behave properly again. *It's Taps for the Japs*, also signed Im.Ho, depicts a little yellow-skinned Japanese marine with spectacles, of course, who tumbles to the sound of a bugle.

One of the most original cover drawings is that of *Fud-g-ama*. Whereas in the foreground eight people as the representatives of the American people are marching hand-in-hand, in the upper part of the cover two cannons are shooting at the top of Mount Fuji, from which the top of the mountain falls off and the head of a Japanese soldier appears with the Japanese navy's flag in his mouth and his cap falling off.

If we look at how the Japanese were called in the titles of these 73 songs, the result is obvious. Twenty song titles mention the "Jap" or the "Japs," in one song even as "dirty little Jap." At the time of the Pacific War, compared to the Russo-Japanese War, "Jap" was no longer a nice denomination for the Japanese but together with "Nip" or "Nippy" from Nipponese a very disdainful one. "Nip," though, does not appear in the titles of the songs. The correct "Japanese" is not to be found in a single song title. Other words for the Japanese in the songs' titles are "cowards," "Satan's Angels from the Rising Sun," "little son of an Oriental," "yellow fellow," "little yellow bellies," and "sap," which in this context means as much as "idiot." For Japan two times the "rising sun" is used, of course alway with the additional explanation that it is destinated to set down. The only comparison of the Japanese in a song title with an animal is that with a skunk.

The use of denominations for the Japanese in the song texts is similar. I can use the texts of 46 songs, while I do not know the texts of the remaining 27 songs. "Jap" or "Japs" is by far the most common way of speaking about the Japanese (PW05, 08, 11, 14, 15, 16, 24, 26, 30, 38, 41, 42, 45, 54, 57, 61, 63, 64, 66, 67, 69, 73) while "Nip" (PW53) or "little Nippy" (PW32) is seldom used. Whereas the use of "Japs" or "Nips" is widely known, the use of "suki yakis" for Japanese (PW23, 28, 33) is not. *There'll be a Little Smokio in Tokio* speaks of "saki yaki boy," while in *The Cranky Old Yank* one line says "ev'ry Sukiyaki lacky will be lookin' mighty tacky" and the *Salt Water Cowboy*, a synonym for marine, says

---

54 IM-HO stands for Immerman-Holley Art Studio, founded by Robert M. Holley (1913-1977) and Sol Immerman in the late1930s. See also Martin Klamkin, *Old Sheet Music: A Pictorial History* (New York: Hawthorn Books, 1975), 182-183.

Fig. 6.9   PW16 *It's Taps for the Japs*. Words and music by Rev. James R. Cox. Pittsburgh, PA: Rev. James R. Cox 1942. Author's collection

"Get along, sukiyaki, ... I'm gonna brand your carcass with a star-striped U.S.," which indicates that the Japanese dish Sukiyaki was already well known in the US at the time of the Pacific War. Sukiyaki as a pejorative term for Japanese reminds one of the term Krauts for Germans or Frogs for the French, all terms derived from the imagined eating habits of the people of these nations.

One problem, which one encounters, when one tries to discover the image of the Japanese Army in American war songs is the unspecific nature of the word "Jap," or "Japanese." The American soldiers in the song texts fight the "Japs" and not the "Japanese soldiers" or the "Japanese marines," but in reality the American enemy is the Japanese military and not the Japanese children, women or elderly, the civil population, even though in some American propaganda texts it is stated that the whole population of Japan shall be extincted.[55] Since the US soldiers were fighting the Japanese, the "Japs," "Japanese," or "Nips" in the song texts have to be understood as the Japanese Army and Navy. All statements about the Japanese can be equally understood as statements about the army.

Here, I would like to look at the song texts of the 73 songs, but I can say nothing about the 27 songs which I know only from the title and which I could not look at. Of the remaining 46 songs 26 deal with the US army and what it will do, and therefore they contain no judgements about the Japanese. Finally, only 20 songs out of 73 remain for a content analysis of the image of the Japanese Army.

If we start with the bodily qualities of the Japanese, there are surprisingly few negative qualities mentioned. As might be expected, "yellow" is mentioned most often, but by far not in all songs. "I'll stick their yellow nose in the ground" (*Here I Go to Tokio* (*Said Barnacle Bill, The Sailor*), and "those yellow faces" (from *Uncle Sam's The Japanese Sandman*) are still more neutral, while "the dirty yellow louses" (from *Uncle Sam's The Japanese Sandman*), "that yellow scum of the sea" (*Remember Pearl Harbor*) or "We'll skin the streak of yellow from the sneaky little fellow" (*We're Gonna Have to Slap, the Dirty Little Jap*) nowadays are to the utmost politically incorrect. "Yellow" seems to have been a much more injurious skin colour than "brown," as we can see from the Japan-friendly Russo-Japanese war song *Little Brown Man of Japan*. In *Remember Pearl Harbor* by Frank Luther one line says: "we used to call them our 'little brown brothers,'"

---

55 An American propaganda postcard carries the announcement "We'll blow the Jap off the map." See Linhart, *"Dainty Japanese" or Yellow Peril*, 128, similar to 'wipe the Jap from the map' in *Remember Pearl Harbor* (PW30) by Frank Luther or to "we'll wipe the Axis right off the map" in *You're a Sap, Mister Jap* (PW73). See also "Uncle Sam's gone to slap the treacherous Jap and wipe him from creation" and "we'll wipe him off the earth" in *Japan and the United States* (PW18).

Fig. 6.10   PW73 *You're a Sap, Mister Jap.* Words and music by James Cavanaugh, John Redmond and Nat Simon. New York: Mills Music 1941. Author's collection

which also shows that brown is accepted but yellow is different. Other body-related qualities to be found in the songs are slant-eyes and buck-teeth, but compared to visual materials, on which the Japanese soldiers are always depicted as yellow, slant-eyed and with buck-teeth, the song texts are harmless. When compared to animals the Japanese are likened to monkeys in *There'll Be A Little Smokio In Tokio* (PW47): "We're getting all set to sail/ To make all the monkeys wail/ Over the ocean, ahoy." This animal metaphor was widely used in the US for the Japanese during the Pacific War,[56] and it had been already used before by the Germans during World War I.[57] Other songs call the Japanese "louses" (see above), "rats" (*Remember Pearl Harbor* (PW30) by Frank Luther), or "ratzes," probably a contraction of rat and Nazi (*We'll Have a Rodeo in Tokyo*, PW56), "vultures" (*Remember Pearl Harbor* (PW30) by Frank Luther), "swine" (*Modern Cannon Ball*, PW23), a "stray dog" or worse than a "rattlesnake" (both from *Pearl Harbor Blues*, PW28). In *Get Your Gun and Come Along* (PW09) the Japanese are compared to a skunk. Anyway, there is not one single animal to which the Japanese are compared constantly. Here again a problem appears. All the animals enumerated are animals which are kept in contempt, and it can hardly be made understandable that the US have to mobilize their navy and airforce to fight an foreign army compared to louses, rats, monkeys, skunks, rattlesnakes, and vultures.

More important than the bodily characteristics are the mental or spiritual characteristics or, stated otherwise, the Japanese character as mentioned in the songs. The Japanese attack on the US Pacific Fleet in Pearl Harbor must have been a real shock for the US, and thus by and again the song texts remember that "the Japanese attacked without warning," and therefore they are "backstabbers." The Japanese had already started the Russo-Japanese War with a surprise attack on Port Arthur, but at that time this was not considered to be a disreputable deed of barbarians. Therefore, the Japanese were accused of being "worse than a rattle-snake," which does not attack without warning. The denomination of the Japanese as "cowards" can probably also be linked to the Pearl Harbor surprise attack. An honorable enemy would have sent out a warning that he was going to attack. To shoot a person from behind is one of the worst crimes in American Western movies, something only cowards would do, while to shoot one's enemy face to face was considered honorable. Since

56   Dower, *War Without Mercy*, 81-83.

57   Sepp Linhart, "The "Yellow Monkey": Japan's Image in Germany and Austria-Hungary after the Outbreak of the German-Japanese War in 1914 as Seen on Picture Postcards," *The East Asian Dimension of the First World War: Global Entanglements and Japan, China and Korea, 1914-1919*, eds. Jan Schmidt and Katja Schmidtpott (Frankfurt/New York: Campus Verlag, 2020) (forthcoming).

the Japanese "have thrown all scruples off," they could resort to such dishonorable tactics. But it could also be that the fact that the Japanese are "heathens" was responsible for their misbehavior. Given the bad character of the Japanese, Sunny Boy Williams in his *Win the War Blues* (PW71) even utters the fear that the Japanese might be "slippin' in through my baby's back door," a fear that was also stirred by the American WWII propaganda posters series "This is the Enemy," on which a yellow man is stealing or attacking a white woman. In *Tell Them all in Tokio We're Coming* (PW39) the Japanese are accused of murdering "men and women and the babes up on the breast." Doctor Clayton in his *Pearl Harbor Blues* (PW28) calls the Japanese "ungrateful," an allegation against the Japanese which was also very widespread in Germany during WWI, when Japan attacked the German colony Tsingtao. Clayton is especially upset because the US sold Japan "brass and scrap iron" which the Japanese used to produce bombs and shells which they "dropped on Pearl Harbor."

Other bad characteristics of the Japanese are that they are "cruel," destructive," "dirty," "evil," "full of hate," "rotten," "ruthless," "sneaky," and "stupid." They are "spying," "treacherous," and "their word is not worth a snap." When doing bad things they even "grin with great delight" (PW08).

One of the most racist songs *We're Gonna Have to Slap, the Dirty Little Jap* (PW61) is the only one which gives an explanation why the Japanese are fighting the US, when it says "Their alibi for fighting is to save their face/ For ancestors waiting in celestial space," a reference to Japanese ancestor worship. All the other songs are not interested in the reason for the Japanese attack or they simply state that the Japanese are "stupid" because they have attacked a giant enemy like the US.

Finally, it has to be stressed that only in two songs statements about the Japanese soldiers' fighting abilities are made. In *Pearl Harbor Blues* (PW28) Joe Clayton says "Some say the Japanese is hard fighters," but he at once adds that they are fighting in an unfair way, and in *You Can't Win This War Through Love* (PW72) the enemy is said to be rough and tough. It seems that positive remarks about the fighting abilities of the Japanese or even calling them a dangerous enemy would have been seen as destructive and as demoralizing for the US forces, even though the Amerian soldiers as well as their war leaders certainly did have a lot of respect for the Japanese forces.

Conclusion

When the war between Japan and Russia started on February 8, 1904, the Americans as neighbours of the two combatants were interested observers of this conflict. Already before the war broke out, many songs about Japan had been published in the US, and after the war had begun a small number of songs about the Japanese soldiers, who had to fight the Russians were published as sheet music in the US. Even though the racial conflicts between white Americans and Japanese immigrants had already begun in California, the songs about the Russo-Japanese War, usually published on the East Coast, were without any exception sympathetic with the Japanese case. The soldiers were described as good fighters, as brave men with a long tradition of heroism, with a profound love for their country and for the *tennō*.

During the Pacific War, only three and a half decades after the Russo-Japanese War, many more songs on Japan were published as sheet music or sold as records. Now the Americans were no longer bystanders, but involved in the war as the defending ones. The Japanese troops, under the supreme command of Prime Minister Tōjō and *tennō* Hirohito, were the aggressors, and accordingly the vocabulary and with it the image of the Japanese military changed radically. All the good characteristics ascribed to the Japanese soldiers in 1904-05 were substituted by evil characteristics. These characteristics were no longer attributed to the Japanese soldiers, but to the Japanese people as a whole.

There are only two attributes or denominations, which seem to have survived from the Russo-Japanese to the Pacific War, namely the name "Jap," which underwent a complete change of meaning, as can be easily seen if comparing the titles *Happy Jappy Soldier Man* and *We're Gonna Have to Slap, the Dirty Little Jap*, and the attribute "little." In songs like *Little Brown Man of Japan, Little Fighting Soldier Man, Little Japan, One Little Soldier Man*, or *The Little Jap* from the years 1904-05 "little" is an attribute which expresses sympathy and worry for the little Japanese soldiers, who have to fight the "big" Russians. In contrast, the usage of "little" in phrases like "little punk" (PW09), "little son of an Oriental" (PW27), "little Nippy" (PW32), "this sneaky little fellow," "the dirty little Jap" (PW61), "those little yellow bellies" (PW68) is full of contempt for the "stupid little" Japanese who dared to attack the "big" Americans.

It seems that the producers of the war songs against Japan by intent did not want to write anything about the Japanese military besides that the Japanese were unfair fighters, backstabbers etc., and of course that they were bad and evil because they sided with Nazi Germany and Fascist Italy. The songs probably had the function to quieten the American population. Any reference to the Japanese Army as filled with great fighting spirit or as being a dangerous enemy could have had negative effects on the American morale. Therefore, the image of the Japanese military in the songs between 1941 and 1945 is totally different from that of the songs between 1904 and 1905. The time span of thirtyfive years, more than one generation, was long enough that people who had observed the Russo-Japanese War from afar and through popular songs did no longer remember what had been said back then about the Japanese soldiers, and thus saw no contradiction in them to the anti-Japanese songs from the Pacific War.

Works Cited

Authentic History Center (AHC): *Primary Sources from American Popular Culture: World War II in American Music*. Accessed November 21, 2016. http://www.authentichistory.com/1939-1945/3-music/index.html

Bernardi, Joanne. *ReEnvisioning Japan: Japan as Destination in 20th Century Visual and Material Culture*. Accessed December 6, 2016. http://humanities.lib.rochester.edu/rej/.

Dower, John W. *War Without Mercy: Race and Power in the Pacific*. New York: Pantheon Books, 1986.

Erenberg, Lewis A. und Susan E. Hirsch, eds. *The War in American Culture: Society and Consciousness During World War II*. Chicago and London: Chicago University Press, 1996.

Jacob, Frank. *Tsushima 1905: Ostasiens Trafalgar* (Paderborn: Schöningh, 2017).

Jones, John Bush. *The Songs that Fought the War: Popular Music and the Home Front, 1939-1945*. Waltham, MA: Bandeis University Press 2006.

Linhart, Sepp. *"Dainty Japanese" or Yellow Peril? Western War Postcards 1900-1945*. Vienna: LIT, 2005.

———. „The "Yellow Monkey": Japan's Image during the First World War as Seen on German Picture Postcards". In *The East Asian Dimension of the First World War. Global Entanglements and Japan, China and Korea, 1914-1919*, eds. Katja Schmidtpott and Jan Schmidt. Frankfurt, New York: Campus Verlag (forthcoming).

Mac Dougall, Robert. "Red, Brown and Yellow Perils: Images of the American Enemy in the 1940s and 1950s". *Journal of Popular Culture* 32:4 (1999), 59-75.

Miles, Hannah. "WWII Propaganda: The Influence of Racism." *Artifact* (A Journal of Undergraduate Writing of the University of Missouri) 6 (2012). Accessed July 31, 2019. https://artifactsjournal.missouri.edu/2012/03/wwii-propaganda-the-influence-of-racism/.

Moon, Krystyn R. "'There's no Yellow in the Red, White, and Blue': The Creation of Anti-Japanese Music during World War II." *Pacific Historical Review* 72:3 (2003), 333-352.

Sheppard, W. Anthony. "An Exotic Enemy: Anti-Japanese Musical Propaganda in World War II Hollywood." *Journal of the American Musicological Society* 54:2 (2001), 303-357.

Smith, Kathleen E.R.: *God Bless America. Tin Pan Alley Goes to War*. Kentucky: The University Press of Kentucky 2003.

The Parlor Song Academy. "Far Away Places with Strange Sounding Names. Tin Pan Alley Goes to Asia," (2003). Accessed July 31, 2019. http://parlorsongs.com/issues/2003-1/thismonth/featurea.php.

The Parlor Song Academy. "Music About Asian Places, Page 2," (2003). Accessed July 31, 2019. http://parlorsongs.com/issues/2003-1/thismonth/featurea.php.

Townsend, Peter. *Pearl Harbor Jazz. Change in Popular Music in the Early 1940s*. Jackson: University Press of Mississippi, 2007.

Young, William H, and Nancy K. Young, *Music of the World War II Era*. Westport, CT/London: Greenwood Press, 2008.

Postscript: Some days before I got the galley proofs for this article I got notice of W. Anthony Sheppard's new book Extreme Exoticism: Japan in the American Musical Imagination. New York: Oxford University Press 2019, too late to incorporate its findings in my essay. I recommend all readers interested in this topic to read especially the section "The Yankees of the Far East": Representations of the Russo-Japanese War, pp. 90 to 94.

CHAPTER 7

Monsters or Men? Popular Perceptions of Japanese POWs on American Soil

Adam S. Rock

Introduction

Despite efforts to market the noble Japanese soldier to Western audiences during the opening decades of the 20th century, most Americans continued to question the civility and benevolence of a territorially aggressive, and racially different "other" directly challenging the United States. Fuelled by racially explicit propaganda Americans became preoccupied with the image of Japanese soldiers as menacing "ape-like" invaders, while others respected a worthy advisory humanized through pre-war relationships or personal interaction with Japanese POWs in the United States. Highlighting these conflicting images offers a more comprehensive view into American perceptions of the Japanese military during the war, while uncovering the effectiveness of domestic propaganda in continually influencing those views. Before the war most Americans knew very little about Japan or the nearly 75 million people residing far across the Pacific. Public opinion varied considerably during the war ranging from, "There are lots of good Japs regardless of what people say," and "The [Japanese] leaders are basically to blame. I read a piece in *YANK* magazine just last night about what the Jap G.I. goes through in his basic training, and after reading that I can see what I couldn't see before." to increasingly judgmental and punitive sentiments classifying the Japanese as "a cruel race, abusing even their own people, especially the women," as well as "the leaders are ambitious and the people are uneducated."[1] Although racist perceptions of the Japanese permeated throughout American society during the war, others overlook or overcame these misconceptions, extending cooperation, compassion, and occasionally even friendship, toward the Japanese people. With the exception of those serving in uniform throughout the Pacific, most Americans had almost no previous exposure to the Japanese, relying on derogatory propaganda to construct personal opinions; however, a relatively small number of Japanese

---

1   National Opinion Research Center, "Japan and the Post-War World," Report No. 32 (University of Denver, Aug 1946), 11.

© VERLAG FERDINAND SCHÖNINGH, 2020 | DOI:10.30965/9783657702930_008

prisoners of war (POW) held in a series of POW camps throughout the United States offers a unique opportunity to explore the effectiveness of this medium on the American people, as well as the influence of this racist campaign on the thousands of Japanese fighting men adjusting to captivity in the U.S.

Unlike the 400,000 German and Italian prisoners of war detained in America between 1941 and 1946, there have been few studies of the 5,000 soldiers and sailors from the Empire of Japan detained within the borders of the United States, limiting our perceptions of race on the treatment of these racially different POWs.[2] The first historical analysis of the Japanese POWs held in the United States published in English, Arnold Krammer's fascinating 1983 article "Japanese Prisoners of War in America," provides readers with a concise overview of the program including capture, treatment, and repatriation, of Japanese POWs. Although primarily focusing on U.S. interrogation practices and their results, Krammer argues that Japanese prisoners seemed to experience visibly different treatment compared to Italian or German POWs in American camps; however, the article only begins examining how these fluctuations in treatment, labor, and education. Building upon Krammer's seminal study, Ulrich Straus' 2003 monograph, *The Anguish of Surrender: Japanese POWs of World War II*, expands Krammer's examination and further highlights the psychological issues often associated with the transition from warrior to captive. Straus also focuses on the controversial extended interrogation process that Japanese POWs appeared to endure at considerably higher rates when compared with German or Italian prisoners.[3] Considering the racial dynamics of the Pacific War, discrepancies in treatment and variations in policy between the Asian and Caucasian POWs in American hands seems to have an easy explanation. John Dower's influential study of the racial influences in the Pacific theater fittingly titled *War Without Mercy: Race and Power in the Pacific War*, argued that racial fear and hatred were major factors that determined how

---

2 The exact number of the Japanese prisoners is debated according to official sources, ranging from 569 in the U.S. Army publication by George G. Lewis and John Mewha, "History of Prisoner of War Utilization by the United States Army, 1776-1945," U.S. Dept. of the Army Pamphlet No. 20-213 [Washington, D.C., June 1955], 148; to 3,260 referenced within the "Investigations of the National War Effort," H. Rep. 728, 79 Cong., 1 sess., (June 12, 1945). Ultimately the most accurate number comes from the Records of the Provost Marshal General's Office (Record Group 389), at the Modern Military Branch of the National Archives II Washington, D.C. (henceforth cited as MMB-NA II). These records indicate the total number of Japanese POWs detained within the continental United States at 5,424. Arnold Krammer also uses this number in "Japanese Prisoners of War in America," *Pacific Historical Review* 52:1 (1983), 67.

3 Ulrich Straus, *The Anguish of Surrender: Japanese POWs of World War II* (Seattle, WA: University of Washington Press, 2003), 116, 135, 139.

both Japanese and Anglo-Americans perceived and dealt with an enemy they viewed as the "inferior other."[4] While Dower's work highlights the influence of this relationship overseas, the American home front seems complacent if not culpable with the forced relocation of over 100,000 Japanese Americans in accordance with President Roosevelt's Executive Order 9066. Because Americans of German and Italian descent escaped this extralegal measure, it appears that influence of racism extended far-beyond the battlefield. Despite these factors, many historians continue to overlook the importance of understanding the war through this powerful lens. Part of the blame lies in Western preoccupation with the fighting in Europe that often glosses over the underlining origins of the war in favor of a triumphant narrative driven by conquest and liberation. In the Pacific, however, the influence of race on the war is almost undeniable. John Dower skillfully argues racial fear and hatred were major factors that determined how both Japanese and Anglo-Americans perceived and dealt with an enemy they viewed as the inferior other. Using the story of Japanese POWs in the United States to uncover American perceptions of the Japanese fighting-man, as well as influence of domestic propaganda, this chapter argues that although personal interaction with Japanese POWs could occasionally change the preconceived ideas of stateside personnel and local residents, racist propaganda, embellished accounts from the front, and xenophobia, effectively alienated and vilified the Japanese people beyond redemption.

Preconceived Notions of the "Inferior Other"

American prejudice toward the Japanese originated with the anti-Asian sentiment and xenophobia occurring during the first major waves of Asian immigration in the mid to late nineteenth century. When war between these two empires broke out in December 1941, most Americans still knew very little about Japan and lacked communalities with its people, who appeared vastly differed in almost every aspect including language, history, politics, religion, culture, and race. When Fortune magazine asked Americans in 1944 if they knew the population of Japan, and what percentage of the nation could, "Read their own language?" less than 15% responded with the correct answers of nearly 75 million literate Japanese.[5] Furthermore, in the late spring of 1945 and after four years of desperate fighting, nearly half of Americans could not even

---

4   John W. Dower, *War Without Mercy: Race and Power in the Pacific War* (New York: Pantheon Books, 1986), 10.

5   NORC, "Japan and the Post-War World," 13.

name the Japanese Emperor.[6] What little Americans did know was often based
on propaganda and racist caricatures portraying Japanese people as collectively driven, fiercely aggressive, dull-witted, bucked-toothed, physically weak,
with poor eyesight, and frequently depicted using thick "coke bottle" glasses.
In fact, U.S. propaganda often portrayed the Japanese as bats or primates.[7] The
surprise attack on the Pacific fleet docked at Pearl Harbor on 7 December 1941,
strengthened these misconceptions and seemed to galvanize Americans hatred for Japanese men and women perceived as racially inferior. The outbreak
of war intensified the existing racial hatred dating back to the nineteenth
century. Like other Asian immigrants in the United States before the war, the
Japanese experienced overt racism and legal barriers intended to exclude and
control them. Many of these laws focused on depriving Japanese immigrants
of American citizenship and the ability to own land. Several organizations
throughout the Pacific Northwest including the Japanese Exclusion League
of California, Native Sons and Daughters of the Golden West, the California
Farm Bureau, and many others, relentlessly worked to deprive Japanese immigrants of basic human rights.[8] Home to the largest population of Japanese
immigrants, California was also perhaps the most assertive in restricting their
basic freedoms, even passing the "Alien Land Law" in 1913, legally preventing
Japanese citizens from owning land within the state.[9] Following the attack at
Pearl Harbor, existing American hatred and fear of the Japanese intensified to
the point where President Roosevelt issued his infamous order requiring the
forced relocation of all Japanese Americans living in western states. This order
gave the federal government power to prohibit any person from any area of
the country where national security was considered threatened. Although the
measure did not explicitly apply to Japanese Americans or require imprisonment, nearly all persons of Japanese descent along the west coast were forc-
ibly relocated to War Relocation Centers away from the Pacific seaboard.[10] The
internment of Japanese Americans highlights an additional example of the
United States tumultuous racial history, only decades removed from the institu-
tion of slavery, and where many state governments still supported exclusionary

---

6   Ibid., 21.
7   Dower, *War Without Mercy*, 81.
8   Edwin E. Ferguson, "The California Alien Land Law and the Fourteenth Amendment,"
      California Law Review 35:1 (1947), 61.
9   Brian Niiya, ed. *Japanese American History: An A-to-Z Reference from 1868 to the Present*
      (Los Angeles, CA: Japanese American National Museum, 1993), 110.
10   Francis Feeley, *A Strategy of Dominance: The History of an American Concentration Camp
      Pomona, California* (St. James, NY: Brandywine Press, 1995), 7.

Jim Crow segregation laws.[11] These controversial interment camps were not the only holding facilities for prisoners of Japanese lineage however, with the U.S. War Department eventually holding over 5,000 Japanese POWs from across the Pacific within the United States during the war. Much like the war itself, the U.S. Government seemed unprepared for this great influx of enemy prisoners that came flooding into the United States, and in the winter of 1942 American officials rushed to outline regulations given that the nation lacked existing policy on the treatment of POWs. Springing together virtually overnight, the War Department delegated responsibility onto several departments. Unfortunately, these overlapping bureaucratic command structures heavily relied on stateside commanders and guards to implement oversee daily operations, in addition to various educational and labor programs. Although American officials outwardly projected fair and equal treatment for all POWs held in the United States, deeply engrained racial stereotypes of Orientals reinforced through a vicious propaganda campaign aimed at dehumanizing the Japanese made this task nearly impossible.

Racism and Equal Care

In early 1943 American personnel began receiving the first large shipments of POWs as a result of the Anglo-American agreement made the previous year, which outlined the transfer of all captured prisoners of war to the continental U.S. The transfer was thought to alleviate already stressed British forces from the problems of guarding, holding, feeding, and caring for large numbers of captured enemy combatants. In August 1942, the Joint Chiefs of Staff chose to accept 50,000 POWs and requested the additional 100,000 be sent to Canada, as the sudden infusion of 150,000 enemy prisoners into the United States appeared too large of a security threat. However, after further consideration, the Joint Chiefs decided that it was impractical to split the shipment of prisoners and accepted them all, provided American personnel were given at least one month to make preparations.[12] Over the next three years, an unprecedented number of enemy prisoners arrived on American shores,

---

11   Michael J. Klarman, From Jim Crow to Civil Rights The Supreme Court And the Struggle for Racial Equality (Oxford: Oxford University Press, 2007), 58.

12   Extract from Minutes, JCS-32d meeting, 8 Sep 42, Item 5; Report by the Joint U. S. Staff Planners, 7 Sep 42, sub: Acceptance of Custody of Prisoners of War taken by the United Nations. JCS 64/2. All in OPD 383.6 (POW) Sec. I, Case 21 (S). DRB, TAG. in George G. Lewis and John Mewha, "History of Prisoner of War Utilization by the United States Army, 1776-1945," U.S. Dept. of the Army Pamphlet No. 20-213 [Washington, D.C., June 1955], 84.

growing from less than two thousand in January of 1942, to over 360,000 in December of 1944, and eventually peaking in June of 1945 at nearly 426,000 prisoners of war.[13] Although the U.S. War Department detained POWs from all major Axis nations within the United States during the war, the proportions of American-held prisoners were far from an equal mix of fighting men from Germany, Italy, and Japan. All records indicate that a clear majority of POWs held by American personnel were German. During the war German POWs outnumbered their Italian and Japanese comrades at least 2:1 and often higher, reaching 6:1 in the summer of 1945.[14] Several factors account for such a large variation in the representative size of POW populations within the continental United States. One was the Japanese preference to die fighting rather than surrender, combined with American soldiers' clear reluctance in offering quarter to those who attempted to surrender. Another reason is the official agreement made by the War Department to pay the Australian and British governments to house and care for a majority of Japanese prisoners captured by American forces in the Pacific. These factors partially explain the glaring discrepancy between such large numbers of German POWs held in the United States and the considerably smaller proportion of Japanese prisoners detained within the U.S. mainland. Although the vast majority of Japanese POWs were held in Australia or surrounding islands in exchange for lend-lease aid, a select few, who were deemed of particular use to stateside intelligence officers, were transferred to camps within the United States.

Unlike soldiers and sailors from Western European nations who were aware of the protections offered within the Geneva Convention to surrendering forces, Japanese combatants were generally unaware of this possibility, and rarely viewed surrender as an acceptable alternative to death at enemy hands. Japanese military culture of the early twentieth century revived traditional notions of the samurai and promoted the warrior mentality of Bushido, which regarded surrender as a fate worse than death and one that would bring shame upon themselves and their families for generations. During the Second World War, every Japanese Army soldier was issued a copy of the "Code of Battlefield Conduct" or *Senjinkun*, intended to bolster morale and reinforce the warrior spirit. This regulation was intended to improve discipline within the Japanese Army and, most importantly, prohibited solders from surrendering.[15] While

---

13   Monthly Census of Prisoners of War Interned in Continental United States: ASF WD
       Monthly Progress Reports, sec. 11, Administration, "Historical Monograph, Prisoner of
       War Operations Division, Historical File, 1941-1958," In "Prisoner of War Operations, vol. I,"
       Folder, "Prisoners of War Operations," RG 389, Entry 459A, Box 36, (PMGO) MMB-NA II.
14   Ibid.
15   *Senjinkun* (Tokyo: Imimi-Kan, 1941).

the document did not apply to sailors in the Japanese Navy, they too were expected to spare themselves the indignity of falling into enemy hands alive. This preference to die an honorable death rather than live in shame, combined with the merciless nature of fighting in the Pacific and ultimately resulted in a considerably lower number of Japanese prisoners. All too often, less than 100 Japanese POW were taken after major battles in the Pacific, while ten or even twenty times that number were killed or committed suicide. During the Burma campaign alone, Allied forces captured a total of 142 prisoners while recording over 17,000 enemy dead, while the combined actions of the Coral Sea, Midway, Guadalcanal, and Tarawa, some of the largest battles in the Pacific, American forces netted fewer than 600 Japanese POWs.[16] Although Japanese notions of honor and self-sacrifice in defense of the Emperor played an influential part in limiting the numbers of POWs taken by American forces, it was only one side of the story. Unlike the ongoing fighting in Western Europe, the brutal nature of the Pacific war often led both American and Japanese combatants to offer no quarter to surrendering enemy troops. John Dower highlights this key factor, arguing that American soldiers, sailors, and marines generally refused to take prisoners even if the opportunity arose. Often American commanders resorted to bribing troops with liberty-passes and even ice cream in order to bring in the first Japanese prisoners.[17] Ultimately the combination of Japanese culture and American hatred resulted in staggeringly low numbers of prisoners captured during the majority of the Pacific War. Unfortunately, these engrained racial prejudices often extended far beyond the battlefield, heavily influencing the way average Americans perceived the Japanese military as well as the common people. Further examining the inconstancies between the treatment of Asian and European POWs in America, it becomes apparent that despite the U.S. War Department making considerable effort to ensure equal accommodations among racially different populations, Japanese prisoners were frequently denied access to rewards and privileges available to white European POWs, in addition to more frequent exposure to physical and verbal abuse at the hands

---

16   Arnold Krammer, "Japanese Prisoners of War in America," *Pacific Historical Review* 52:1 (1983), 69.

17   John Miller, Jr., Guadalcanal: The First Offensive (Washington, D.C., U.S. Dept. of the Army, Historical Division, 1949), 310. In a frank, confidential intelligence memo on the problems of interrogating Japanese prisoners of war, the army conceded, "it took the promise of three days leave and some ice cream [to tempt U.S. soldiers] to bring in the first live prisoner." U.S. Fourth Army, Headquarters, Office of the Assistant Chief of Staff, G-2, "Interrogation of Japanese Prisoners in the Southwest Pacific," Intelligence Memo no. 4, July 22, 1943, Information Derived from Japanese POWs, Record Group 165, Records of the War Department, General and Special Staffs. MMB-NA II.

of American personnel fuelled by a network of Anti-Japanese propaganda and engrained racial stereotypes.

Although the later years of the war would see an increase in the number of Japanese taken captive by American forces, this figure never equaled the percentages of the German troops surrendering in Europe. Unlike their Japanese counterparts, European soldiers and sailors knew about the basic rights guaranteed to them by the Geneva Convention and frequently chose surrender rather than death. With large numbers of enemy prisoners arriving on American shores in the spring of 1943, this massive influx of German POWs combined with an increasing number of Japanese prisoners, begin filling the hastily organized system of POW camps springing up throughout the nation bustling with thousands of young men from as far away as Frankfurt, Venice, and Osaka. Unlike the massive numbers of German POWs arriving in port cities up and down the eastern seaboard, nearly every Japanese prisoner's first steps on American soil took place at Camp Angel Island in route to Camp Tracy, California. This U.S. intelligence center operated within the gray areas of the Geneva Convention by subjecting Japanese POWs to secret and prolonged interrogation practices, which at the very least violated the intentions, if not the actual provisions of the 1929 Convention.[18] The length of time each prisoner spent at Camp Tracy depended on the quality and quantity of information the prisoner supplied American intelligence personnel. Once they were no longer of use to Army intelligence, nearly all Japanese POWs were transferred to one of three detention centers, Camp Clarinda in Iowa, Camp Kennedy in Texas, and Camp McCoy, Wisconsin. In comparison, German POWs were rarely subject to interrogation of any considerable degree aside from separating members of the criminal organization know as the SS or *Schutzstaffel* from regular German units. Although the massive numbers of European prisoners falling into Allied hands compared to the relatively small population of Japanese POWs might also be an influential factor, the fact that German troops unlike their Japanese allies, understood the Geneva Convention protected them from prolonged interrogation can not be entirely overlooked.[19]

---

18   For detailed look at the utilization of Japanese POWs by U.S. psych ops see; *You Can't Fight Tanks with Bayonets: Psychological Warfare against the Japanese Army in the Southwest Pacific*, by Allison Gilmore and Alexander Corbin's, *The History of Camp Tracy: Japanese WWII POWs and the Future of Strategic Interrogation*.

19   Krammer, *Nazi Prisoners of War in America*, 14, 16.

Bunking with Bigotry

Upon arrival to the POW Camp, each prisoner was issued basic toiletries and a set of work clothes to be worn while about camp or on work detail.[20] The men of supply-starved armies in North Africa and remote Pacific islands were amazed when they saw what was awaiting them in the cafeteria on their first days in camp. Prisoners often recalled hiding what food they could not manage to eat during the first few weeks, in fear of having rations cut in order to reduce waste.[21] Initially, some prisoners had difficulties adapting to the strictly American cuisine, and soon a mixture of ethnic and American meals were being provided to POWs. Japanese prisoners were given increased portions of rice and fresh vegetables; Germans more fish, soup, and pork, while Italians received a greater quantity of spices, olive oil, and spaghetti.[22] In addition to the meals provided in the mess halls, prisoners were encouraged to supplement their own diet with additional items available within the Camp Canteen and produce grown inside the camp or purchased from local markets when available.[23] Prisoners were encouraged to improve their camps, through planting trees and flowers as well as building recreational facilities for soccer and baseball. POWs also constructed theaters for performances and outdoor gazebos for music concerts in which all prisoners were expected to attend. Much like other prisoners, the Japanese POWs were encouraged to occupy themselves through a wide variety of activities, games, and sports. American personnel believed providing prisoners with recreational activities would constructively fill large blocks of leisure-time that could otherwise be directed at causing disciplinary problems for guards or planning escapes.[24] At Camp McCoy, Japanese POWs planted gardens and shrines to Buddha around the camp in order to make their imprisonment more tolerable. They also received colored paper and thin wire to make artificial flowers, Mah-Jong sets, and even constructed a tennis court.[25] Prisoners were able to transform many of these drab and cold structures into places that were almost enjoyable, especially compared with the combat conditions most experienced prior to capture. Many prisoners took great pride in the work they did, and their actions were encouraged by the War Department because prisoners who were preoccupied

---

20 Straus, *The Anguish of Surrender: Japanese POWs of World War II*, 16.
21 *Nazi POWs in America*, Sharon Young director, A&E Television Network, 2002, DVD.
22 Krammer, "Japanese Prisoners of War," 71.
23 Krammer, *Nazi Prisoners of War in America*, 48.
24 Robert Devore, "Our 'Pampered' War Prisoners," *Collier's*, October 14, 1944, 57.
25 "POW Special Projects Division, Administrative Branch, Decimal File, 1943-46," box 1618: "Camp McCoy to Camp Orlando," folder: "Camp McCoy" RG 389 (PMGO) MMB-NA II.

with camp improvement would be less likely to cause trouble. In an effort to reassure concerned citizens in nearby towns and avoid unwanted inspections from superiors, POW Camp commanders projected an atmosphere of quiet and orderly discipline within the camp. American officials believed prisoners could not escape or take part in riots if internal discipline was maintained through occupying prisoners' idle time. Ultimately these measures seemed successful and through an elaborate system of required camp maintenance, educational programs, recreational activities, and paid labor, American personnel successfully avoided major incidents while detaining over 470,000 Axis POWs during the war.

While Japanese POWs experienced the same general treatment in American camps, upon closer inspection, German prisoners frequently enjoyed greater freedoms and more access to a wider variety of leisure activities then their Japanese counterparts. The War Department restricted the sale of various items within the camp exchange for a variety of reasons that frequently included fear of self-harm. For example, the War Department ordered that the razorblades available for purchase in the Camp Exchange could only be sold to German and Italian prisoners.[26] The rationale behind this was to prevent the Japanese from taking their own lives, despite having access to more effective means, such as knives, cutlery, and blades, while working in the camp kitchen, lawn-maintenance, or even eating at the cafeteria. Although reports confirmed Japanese prisoners no longer displayed a desire to harm themselves once in captivity, American officials often overlooked or ignored these statements. One such report observing prisoners at Camp McCoy, Wisconsin described Japanese POWs as, "responding well to good treatment," being "quite cheerful," and seemed to "enjoying living."[27] Additionally, Japanese POWs were housed together in segregated barracks with no distinction between rank or service, whereas their fellow German and Italian prisoners were separated by branch of service and only supervised by officers and non-commissioned officers (NCOs) from within their own branch. Despite regularly documented issues of disorder that arose from inter-service rivalries at Camp McCoy, this practice of combining Japanese sailors and soldiers would continue for the duration of the war.[28] While initially, many of the safety precautions instated by

---

26   Hata Ikuhiko, *Nihonjin horyo: Hakusonkō kara Shiberia yokuaryū made*, 2 vols. (Tokyo: *Harashobō*, 1998), 198. also cited in; Ulrich Straus, *The Anguish of Surrender*, 204.

27   Memo, Army Service Forces, from Captain Separd Traube to Major Paul Horgan, Morale Services, War Department, June 8,1944, "POW Special Projects Division, Administrative Branch, Decimal File 1943- 46," folder: "255. Cp. McCoy," Entry 459A, Box 1624, RG 389 (PMGO) MMB-NA II.

28   Krammer, "Japanese Prisoners of War," 80.

the American officials seem somewhat justified, often such drastic restrictions were based on little to no substantial evidence and led to adverse reactions among many Japanese POWs. Considering that the majority of Americans perceived the Japanese people as racially inferior, it comes with little surprise that racial prejudice seems ultimately responsible for the unequal treatment of POW populations within the continental United States. What is surprising, however, was the number of additional factors that may have contributed to large variations in the treatment of the racially different POW populations.

Despite uniformity within the official policy for treatment of racially different enemy POWs, the organization of the camp system allowed for considerable interpretation of vague regulations. American personnel overwhelmingly seem to view the Japanese POWs as inferior to their German campmates and the only logical explanation for this preference is racism. In addition to racial stereotypes, other factors such as the considerable latitude given to camp commanders through an absent command structure and personal prejudices as a result of combat action, may have also influenced American treatment. Further investigating these variations between racially different prisoner populations in the utilization of POW labor and availability of educational programs to Japanese prisoners, provides additional avenues to explore the causes behind unequal treatment, while highlighting the American perceptions of the Japanese military as well as the Japanese people. Racism clearly influenced American military personnel and considering the latitude given to individual Camp commanders, these personal prejudices often resulted in unequal treatment. Similarly to Camp McCoy and Camp Kennedy, Camp Clarinda, contained Japanese and German POWs, offering a unique opportunity for comparison. When asked by a reporter from the *Des Moines Register* regarding which race of POW was more disciplined, Lt. Colonel Ball rather bluntly responded, "[h]andling these little yellow monkeys is a lot different than handling German prisoners.... The German was far more desirable, they looked you in the eye, the Jap doesn't."[29] These individuals were allowed considerable control in the implementation of official policy. It is obvious that without frequent supervision by the senior officials, race may have played an equally influential role as any other in dictating the specifications of treatment regardless of the national POW policy. Moreover, U.S. camp personnel clearly

---

29   Lt. Col. Ball in "Tough with Japs at Clarinda," Des Moines Register, 8 April 1945, quoted in Patrick C. Miller, "Camp Clarinda: A POW Camp in Southwest Iowa" (M.A. Thesis, Bowling Green State University, 1993), 78–79. cited in: Matthias Reiss, "Bronzed Bodies behind Barbed Wire: Masculinity and the Treatment of German Prisoners of War in the United States during World War II," *The Journal of Military History* 69:2 (2005), 502.

demonstrated an affinity for German troops. Colonel Harold G. Storke, the officer in command of Camp Fort Devens, Massachusetts explained to a reporter that he could, "Change [German POWs] uniforms and you would hardly know them from our own men."[30] Comments like these from Colonel Ball and Colonel Storke provide valuable insight into the racial views of senior camp officials. After considering the latitude given to camp commanders, and the influence of racial prejudices on American personnel, it becomes evident that although absent from official POW policy, race clearly effected its implementation within the Camps themselves.

Additionally, the service record or prior combat experience of camp commanders and guards may also account for such variations in treatment. One glaring example occurred at Camp Kennedy in Texas during the spring of 1945. A veteran of Pearl Harbor, Captain Taylor viewed his Japanese POWs as problematic, and became a strict enforcer of all official regulations that could make life as hard as possible for the Japanese in his care. When Ensign Kazuo Sakamaki, normally a model prisoner with no history of disobedience was transferred to Camp Kennedy from Camp McCoy, a penknife was discovered in Sakamaki's belongings during an initial inspection. This item was a typical addition to pen-sets of the era, often used to cut or sharpen the tip of a quill in order to make a pen nib. The knife was never taken from Sakamaki during his previous four years of imprisonment, and also frequently found among the personal effects of German officers. Despite his clean disciplinary record, Ensign Sakamaki eventually received a week in solitary confinement and placed on a ration of bread and water for the minor violation.[31] This example highlights the variation between what regulations different camp commanders enforced and how race may have influenced that decision. Japanese POWs also experienced unequal punishment for their failure to obey orders issued by U.S. officials. In May of 1944, Colonel Rogers ordered all able-bodied enlisted POWs detained at Camp McCoy to participate in a forty-hour workweek. Because of the fear of violence between civilians and Japanese prisoners, Rogers ultimately mandated that the Japanese POWs only be allowed to perform labor within the camp. This restriction sparked unrest among the Japanese prisoners who were unhappy at the lack of coveted outside labor opportunities, ultimately resulting in a work slow down. In response, Rogers placed the reluctant Japanese on a diet of bread and water, although this measure failed to motivate the POWs within the camp. Seeking to maintain labor output numbers and avoid an unscheduled visit from his superiors, Rogers eventually ordered guards to use

---

30   Ibid., 485.
31   Hata Ikuhiko, *Nihonjin horyo*, 198.

force in order to persuade the Japanese back to work. Following the separation of Japanese non-commissioned officers involved in the incident from the rest of the men, and several Japanese prisoners being treated for minor bayonet wounds, the POWs soon reluctantly returned to work.[32] Unfortunately the report fails to mention exactly what "minor bayonet wounds" entailed; however, no formal complaints from prisoners were reported to the International Red Cross. It should also be noted that German POWs were never subject to similar violence when refusing to work.

The Logistics of Labor

Initially, POWs were employed on various tasks within the camp such as clerks, laundry attendants, and as laborers, but the growing number of workers quickly exceeded the amount of available jobs. To complicate this issue, civilian contractors throughout the United States clambered for an opportunity to access the growing numbers of able-bodied POWs for outsourced labor in the agriculture and manufacturing industries. While the Geneva Convention allowed POWs to be used in any labor that was not considered hazardous, degrading, or directly related to the war effort, it failed to provide detailed explanations as to what types of jobs prisoners could and could not perform. When the Office of the Provost Marshal General began drafting the official regulations outlining treatment for the growing number of Axis prisoners arriving from Europe and the Pacific in the beginning of 1943, the topic of POW labor was a primary concern. Again the War Department simply expanded upon the provisions of the 1929 Geneva Convention that also outlined out the basic provisions regarding POW labor, although these provisions still needed clarification in several key areas including specifically what jobs constituted labor related to prohibited "war operations" and what wage-scale would be used to compensate prisoners for working while in captivity.[33] The 1942 Army manual, "Civilian Enemy Aliens and Prisoners of War" eventually supplemented the provisions of the Geneva Convention, addressing these issues among many others. According to Article 34 of the 1929 convention, prisoners should be compensated for their labor and the War Department agreed to a minimum pay rate for POW labor set at 80 cents per day, per prisoner. After addressing issues over paying POWs, the Office of the Provost Marshal General next sought to establish what types

---

32 "Report on visit to Prisoner of War Camp McCoy, Wisconsin, by Señor Gonzalles." cited in Arnold Krammer's "Japanese Prisoners of War," 83.

33 "Civilian Enemy Aliens and Prisoners of War," 1942, I, 38-39. RG 389, (PMGO) MMB-NA II.

of jobs constituted "dangerous" or "demeaning work," specifically prohibited by Articles 31 and 32 of the 1929 Convention. American policymakers examined the vague bylaws of the Convention and concluded that the definition of jobs considered hazardous, demeaning, or directly related to the war effort, was ultimately left to the discretion of the captors.[34] Clarifying Articles 31 and 32, local camp commanders now required all able-bodied enlisted POWs to work up to ten hours a day on approved jobs in addition to any required administration, beautification projects, and maintenance duties within the camp.[35] Initially only small numbers of selected POWs were permitted to work outside of the wire under guard, performing minor tasks and expressly prohibited from interacting with curious local civilians. This arrangement soon evolved as the influx of prisoners grew from just over 5,000 in April 1943 to over 130,000 by the end of August, all available labor opportunities within the camps were exhausted and officials needed to identify more jobs for POWs.[36]

With large numbers of able-bodied American men in the military, many small towns throughout the nation sought POW labor.[37] Civilian contractors and agriculture were particularly eager to employ prisoners, as the War Department announced outsourced POW labor would cost fifty to seventy percent less than the going rate for civilian workers to account for "nuisance factors."[38] Over the course of the war, the United States Government profited greatly from POW labor, bringing in over a $100,000 in 1944 alone.[39] During the period between 1943 and December of 1945, POWs performed over 90,629,233 paid man-days of labor on military instillations throughout the United States.[40] Realizing the potential for profit early on, the Office of the Provost Marshal General and the Prisoner of War Employment Reviewing Board set out to further refine POW labor regulations in order to better incorporate

---

34 Krammer, *Nazi POWs in America*, 81.

35 AG Ltr, 10 Jan 43, subject: "War Department Policy with Respect to Labor of Prisoners of War." (10-30-42) (1). RG 389, Entry 467, Box 1516, "Prisoner of War Operations Division, Legal Branch" (PMGO) National Archives II, MMB.

36 Monthly Census of Prisoners of War Interned in Continental United States: ASF WD Monthly Progress Reports, sec. 11, Administration, "Historical Monograph, Prisoner of War Operations Division, Historical File, 1941-1958," box 36: "Prisoner of War Operations," vol. 1, folder: "Prisoners of War Operations," vol. 1 of 3, MMB-NA II.

37 Army Service Forces, ASF Circular No. 155 (Washington 25, DC: GPO, May 1,1945), p. 4-5, in Office of the Provost Marshal General, *Historical Monograph*. RG 389, MMB-NA II.

38 George G. Lewis, John Mewha. *History of Prisoners of War Utilization by the United States Army 1776-1945*. Department of the Army Pamphlet No 20-213. (Washington D.C.: Department of the Army, 1955). 104.

39 "Prisoner of War Fact Sheet," box 22: "Technical Information Officer Publicity File 1942-1945," folder: "Prisoner of War Fact Sheet BPR," RG 389, Entry 440, MMB-NA II.

40 Minutes of the 79th U.S. Congress, "Investigation of the National War Effort." June 12, 1945, 8.

civilian contract work. In May 1943, the chairman of the newly established War Manpower Commission suggested to the Secretary of War that POWs should be used within the food processing, lumber, and railroad industries, to help alleviate critical manpower shortages.[41] In order to address this new directive, the Provost Marshal General and the Manpower Commission met to formulate the official policy for POW contracted labor to civilian authorities. The August Directives, as they would come to be known, organized POW labor into three distinct categories. Priority I work consisted of "essential work" conducted within the prison camp or military instillation itself. These jobs often included working in the laundry, cooking, and kitchen, in addition to improvements and maintenance of the POW complex. Priority II work related to outsourced contract labor employed in various civilian industries, primarily agriculture. Finally, Priority III labor included "useful but nonessential work" on U.S. military instillations not directly related to the Allied war effort.[42] In addition to organizing the three classes of labor and clarifying official regulations, the Manpower Commission also recommended future sites that could provide POWs for necessary work.[43] In order to ensure the safety of POWs performing paid labor, prisoners were directly supervised by their own officers and NCOs while under the watchful eye of armed guards with orders to fire on any prisoner attempting to escape. Initially most POWs failed to notice anything had changed because many camp commanders had been putting prisoners to work on similar jobs without payment under the classification of "maintenance" and "improvement" as specifically permitted by the Geneva Convention. Despite American commanders' early reservations about thousands of enemy soldiers recently removed from combat causing havoc on U.S. military instillations, very few incidents involving POW labor eventually materialized. American commanders were quick to notice the added benefits of POWs performing various essential jobs on military bases that kept prisoners busy and freed thousands of American personnel for the Allied war effort, who would otherwise be forced to perform these duties.[44] Whatever concerns camp commanders expressed with employing POWs quickly diminished as

---

41 Letter, Paul V. McNutt, Chairman, WMC, to SW, 24 May 43. PMGO 383.6, "Labor P/W." MMB-NA II.

42 George G. Lewis, John Mewha. *History of Prisoners of War Utilization by the United States Army 1776-1945*. Department of the Army Pamphlet No 20-213, 121.

43 Letter, AG to CG's, all service commands, 24 Aug 43, sub: Employment of Prisoners of War off Reservations. G-1 383.6 "Labor" (1 Apr 43), "General Policies, Procedures, Regulations" MMB-NA II.

44 Report: "Earnings From Labor of Prisoners of War," RG 389, Entry 440, Box 22, Executive Division "Technical Information Officer, Publicity File 1942- 1945, Labor POW to Newspaper Articles." (PMGO) MMB-NA II.

the first few thousand prisoners worked without any major incidents. Even at the height of the program, when the United States held 420,000 prisoners, only three escapes per month for every 10,000 POWs occurred.[45] The United States War Department even boasted about achieving a lower ratio of escapes than the federal penitentiary system with its permanent walls and state-of-the-art security devices.[46] In comparison, Japanese POWs generally restricted in work assignments and more closely supervised, eluded camp guards fourteen times over the course of the war; however, prisoners never got too far and usually returned to the camp on their own after exploring the surrounding countryside.[47] When the War Department realized the benefits of POW labor, American officials soon encouraged all local service commands to employ any available prisoners on tasks where POWs had not been already used. As a result of this push, camp commanders only calculated how many workers they would be able to assign and need not consider if the job was approved for POWs.[48]

While Japanese and German prisoners all received the same basic pay and had access to generally equal job opportunities on military installations, racism and inequalities were prevalent throughout the POW labor program. American officials and commanders alike expressed a greater concern for escape and sabotage from the 340 Japanese prisoners working at the height of Priority I and Priority III labor utilization in March of 1944 than they did from nearly 200,000 German POWs who also held the same jobs.[49] Commanders whose camps held Japanese POWs frequently warned personnel and local townspeople about Japanese prisoners, "The Japanese, with their reputation for trickiness and sneakiness, are apt to make a greater attempt to disturb our home front security than the Germans ever did."[50] In reality, however, Japanese POWs accounted for a smaller percentage of escapes than their Germans counterparts due to commanders restrictive attitude toward Japanese in terms of available labor assignments, a more substantial language barrier, and greater difficulties blending into the largely Caucasian or African American civilian

---

45   Martin Tollefson, "Enemy Prisoners of War," *Iowa Law Review* 32 (1946), 63.

46   "Investigations of the National War Effort," *H. Rep.* 728, 10. cited in Arnold Krammer, "Japanese Prisoners of War," 84.

47   Tollefson, "Enemy Prisoners of War," 63.

48   Minutes from a Conference held in Gen Styer's office, 1 Oct 45, "Conference on Employment of Prisoners of War." Military Police Command, AFWESPAC, 383.6 Prisoners of War, Book III. MMB-NA II.

49   Monthly Census of Prisoners of War Interned in Continental United States: ASF WD Monthly Progress Reports, sec. 11, Administration, "Historical Monograph, Prisoner of War Operations Division, Historical File, 1941-1958," RG 389, box 36: "Prisoner of War Operations," vol. 1, folder: "Prisoners of War Operations," vol. 1 of 3 (PMGO) MMB-NA II.

50   *Sparta Herald*, (June 11, 1945), 2. quoted in Krammer, "Japanese Prisoners of War" *P* 84.

population. Additionally, American commanders and guards alike displayed a clear affinity to German POWs and publicly admired their work ethic. Unlike soldiers supervising Japanese prisoners, American guards frequently broke regulations when handling German POWs on work assignments, as they grew more comfortable with them. Alfred Klein, a German prisoner of war held at Camp Rucker, Alabama, recalled, "I remember a number of times I was sent to work at Fort Rucker, and the guard would ask me to hold his rifle until he had climbed in or out of the truck. Almost as an after-thought, he would ask me to hand it up to him a few minutes later."[51] Civilians, too, who worked in close contact with German POWs, experienced the same surprising transformation as east Texas farmer Lloyd Yelverton stated, "They were just the best bunch of boys you ever saw in your life. You enjoyed being around them."[52] Not surprisingly, this cordial relationship did not extend to the more than five thousand Japanese POWs who were also entitled to equal working conditions. Civilians living or working near camps holding Japanese prisoners were warned that POWs would try to steal from local farmers and to be extra vigilant as, "these men, with their strange philosophy of 'dying for the Emperor,' could cause a great deal of damage."[53] Many of these warnings appeared unfounded, with no major incidents of violence or suicides among the Japanese POW population held on American soil reported during the war. Many Americans believed the Japanese were racially inferior as a result of engrained stereotypes combined with the ongoing propaganda campaign, and the results of these attitudes are consistently evident at the local level. While guards and commanders often treated Japanese POWs differently, the POW labor program was generally equal in terms of Priority I and Priority III work; however, race-based discrimination was evident in the implementation of the contracted labor program – Priority II work. By the middle of 1945, for every 1,000 POWs held within the United States, 965 were employed in some form of paid labor. What made Priority II labor so appealing to the War Department was the fact that outside contractors would essentially cover at least two-thirds of the wages paid to prisoners, further expanding the profit margin from POW labor. The prisoners themselves seemed to favor this type of work over jobs on military installations or around camp, as they had the ability to make extra money through incentive pay and enjoyed working around the neighboring countryside among the civilian population.

---

51   Letter from John Schroer, May 20,1976. cited in Arnold Krammer *Nazi POWs in America*, 84.
52   Robert Warren Tissing, "Stalag-Texas, 1943-1945: The Detention and Use of Prisoners of War in Texas During World War II," *Military History of Texas and the Southwest* 13 (1976), 29.
53   *Monroe County Democrat*, 5 July 1945, 1.

Unlike European prisoners, Japanese POWs did not receive this incentive pay because they were excluded from civilian contract labor opportunities.[54] The official regulations from the Office of the Provost Marshal General directed all service commands to use only German and Italian POWs for civilian contract work, suggesting that race affected labor policies.[55] American personnel attempted to justify this unwritten policy by explaining that it was intended to save Japanese prisoners from exposure to civilian violence, despite lacking any substantial reasoning for this claim and overlooking the detachment of armed guards accompanying the POWs that provided security for the prisoners while working. Although the war department had no real idea how American citizens might react to Japanese POWs working outside the camp among civilian populations, Japanese prisoners had been previously employed on similar conditions in the Philippines without issue.[56] It seems far more likely that Filipinos who experienced harsh Japanese occupation, would harbor more animosity and thus pose a more viable threat.[57] Additionally, considering the relative location of the Philippines to Japanese forces, the risk of escape would also appear greater. Ignoring these examples of Japanese working outside POW Camps without serious incident, commanders within the United States were instructed to withhold their Japanese POWs from Priority II labor opportunities during the war. This exclusion may have been particularly unwise because of the potential benefits of Japanese labor. Almost immediately following V-J day groups of Japanese POWs began relocating to camps near the Pacific coast in preparation for repatriation. In response to the shortage in agricultural labor in the area, Japanese POWs were used in cotton harvesting outside the camp and in close proximity to civilian workers. Despite California Governor Earl Warren (1891-1974), making a considerable effort to keep Japanese POWs out of his state, three sub-camps in the San Joaquin Valley were filled with the former Japanese prisoners from McCoy in October of 1945. During several months of outside labor, reports of hostility or violence toward Japanese prisoners failed to materialize and Japanese laborers even outperformed German POWs in pounds of cotton picked per day at a rate of nearly 2:1.[58] Whatever

---

54   George G. Lewis, John Mewha, *History of Prisoners of War Utilization by the United States Army 1776-1945*. Department of the Army Pamphlet No 20-213, 150.

55   Ibid.

56   Ōoka Shōhei and Wayne P. Lammers, *Taken Captive: A Japanese POW's Story* (New York: J. Wiley & Sons, 1996), 216-217.

57   Frank Dexter, "Appalling Stories of Jap Atrocities: 1,400 Civilians in Manila Were Murdered." *The Argus*, (Melbourne, Australia; April 3, 1945), 16.

58   See figures of cotton picked by Japanese at Camp Lamont California and German POWs at Camp Ruston Louisiana, comparing the Japanese average at 70 to 80 lbs to the Germans

reservations American personnel may have had about employing the vast numbers of enemy POWs quickly subsided as fears of escape and sabotage failed to occur. After the Army Service Forces issued orders to all service commands instructing them to take a "calculated risk" with guarding prisoners, it was clear that security was no longer the paramount factor when deciding POW labor policy.[59] With this in mind, relying on the original justifications for withholding Japanese prisoners from Priority II work out of concern for the safety of the POWs appeared less creditable. Unlike German prisoners, who were increasingly employed in contract work under an ever-shrinking detachment of guards, racial stereotypes and cultural differences continued to drastically limit equal employment opportunities for Japanese POWs. Additionally, the overwhelming majority of guards, commanders, and policy makers alike failed to make equal attempts to accommodate and motivate Japanese POWs in terms of labor production. When supervising German POWs, American personnel eventually learned that relaxing the number of guards and assigning more rigorous work-schedules, in addition to pitting small groups of prisoners against each other in competition while performing tasks, combined to produce greater output.[60] On the other hand, American personnel failed to make similar efforts to better understand ways of motivating Japanese prisoners and simply classified them as poor and ineffective workers. These commanders did not recognize how factors such as language barriers and ineffective leadership that stemmed from rivalries due to the inter-service grouping of Japanese POWs were influential in lowering motivation and possibly responsible for discrepancies in labor production. Although camp maintenance and paid labor occupied the majority of prisoners' free time, individuals in the War Department continued to search for other avenues that could keep POWs busy after returning from work and on the weekends. The answer to the Army's problems seemed to lie in Article 17 of the 1929 Geneva Convention that required captors to provide and encourage prisoners with intellectual pursuits. This vague provision eventually evolved into a clandestine effort to re-educate select numbers of POWs housed in the United States during the Second World War.

---

who averaged only 30 to 40 lbs in: Yoshiteru Kawano, "Experiences with Japanese Prisoners of War," unpublished memoir, n.p., n.d., cited in Ulrich Straus's *The Anguish of Surrender: Japanese POWs of World War II*, 226. and "War Prisoners Working on Southwest Farms," *New York Times*, 8 August 1943.

59   Lewis and Mewha, Pamphlet No 20-213, 118.

60   Headquarters, ASF, *Army Service Manual*, M-811, *Handbook for Work Supervisors of Prisoner of War Labor* (July, 1945), 7, 15.

Race and Reeducation

With most of the basic problems regarding the treatment and employment of nearly 340,000 enemy prisoners of war held within the United States largely solved by the Fall of 1944, most American personnel appeared generally content with POW operations, although a few of these officials feared releasing nearly half a million pro-fascist foot solders back to war-torn areas without some form of political reeducation once the war ended. The Geneva Convention specifically forbade attempts to indoctrinate prisoners of war, but also required captors to provide and encourage enemy POWs with intellectual pursuits. American personnel would eventually use this stipulation as a cover to introduce a clandestine program aimed at indoctrinating German and Japanese POWs. Examining the American reeducation program and how it varied in content and implementation between German and Japanese prisoners provides a final opportunity to observe American perceptions of the Japanese, and highlight the influence of racism in the treatment of Japanese POWs. In addition to outlining housing, diet, recreational activities, and labor requirements for prisoners of war, the Geneva Convention also required signatory nations to provide POWs with educational materials that encouraged their intellectual pursuits. While the provisions outlined in Article 17 intended to provide prisoners with access to newspapers, books, newsreels, classroom instruction, and other forms of educational diversion, its vaguely wording ultimately gave captors the power to decide what material was appropriate and how it would be disseminated among POWs.[61] Under the pretenses of providing the required intellectual opportunities, the War Department began developing its controversial reeducation program in March of 1943 as the first large groups of POWs began arriving in the United States.[62] Although General Marshall appeared interested in the possibilities of a program, which, "prisoners of war might be exposed to the facts of American history, the workings of democracy and the contributions made to America by peoples of all national origins," might have on repatriated POWs after the war, the Provost Marshal General initially considered the idea "inadvisable" and filed it away pending further investigation.[63] The American public held vastly different views when the topic of re-educating enemy POWs first surfaced. Some seemed supportive and hoped to successfully rehabilitate German and Japanese prisoners; others

---

61   *Convention Relative to the Treatment of Prisoners of War* (Geneva: 1929), Article 17.

62   Krammer, *Nazi Prisoners of War in America*, 195.

63   Judith M. Gansberg, *Stalag: U.S.A.: The Remarkable Story of German POWs in America.* (New York: Crowell, 1977), 59-60.

rejected the idea on grounds that the task was impossible. A 1946 Gallup public opinion poll highlighted a wide range of American perception including
the mildly optimistic, "The Japanese should be educated in our ways of living.
After about 100 years they might be ready to assume some responsibility," and
"Find the right thinking people in Japan and work with them in training the
others to live right.[64] These sentiments highlight the conflicting desire to educate POWs on the workings of American democracy and a belief that doing
so was a very real possibility. However, another commentator in the same poll
argued Americans should "Annihilate the whole Japanese race. Get rid of every
last one, women and children too," rejecting any notion that reeducation was
worthwhile.[65]

Ultimately several leading Academics, journalists, politicians, and military
officials weighed in on this issue, and were clearly divided on the idea of indoctrination. Although many believed the program could have some influence
among Germans, most American officials were less than optimistic about the
possibility of including the several thousand Japanese prisoners in the reeducation effort. Overall several factors appear to contribute to the American perception that Japanese prisoners could not be re-educated including, pre-war
racial stereotypes, the brutal nature of the Pacific War, as well as the fanatical
sense of collective identity and devotion to the Emperor. While the general
consensus appeared in favor of excluding Japanese POWs from the formal reeducation program, this feeling was not unanimous. Although officials initially excluded Japanese prisoners from indoctrination efforts within the United
States, efforts had already been underway in Burma and China that yielded
surprising results. John Emmerson, a State Department officer assigned to the
China-Burma-India Theater during the war noted the large amount of valuable information provided by Japanese forces captured in Burma.[66] Emmerson
wrote, "There seems to be no feeling that he is a traitor to his country, but rather that he no longer belongs to a country." The reasoning behind this statement
ties back to the psychological make-up of Japanese troops who believed they
could never return home after suffering the immense shame of surrender.[67]
Japanese POWs in captivity seemed to embrace the principals of spiritual re-
birth contained within their Buddhist religious beliefs, and despite being in
the clear minority, whose members saw the potential for including Japanese

---

64   NORC, "Japan and the Post-War World," 18, 19.
65   Ibid., 16.
66   Straus, *Anguish of Surrender*, 218.
67   John K. Emmerson, *The Japanese Thread: Thirty Years of Foreign Service* (New York: Holt,
      Rinehart and Winston, 1978), 216.

into the reeducation program, American officers like John Emmerson were not alone. Although official regulations did not sanction indoctrination efforts prior to the fall of 1944, several camp commanders experimented with unofficial efforts including Otis Cary, an assistant POW camp commander located near Pearl Harbor, Hawaii. Unfortunately, Cary represents a minority segment within the American military who shared a much more optimistic view of the Japanese people; having grownup in Japan to long-time missionary parents, and spending considerable portions of his formative years captivated with the Japanese way of life. Through Cary's hands-on encouragement, a small group of Japanese POWs worked in conjunction with civilian educators and utilized Japanese language texts from the local Nisei community and the University of Hawaii at Honolulu to begin an unofficial democratization program later known as the "Hawaii College."[68] Without official orders, this influential group of Japanese prisoners began reading and translating material that might help to democratize post-war Japan. Under Cary's guidance, Japanese POWs taught their fellow prisoners classes in the English language, history, and politics, with each lecture identifying the ways Japan would need to adapt in the postwar world. After lecture, prisoners engaged in a wide-ranging discussion on the idea presented within the each topic. In addition to classroom instruction, lecture, and assigned readings, Japanese POWs in Hawaii published a pro-democratic Japanese language newspaper that was largely seen as unbiased, as it came from the prisoners themselves. The willingness of American personnel to allow Japanese POWs to play an active role in creating the curriculum, translating material, and administering the lectures greatly contributed to the initial success of the program in Hawaii – over a year before similar efforts for Japanese POWs were in place stateside.

While American officials initially expended little effort to reeducate prisoners; they seemed willing to violate the Geneva Convention and use prisoners to help improve propaganda efforts. Despite disregarding the results of Otis Cary's unofficial, prisoner-led indoctrination program at Pearl Harbor, orders were given to transfer a select few of its instructors to help improve American propaganda directly linked to the war-effort.[69] Unlike other aspects of POW treatment, using Japanese prisoners on projects directly related to the American war effort was a clear violation of Article 31 in the Geneva

---

68   Straus, *Anguish of Surrender*, 211, 212.

69   For a more detailed account of Japanese POWs covertly assisting the U.S. Psychological Operations program during WWII see, Allison Gilmore. *You Can't Fight Tanks With Bayonets: Psychological Warfare against the Japanese Army in the Southwest Pacific,* (Lincoln: University of Nebraska Press, 1998).

Convention. At Iroquois Point, an island adjacent to Ford Island in Pearl Harbor, a group of thirty Japanese prisoners, monitored by Cary, set to work improving American propaganda being used in the Pacific. Unlike a majority of U.S. personnel clouded by ignorance, or misguided racial propaganda, Cary seemed determined to treat Japanese prisoners not as enemies but as "human beings, individuals who deserved to have a bright future aiding the reconstruction of a new, democratic Japan."[70] One of the first operations that POWs at Iroquois Point worked on was to improve the effectiveness of the *Mariana Jiho*, a propaganda newspaper used to undermine the morale of Japanese forces on the front lines. Initially, this leaflet was largely ineffective, as it suffered from translation errors and lacked a sense of connection to Japanese combatants. Prisoners worked to create content originating in Japanese, bypassing the need for articles translated from English that had made it less affective. Additionally, prisoners added creditability to *Mariana Jiho* by fabricating advertisements from prominent Tokyo department stores. Japanese POWs working with the psychological operations program also helped improve various other aspects of American propaganda, including translating the Potsdam Declaration for leaflets dropped by B-29s over Japan.[71] The document laid out Allied plans for the post-war world and provided terms for Japanese surrender, but was not published in its entirety to the Japanese people. American leaflets informed citizens of the relatively lenient Allied terms that may have contributed to the Japanese government's final decision to capitulate on 2 September 1945. The use of Cary's POWs at Iroquois Point attests to the receptiveness of Japanese to American reeducation efforts as well as, American willingness to violate the Geneva Convention. Both factors suggest that the motivating factor behind the different educational opportunities and reeducation policies came down to race, since American officials were willing to blatantly violate the Geneva Convention when it came to Japanese prisoners but not German POWs.

Despite Cary's initial successes reeducating Japanese POWs in Hawaii and reports showing the Japanese at Camp McCoy were just as responsive to indoctrination as German prisoners, the Provost Marshal General and Army Service Forces remained convinced that the formal indoctrination program should only include German POWs.[72] Over the next year, and despite repeated requests from a variety of civilian and military personnel, the U.S. War Department

---

70   Straus, *Anguish of Surrender*, 213.
71   Ibid., 217.
72   Memo, "Prisoner of War Special Projects Division, Interoffice communication," from Major Maxwell S. McKnight to Major Neuland, Subject: "Camp McCoy," March 28, 1945, "POW Special Projects Division, Administrative Branch, Decimal File 1943- 46," folder: "255. Cp. McCoy," Entry 459A, Box 1624, RG 389 (PMGO) MMB-NA II.

made no effort to expand the program to include Japanese prisoners. The un-authorized Navy reeducation program underway at Pearl Harbor should have given American officials more than enough evidence to demonstrate the feasi-bility of reeducating Japanese POWs, especially as prisoners themselves con-structed and implemented it. In addition to the Hawaii-based program, the Provost Marshal had other examples attesting to the Japanese prisoners' re-ceptiveness toward reeducation efforts. One such report came in June of 1944, when Captain Shepard Traube conducted a preliminary visit to Camp McCoy in Wisconsin to observe German prisoners in preparation for the Special Projects Division's reeducation program. In addition to reporting on German POWs, Traube noted that reports claiming Japanese prisoners displayed in-tense hatred toward American personnel, made any attempt to avoid work, and faked wounds and illnesses were inaccurate. In his report, Captain Traube showed Japanese POWs responded to fair treatment by American personnel at McCoy positively and even appeared to enjoy themselves. He went on to ex-plain how, "The Japanese played baseball during recreation, practiced gymnas-tics, and even put on a theatrical show, to which only the camp C.O. was invited from the American officers."[73] By March of 1944, examples like the prisoner-led program at Pearl Harbor, reports from officers like Shepard Traube docu-mented, and continuous lobbying from civilian academics, eventually led the War Department and the Provost Marshal General to reconsider their deci-sion to exclude Japanese prisoners from official reeducation efforts.[74] When the Special Projects Division finally decided to include Japanese prisoners into the official reeducation program in the summer of 1945, officials immediately started screening over 5,000 Japanese POWs in American camps. Soon after, 200 of the most qualified prisoners were selected for the Japanese reeduca-tion program and sent to one of three POW camps in Texas.[75] By mid- June, these Japanese prisoners successfully relocated to Camps Huntsville, Kennedy, or Hearne, and awaited further instruction. Although the War Department had been conducting its reeducation program on Germans prisoners for over

---

73   Memo, Army Service Forces, from Captain Separd Traube to Major Paul Horgan, Morale
      Services, War Department, June 8,1944, "POW Special Projects Division, Administrative
      Branch, Decimal File 1943- 46," folder: "255. Cp. McCoy," Entry 459A, Box 1624, RG 389
      (PMGO) MMB-NA II.

74   Letter to the Secretary of State from the Secretary of War, June 25, 1945. "POW Special
      Projects Division, Administrative Branch, Decimal File 1943- 46," folder: "291.1 (Japanese)
      Gen." Entry 459A, Box 1624, RG 389 (PMGO) MMB-NA II.

75   Memo, "Repartition of Korean and Japanese Prisoners of War," to the Director, Provost
      Division, Attn. Major Monett," December 6, 1945, "Internal Security Division, Coordination
      Branch, Subject File 1937-46," "Investigation Program, POW Intelligence, Food & Canteen
      Restrictions to Safe-haven Project," Entry 468, Box 1846, RG 389 (PMGO) MMB-NA II.

nine months before the first Japanese POWs began, to form classes in Texas, American officials failed to incorporate the most successful aspects of the German program, when creating a parallel Japanese program.

While the Special Projects Division utilized cooperative German officers to help construct the program's curriculum and even lecture to fellow POWs, the content and specifics of the Japanese program were left strictly to American service personnel and select academics at Sam Huston State Teachers College. The senior American officer selected to supervise the Japanese reeducation program was Lt. Colonel Boude C. Moore, an American born to missionary parents in Japan who received his education in the United States and returned to live in Japan from 1924 to 1941. Assisting Colonel Boude in outlining the Japanese reeducation program, the Provost Marshal assigned Dr. Charles W. Hepner, a well-known veteran of the Far Eastern Branch of the Office of War Information and thirty-year resident of Japan. These two men would construct a series of lectures on various topics ranging from studying the English language and American history, to discussions comparing Japanese and American literature, books, and magazines. Unlike the instructors who had been carefully selected by the Special Projects Division and were fluent in German, instructors used in the Japanese program relied on prisoners to translate lectures to the class because they could not speak the language. This language barrier also extended to other aspects of the Japanese reeducation program such as shortages in textbooks, magazines and other published material, as well as what films could be made available to prisoners. Under the watchful eye of camp officials, Japanese POWs in Texas worked to translate written material that could be distributed to the remaining prisoners not selected for reeducation. Like the German program, the Special Projects Division worked with Japanese POWs to create a pro-democratic Japanese-language newspaper that could be distributed to Japanese POWs nationwide.[76] American officials also encouraged Japanese POWs to attend Christian religious services in an effort to break them from "traditional emperor-worship."[77] While camp personnel encouraged the religious transformation of Japanese POWs, this was not about conversion; instead, these officials intended to lead prisoners away from their feelings of group mentality and intense nationalism. In addition to written material and religious services, the Special Projects Division made a detailed effort to utilize

---

76   Memo, "Japanese Projects," from Major Maxwell S. McKnight, Acting Director Special Projects Division, to General Leech, June 25, 1945. "POW Special Projects Division, Administrative Branch, Decimal File 1943- 46," folder: "291.1 (Japanese) Gen." Entry 459A, Box 1624, RG 389 (PMGO) MMB-NA II.

77   Krammer, "Japanese Prisoners of War," 88.

movies and newsreels in the indoctrination of Japanese prisoners during the war. Concerns over the availability of approved native-language titles, combined with cultural differences between Japanese and American entertainment, led to a greatly reduced pool of available films for Japanese POWs. Camp officials worked to increase the initial list that included only five films. The Special Projects Division intended to utilize these and other movies in conjunction with a synopsis read aloud beforehand by a POW leader to ensure prisoners had received the intended message.

American personnel believed the use of movies in the Japanese reeducation program would help to, "disassociate the individual from the state and establish the right of an individual to follow his desires within the scope of American accepted social customs," as well as, "Impress the Japanese with the solidarity of their opposition; a solidarity that exists not only in military strength but also in fundamental laws of living and decency."[78] In addition to classroom lectures, reading material, and movies, Japanese prisoners filled their time with recreational activities including table tennis, baseball, American music, and even popular cartoons. Before the Japanese program had a real chance to test itself, the War Department decided that after the surrender, unlike the majority of German POWs who would remain in the United States for continued reeducation and labor, Japanese prisoners were to be repatriated home as soon as possible. Despite the results of the Japanese reeducation program, it appeared American officials remained convinced that only German POWs were worth indoctrinating. While Japanese prisoners had been rapidly deployed home upon V-J day eliminating further opportunities for reeducation, the German effort was expanded in order to attempt to expose more prisoners prior to repatriation. Comparing the numbers of POWs residing within the United States by February of 1946 illustrated this discrepancy, as the total number of German POWs remained over 208,403 compared to only 561 Italians and one Japanese prisoner.[79] Unfortunately, whatever good the 200 former students of the Army's reeducation program could have done upon repatriation will likely never be known, as they arrived home after the military

---

78   Memo, "Reorientation Program for Japanese Prisoners of War," from First Lieutenant James E. Stewart, Film Branch to Acting Director, Prisoner of War Special Projects Division, PMGO, June 27, 1945, 1, "POW Special Projects Division, Administrative Branch, Decimal File 1943-46," folder: "291.1 (Japanese) Gen." Entry 459A, Box 1624, RG 389 (PMGO) MMB-NA II.

79   Monthly Census of Prisoners of War Interned in Continental United States: ASF WD Monthly Progress Reports, sec. 11, Administration, "Historical Monograph, Prisoner of War Operations Division, Historical File, 1941-1958," In "Prisoner of War Operations, vol. I," Folder, "Prisoners of War Operations," RG 389, Entry 459A, Box 36, (PMGO) MMB-NA II.

occupation under General Douglas MacArthur had been established and were excluded by the conservative post-war government.[80] By January 1946, the remaining Japanese POWs in the United States boarded ships in San Francisco Bay headed for Japan and nervously anticipated what type of welcome awaited them. Overall, American officials believed a significant percentage of Japanese prisoners had embraced the principles of American democracy, individualism, and multiculturalism taught to them during their time in Texas. Unfortunately, the detailed system of questionnaires given to German POWs prior to and following repartition home did not extend to reeducated Japanese prisoners, making further comparison difficult.[81]

Conclusions

American treatment of enemy POWs varied in both content and application depending on the race of each prisoner. Despite having additional time to prepare and over nine months previous experience with reeducating German prisoners, the Japanese program lagged behind in both available educational materials and qualified personnel. American policymakers also ignored numerous reports that Japanese POWs responded well to these programs.[82] Although several other potential factors may have led to these inconsistencies including public opinion, language barriers, and shortages in qualified instructors, racism seems the most significant factor behind the variations between the German and Japanese POW programs. Throughout the program's evolution, American officials continually justified their actions when applying different standards to Japanese prisoners. Camp personnel often based important decisions on racial stereotypes and personal bias that led to inconsistencies in general treatment, available work assignments, and access to educational materials between German and Japanese prisoners. Although American officials implemented several precautionary measures that intended to prevent suicides among Japanese prisoners and protect them from being harmed by mobs of angry citizens, closer examination has shown considerable evidence existed that invalidated these claims and was ignored or overlooked by American policymakers. Acknowledging that racism was perhaps the most influential factor

---

80   Straus, *Anguish of Surrender*, 219.
81   Krammer, "Japanese Prisoners of War," 89.
82   Memo, Army Service Forces, from Captain Separd Traube to Major Paul Horgan, Morale Services, War Department, June 8,1944, "POW Special Projects Division, Administrative Branch, Decimal File 1943-46," folder: "255. Cp. McCoy," Entry 459A, Box 1624, RG 389 (PMGO) MMB-NA II.

of the Pacific War, we have seen that American treatment of Japanese POWs provides no exception. While Japanese prisoners experienced treatment that often varied in comparison to German POWs also held within the United States, their captivity remains immeasurably better than conditions American prisoners endured in Japanese hands during the war. American POWs were frequently starved, beaten without provocation, and executed working on slave labor projects or during their time in Japanese prisoner camps. Over the course of the war 27,465 American service personnel and civilians were captured or detained by the Japanese, and from this number over 11,000 would eventually die while in captivity.[83] The widely publicized stories of Japanese atrocities also contributed to anti-Japanese sentiment during the war, and further tarnished the American perception of the Japanese military. Although most Americans had almost no previous exposure to the Japanese before they found themselves searching for Pearl Harbor on a map shortly after news of the surprise attack reached thousands of American homes, an eager public enthusiastically consumed an endless stream of racist propaganda designed to vilify and dehumanize the Japanese people. While it appears that personal interaction often worked to reverse preconceived notions of the Japanese, the relatively small numbers of Japanese POWs in the United States combined with orders to keep these men away from the general public ultimately limited the opportunity to establish the type of personal relationships needed to overcome American propaganda.

Works Cited

Cameron, Craig M. "Race and Identity: The Culture of Combat in the Pacific War," *The International History Review*, Vol. 27, No. 3 (Sep., 2005), pp. 550-566

Cantril, Hadley., and Strunk, Mildred. *Public Opinion 1935-1946*. Princeton New Jersey: Princeton University Press, 1951.

Devore, Robert. "Our 'Pampered' War Prisoners." Colliers, October 14, 1944, 14, 57-60.

Dexter, Frank. "Appalling Stories of Jap Atrocities: 1,400 Civilians.

Dower, John W. *War Without Mercy: Race and Power in the Pacific War*. New York: Pantheon Books, 1986.

---

83   Charles A. Stenger, "American Prisoners of War in WWI, WWII, Korea, Vietnam, Persian Gulf, Somalia, Bosnia, Kosovo and Afghanistan; Statistical Data Concerning Numbers Captured, Repatriated, and Still Alive as of January 1, 2002," prepared for the DVA Advisory Committee on Former Prisoners of War, Mental Health Strategic Group, VHA, DVA, American Ex-Prisoners of War Association, 2003.

Emmerson, John K. *The Japanese Thread: Thirty Years of Foreign Service*. New York: Holt, Rinehart and Winston, 1978.

Ferguson, Edwin E. "The California Alien Land Law and the Fourteenth Amendment," *California Law Review* 35:1 (Mar., 1947).

Gansberg, Judith M. Stalag, U.S.A.: *The Remarkable Story of German POWs in America*. New York: Crowell, 1977.

Grochowski, John M. *Model of Success: Camp McCoy's Prisoner of War Camp during World War II*. Thesis (B.A.) University of Wisconsin-Eau Claire, 2007.

Klarman, Michael J. *From Jim Crow to Civil Rights The Supreme Court And the Struggle for Racial Equality*. Oxford: Oxford University Press, 2007.

Krammer, Arnold. *Nazi Prisoners of War in America*. New York: Stein and Day, 1979.

Krammer, Arnold. " Japanese Prisoners of War in America." *Pacific Historical Review*, Vol. 52, No. 1 (Feb., 1983), pp. 67-91.

Niiya, Brian. Ed. *Japanese American History: An A-to-Z Reference from 1868 to the Present*. Japanese American National Museum, 1993.

Ōoka Shōhei and Wayne P. Lammers. *Taken Captive: A Japanese POW's Story*. New York: J. Wiley & Sons, 1996.

Reiss, Matthias. "Bronzed Bodies behind Barbed Wire: Masculinity and the Treatment of German Prisoners of War in the United States during World War II." *The Journal of Military History* 69:2 (2005), 475-504.

Robert Warren Tissing. "Stalag-Texas, 1943-1945: The Detention and Use of Prisoners of War in Texas During World War II." *Military History of Texas and the Southwest* 13 (1976).

Robin, Ron Theodore. *The Barbed-Wire College: Reeducating German POWs in the United States During World War II*. Princeton, N.J.: Princeton University Press, 1995.

Smith, Arthur L. Jr. *The War for the German Mind: Re-educating Hitler's Soldiers*. Providence: Berghahn Books, 1996.

Straus, Ulrich. *The Anguish of Surrender: Japanese POW's of World War II*. Seattle, WA: University of Washington Press, 2003.

Tollefson, Martin. "Enemy Prisoners of War," *Iowa Law Review*, XXXII (1946).

Waters, Michael R. *Lone Star Stalag: German Prisoners of War at Camp Hearne*. College Station: Texas A & M University Press, 2004.

CHAPTER 8

Reshaping the Images of a Fallen Army: Postwar Narratives of the Imperial Japanese Army and Civilian Massacres in British Malaya

Aiko Otsuka

Introduction[1]

In 1947, five Japanese members of the defeated Imperial Japanese Army (IJA) were tried by the British Forces in Kuala Lumpur in British Malaya. The defendants were charged for war crimes of murdering hundreds of civilians, including women and children, in villages in the southern part of the Malaya Peninsula during World War Two (WWII). One of them was the regimental commander, two were company commanders and other two were platoon leaders from the 11th Infantry Regiment. The court gave four of them the death sentence in 1948.[2] These Japanese were adjudicated in three different trials among a total of 304 cases of British trials.[3] Japan's defeat forced the IJA to

---

1 The research leading to these results has received funding from the European Research Council under the European Union's Seventh Framework Program (FP7/2007-2013) / ERC grant agreement n° 313382. This chapter is part of my PhD thesis; see, Otsuka, "Narratives of a Fallen Army: Japanese Veterans' Concepts of Defeat and War Crimes Responsibility in World War Two," (PhD Thesis, University of Cambridge, 2019). This chapter has retained original terms used by the wartime Japanese military and veterans, such as, "mopping-up" (*shukusei*), "subjugation" (*tōbatsu*), and "safety" (*chian*); however, my usage of these terms does not indicate my endorsement of them, but merely to convey the nuances behind their use. Unless otherwise noted, all publications in Japanese have been published in Tokyo.
2 "Eikoku sensō hanzai saiban gaikenhyō" (The Table of British War Crimes Trials), the National Archives of Japan (NAJ), Hōmu-Hei-11-4B-15-7128, 58, 59.
3 These war crimes trial records are kept in the UK National Archives under "WO235 – Judge Advocate General's Office: War Crimes Case Files, Second World War". Major scholarly works on civilian massacres in Malaya and Singapore include: Yuma Totani, *Justice in Asia and the Pacific Region, 1945-1952: Allied War Crimes Prosecutions* (Cambridge: Cambridge University Press, 2015), 129-155; Hayashi Hirofumi, "The Battle of Singapore, the Massacre of Chinese and Understanding of the Issue in Postwar Japan," *The Asia-Pacific Journal Japan Focus* 7 (28):4 (2009). Accessed August 5, 2019. https://apjjf.org/-Hayashi-Hirofumi/3187/article.html; Hayashi Hirofumi, *Sabakareta sensō hanzai: Igirisu no tainichi senpan saiban* (Adjudicated War Crimes: British War Crimes Trials Against Japan) (Tokyo: Iwanami shoten, 1998), particularly, 171-253; Hayashi Hirofumi, *Kakyō gyakusatsu: Nihongun shihaika no Marē hantō* (Massacres Against Overseas Chinese: The Malay Peninsula under Control of the

© VERLAG FERDINAND SCHÖNINGH, 2020 | DOI:10.30965/9783657702930_009

be confronted with Allied justice. Their crimes represent the Japanese Army's atrocities conducted as part of wartime military operations, particularly "mopping-up operations".[4]

In spite of the trials, the detailed accounts of brutality remained unknown to the Japanese public while they were overshadowed by dominant narratives which evolved during 1950s Japan: soldiers became rather "victims" of "unjust" trials by the Allied Powers and had actually been "heroes" during the war.[5] From the period onwards, Japanese veterans published internal histories, including regimental war memoirs (*rentai senki*) and war histories (*rentaishi*).[6] Particularly, war histories based on respective units were published more widely from the 1960s onwards.[7]

This chapter revisits group narratives of the infantry regiments of the 5th Division (11th, 21st, 41st, and 42nd Infantry Regiments) and 18th Division (55th and 56th Infantry Regiments) of the 25th Army, major units which committed civilian massacres in the Malaya Peninsula particularly in 1942; and examines how they reconstructed images of the IJA in the postwar period. The first

---

Japanese Army) (Tokyo: Suzusawa shoten, 1992); Takashima Nobuyoshi, Hayashi Hirofumi, and Murakami Ikuzō, *Maraya no Nihongun: Neguri Senbiran-shū ni okeru gyakusatsu* (The Japanese Military in Malaya: Massacres in the Negeri Sembilan state) (Tokyo: Aoki shoten, 1989), which reveals Japanese atrocities through conducting interviews of survivors and examining documents at the National Institute for Defense Studies (NIDS).

4   Most civilian massacres were carried out as a result of orders from the IJA in military operations. See, Hayashi Hirofumi, *Shingapōru Kakyō shukusei: Nihongun wa Shingapōru de nani o shita no ka* (Purges of Singaporean Chinese: What did the Japanese Army do in Singapore?) (Tokyo: Kōbunken, 2007), 218; Hayashi Hirofumi, "Shingapōru Kakyō gyakusatsu" (Massacres of Singaporean Chinese), in *Sensō hanzai no kōzō: Nihongun wa naze minkanjin o koroshita no ka*, ed. Tanaka Toshiyuki (Structure of War Crimes: Why the Japanese Military Killed cCvilians) (Tokyo: Ōtsuki Shoten, 2007), 199; Kasahara Tokushi, *Nihongun no chiansen: Nitchū sensō no jissō* (The Japanese Military's War for Security: Reality of the Sino-Japanese War) (Tokyo: Iwanami shoten, 2010), 20-21, 24-25, 97-100, 112-119; Kasahara Tokushi, "Chiansen no shisō to gijutsu" (Thought and Techniques of War for Safety), in *Senjō no soshō* (Various Sspects on the Battlefield), Iwanami kōza, Ajia Taiheiyō sensō 5, eds. Yoshida Yutaka et al. (Tokyo: Iwanami shoten, 2006), 217; Hayashi Hirofumi, *BC-kyū senpan saiban* (BC-class War Crimes Trials) (Tokyo: Iwanami shoten, 2005), 76.

5   For instance, see, James J. Orr, *The Victim As Hero: Ideologies of Peace and National Identity in Postwar Japan* (Honolulu: University of Hawai'i Press, 2001); Utsumi Aiko and Udagawa Kota, "Sensō to sabaki: Ōsutoraria saiban to hikoku'nin" (War and Justice: The Australian Trials and Defendants), *Osaka keizai hōka daigaku Ajia taiheiyō kenkyū sentā nenpō*, 2015: 2-8; Sandra Wilson, "War, Soldier and Nation in 1950s Japan," *International Journal of Asian Studies* 5:2 (2008), 187-218.

6   Yoshida Yutaka, *Nihonjin no sensōkan: sengoshi no naka no hen'yō* (The Japanese Perception of War: Its Transformation in Postwar History) (Tokyo: Iwanami shoten, 1995), 94-100.

7   Yoshida Yutaka, *Heishitachi no sengoshi* (The Postwar History of Soldiers) (Tokyo: Iwanami shoten, 2011), 124-125.

section examines accounts given by the Japanese defendants of the 11th Infantry Regiment during the 1947-1948 war crimes trials on civilian massacres and how they defended themselves. The regiment is one of a few among infantry regiments whose members were tried for civilian massacres in the peninsula. The following section discusses to what extent narratives have been consistent or added to their postwar accounts made in *The 11th Infantry Regimental History* (*Hohei dai jūichi rentaishi*), compiled in 1993.[8] The final section compares the group narratives of members of the 11th Infantry Regiment with those of other infantry regiments which also participated in the mopping-up operations against civilians in the peninsula and whose members remained untried.

The 11th Infantry Regimental History mentions and admits civilian massacres in Singapore instigated by the Japanese military; however, it seems to have been written in such a way as to blur the regiment's responsibility. Their postwar narratives were also affected by wartime circumstances in which the IJA instigated the massacres after its victories in the first major operations launched against the British forces in 1941 and 1942, part of the IJA's invasive operations in Malaya (*Malaya shinkō sakusen*) – which became part of their postwar narratives of the "glorious deeds" of these regiments. Operational justifications became a major part of the accounts of infantry regiments which fought in the peninsula.

Japanese Convicts' Operational Justifications of Civilian Massacres in British Trials, 1947-1948[9]

Infantry regiments were considered IJA's critical components in fighting in an Asia-Pacific theater. Among hundreds of the regiments mobilized, the 11th Infantry Regiment was considered one of the IJA's "strongest corps" and

---

8 Koi 11-kai, ed., *Hohei dai-11 rentaishi* (Non-commercial, Hiroshima, 1993), the Yasukuni Archives (YA), 80232.396.5i011.7. The history is usually read by the regiment's former members and their families, and is currently only available in a few locations in Japan: the Yasukuni Archives, the Osaka Municipal Library, the Hiroshima Prefectural Library, and the Hiroshima City Library.

9 The trial proceedings have been recorded in English as is some operational terminology unless it was clarified during the trials; for instance, the word "eliminate" and at some occasions "exterminate" were used to indicate "sōtō" (mopping-up operations) in Japanese; see, defense witnesses accounts in the proceedings, "War Crimes Trial', in "WO235/1071 – Defendant: Watanabe Tsunahiko, Iwata Mitsugi, and Goba Itsugo, Place of Trial Kuala Lumpur" (Sept. 22, 1947-Jan. 18, 1948) (hereafter cited as the Watanabe Trial), Sheet No. 135-179.

was recruited for the IJA's invasion of the Malaya Peninsula.[10] Following IJA's capture of Singapore on 15 February 1942, the Japanese Imperial General Headquarters (*daihon'ei*) issued an order on 23 February to the Konoe Division, 18th Division, and 5th Division to conduct prompt "purges" (*shukusei*) in the peninsula, including the 11th Infantry Regiment. The regiment was appointed the South Guard (*Minami keibitai*) to conduct such purges in Negri Sembilan State and Malacca State, located adjacent to the western coast of British Malaya.[11] Under the order, the regiment conducted six "military operations" of purges from 3 to 25 March. As a result of these operations, it is estimated that a few thousand civilians were massacred; the instances of the Japanese aggression were placed under the British trials.[12] The characteristic discourse that the Japanese created in their defense in the British court in the early postwar period reflects wartime propaganda and military education, which indoctrinated Japanese military servicemen in the justification of any actions taken under military orders.

One of the cases against the regiments' members concerned massacres of Chinese in three different locations in the Kuala Pilah District, which were perpetrated by the regiment's 2nd Battalion (5th-8th Companies) as part of the mopping-up operations issued by the South Guard. One of the massacres involved a large-scale massacre of a total of 675 Chinese, including 249 children, and destroying the entire village of Parit Tinggi (north of the Kuala Pilah District) on or around 16 March 1942.[13] For this case, Regimental commander Colonel Watanabe Tsunahiko was convicted for his responsibility in his assignment to these areas and his subordinates' acts of killing civilians, because there was no evidence to prove that he attempted to prevent the massacres.[14] His subordinates from the regiment's 7th Company, First Lieutenant Iwata Mitsugi

---

10   Shin jinbutsu ōraisha, *Nihon rikugun hohei rentai* (The Japanese Army Infantry Regiments) (Tokyo: Shin jinbutsu ōraisha, 1991), 250.

11   "Tai saku mei, dai 140 gō, dai-ichi daitai meirei" (Imperial Army order no. 140, 1st Battalion) in Hohei dai-jūichi rentai, dai-san chūtai (11th Infantry Regiment, 3rd Company), "Jinchū nisshi, dai-4-gō ji Shōwa 17-nen 2-gatsu 1-nichi shi Shōwa 17-nen 2-gatsu 28-nichi [4]" (war diary, February 28 to May 31, 1942), Japan Center for Asian Historical Records (JACAR), Ref. C14110585300 (NIDS), 1704-1705; Hayashi Hirofumi first discovered war diaries of the 11th Infantry Regiment at the Military Archives at the NIDS in the 1987; see, Hayashi, *Kakyō gyakusatsu*, 26-27.

12   Hayashi, *Kakyō gyakusatsu*, 163-166.

13   Ibid., 108-119.

14   Brigadier, D.J.A.G., Far East Land Forces, "War Crimes Trial," in the Watanabe Trial, 2-3; Hayashi, *Sabakareta sensō hanzai*, 237.

(company commander) and Sergeant Major Gōba Itsuto (platoon leader) were also convicted in the same trial as Watanabe.[15]

Watanabe admitted that the 11th Infantry Regiment received the order to "eliminate anti-Japanese elements" in March 1942 and "further instructions" from the Divisional headquarters.[16] He also stated that he passed the 25th Army directives to his subordinate units. Watanabe was aware that the orders he received from the higher command and passed down to his subordinate units included the meaning of killing.[17] He understood "anti-Japanese" to mean those who possessed illegal arms and those who "resisted the Japanese forces."[18] He also said that killing in this case could be justified. While he clarified the word "sōtō" (mopping-up) as meaning "to chase out or to do away with," he answered that it also included killing.[19] He further stated that "if that ['to kill'] was the meaning, then we would have to obey it."[20] While the defendants did not deny the fact of massacres, they provided operational pretexts for these massacres. Furthermore, Watanabe explained that his knowledge of international law (Hague Conventions of 1899 and 1907) was limited. He stated, "[as] to the orders which I handed down, they did not go against this law."[21] His statement not only shows that his legal knowledge was limited, but also reflects the fact that Japanese wartime military and its education disregarded international law.

Watanabe's subordinate Iwata also testified that the orders he received from Watanabe originally came from the 25th Army. Iwata identified his role as a company commander as the "guarding" of Kuala Pilah (1 March 1942 - 10 January 1943), where they claimed to have suspected anti-Japanese activities by Communists and other anti-Japanese elements.[22] At the beginning of the examination against Iwata, he insisted that the order he had received from the regimental commander was "not the order to kill" and that they were told "to attain peace and order in Malaya as quickly as possible" – such rhetoric was

---

15   "Military Court for the Trial of War Criminals," the Watanabe Trial, no page number; for the Parit Tinggi case, First Lieutenant Yokokoji Kiyomi (8th Company Commander) testified that the 8th company was assigned to the area and participated in purging anti-Japanese elements; see the proceedings, the Watanabe Trial, Sheet No. 184-187. Major Gōba Itsuto was not charged with the Parit Tinggi massacre. The 2nd Battalion commander Nishihara died in 1944; see Hayashi, *Sabakareta sensō hanzai*, 244.

16   "Testimony of Watanabe Tsunahiko," in the Watanabe Trial, Sheet No. 176.

17   Ibid., Sheet No. 181.

18   Ibid., Sheet No. 176.

19   Ibid., Sheet No. 180.

20   Ibid., Sheet No. 181.

21   Ibid., Sheet No. 182-183.

22   Ibid., Sheet No. 135-137.

employed by the IJA during the Southern Expansion.[23] Yet, Iwata mentioned that Colonel Watanabe gave him the orders of the 25th Army to "suppress the anti-Japanese elements and the Communists."[24] Iwata admitted that he passed the orders to his soldiers to assist the *kenpeitai* in arresting anti-Japanese elements.[25] He also warned his soldiers "not to commit brutalities or kill or rape," but a member of the *kenpeitai* told him that the *kenpeitai* member "would ask them" to commit such brutalities.[26] Iwata had known the possibility that his soldiers might commit brutalities. He also admitted:

> If one allows the soldiers to kill at discretion then there would be no limit to what they would do. It would mean that since they could not make [*sic*] any difference between anti-Japanese elements and localinhabitants [*sic*] there would be the destruction of civilians. I earnestly believe it is against the laws of humanity to kill people.[27]

Iwata insisted that he made a point of telling his soldiers not to commit brutal acts but at the same time he was aware of the nature of the orders that they had to obey, and the potential negative consequences that their following of orders might bring about. He was told by the battalion commander that they had to obey because they were "operational orders."[28]

These convicted petitioned against their death sentences by emphasizing that disobeying orders would have led to a punishment of death, thereby reasoning that the mopping-up operations were accordingly unavoidable; therefore, they believed that they could be absolved of their charges.[29] Nonetheless, all three were sentenced to death.[30]

Another case judged First Lieutenant Yokokoji Kiyomi (8th Company commander), who was charged with involvement in his unit's bayonetting of 990 civilians (later replaced with, and recorded as, "many") in the Joo Loong Loong village in the Jelebu District on or around 18 March 1942.[31] Yokokoji

---

23   "Testimony of Iwata Mitsugi," in the Watanabe Trial, Sheet No. 151.

24   Ibid., Sheet No. 137-138.

25   Ibid., Sheet No. 138-139.

26   "Ibid., Sheet No. 139.

27   Ibid., Sheet No. 157.

28   Ibid., Sheet No. 163.

29   "Petition against Finding and Sentence," in the Watanabe Trial, no page number.

30   "Military Court for the Trial of War Criminals," the Watanabe Trial, no page number.

31   "Testimony of Yokokoji Kiyomi," Sheet No. 61, and "Military Court for the Trial of War Criminals" and "Charge Sheet," in the "WO235/1096 – Defendant: Yokokoji Kyomi. Place of Trial: Kuala Lumpur" (December 17, 1947- March 31, 1948), NA, (hereafter cited as the Yokokoji Trial).

also explained the chain of command from the 11th Infantry Regiment to his company and the unavoidability of orders. According to him, the regimental commander and battalion commander issued mimeographed orders on 16 and 17 March to "eliminate anti-Japanese elements" in Titi and Kuala Klawang near Joo Loong Loong.[32] Based on the orders, Yokokoji brought his company to the area to conduct the operations, and battalion commander Captain Nishihara Tōichi informed him that the 6th Company was said to have been attacked by guerrilla gunfire in the areas, so the 5th Company and the Machine Gun Unit went out to search for the attackers. These units arrested the suspects and brought them to the Joo Loong Loong village where Yokokoji received orders from Nishihara to guard the arrested Chinese. Yokokoji instructed approximately 30 soldiers, half of his company, to guard a Chinese schoolhouse where those who were arrested were confined. He estimated that 200 Chinese were held in the school.[33]

Yokokoji also received a written order from the 5th Company, originally from the battalion commander, which warned that the Joo Loong Loong village was "infested with anti-Japanese elements" – the source of this information was the military police. Nishihara was instructed "to take appropriate measures to suppress these elements."[34] Yokokoji stated that based on the order, several soldiers from the 5th and 6th companies took the Chinese out to a nearby house to kill them, but he insisted that his duty and that of his 8th Company was to guard the schoolhouse. He asserted: "[t]his operation was carried out in accordance with the orders from my superiors and I do not believe that any responsibility rests with me" and "[w]hen I found out that I was to be a War Crimes suspect I denied all knowledge pertaining to this incident and I believe if anyone, even in this Court, was in the same place as I was they would have done the same."[35] Yokokoji stressed the impossibility of preventing orders from being carried out once they were given.[36] Consequently, the court decided his military "duty" was not directly involved in the killings and was not unlawful. Additionally, two local witnesses testified that Yokokoji helped prevent massacres in other villages. As a result, he received a lenient sentence of 12 years' imprisonment.[37]

In a different war crimes case, a similar stance was taken by another defendant, Second Lieutenant Hashimoto Tadashi (7th Company platoon leader),

---

32   "Testimony of Yokokoji Kiyomi," the Yokokoji Trial, Sheet No. 62.
33   Ibid., Sheet No. 63-64; Hayashi, *Sabakareta sensō hanzai*, 229.
34   "Testimony of Yokokoji Kiyomi," Sheet No. 64.
35   Ibid., Sheet No. 64-66.
36   Ibid., Sheet No. 70-71.
37   Ibid., Sheet No. 77, 81-84.

who fabricated a story to explain his crime. This officer was prosecuted for taking part in the killing of approximately 350 residents in the Sungai Lui village on or around 30 August 1942.[38] Japanese soldiers under his command bayonetted and shot residents and burned down the village.[39] The village is located in the southwest of British Malaya and in the north of the Jempol District.[40] Hashimoto went to the village following a request made by the Kuala Pilah police, who asked for his escorts to investigate the murder of a Malay man in the village vicinity. They suspected the Communists in the village vicinity of having killed the man and of possessing ammunitions and weapons. Hashimoto asserted that there had been a "small-scale battle" against the "enemy" which in his accounts caused the civilian casualties and the destruction of the village as well as explosions and fire.[41] Two police inspectors rejected the idea that such a battle had occurred, thereby opposing Hashimoto's claim.[42] These two prosecuting witnesses also described how Hashimoto was explicit in his hatred towards Chinese and in his intention of killing: they recalled his mentioning, "I want to finish off the Chinese. They are all Communists", and also that the "Chinese people were all bad."[43] Hashimoto perhaps felt his action was justified by a standing order issued by General Yamashita "to get rid of all Communists in Malaya" prior to the massacre.[44] Hashimoto's involvement in the massacre might also reflect his hatred towards the Chinese people, which had been cultivated through wartime military culture and propaganda. Additionally, he extended his justification to operational ones as though the massacre was instigated for revenge and retribution for the "battle" initiated by the enemy. In spite of his refusal, the court regarded witnesses' testimonies highly and sentenced him to death.[45]

The Allied pursuit of justice forced Japanese veterans to redefine military operations and military responsibilities concerning civilian massacres. The Japanese defendants claimed that they were not culpable for the massacres because their involvement in killing resulted from larger military necessity

---

38   "Military Court for the Trial of War Criminals," in the Yokokoji Trial; in the trial records, it
       is written as "Sungei Lui," but correctly, it is "Sungai Lui."
39   "War Crimes Trial," in the Yokokoji Trial, 1.
40   Hayashi, *Kakyō gyakusatsu*, 67.
41   "Testimony of Hashimoto Tadashi," in "WO235/1070 – Defendant: Hashimoto Tadashi
       Place of Trial: Kuala Lumpur" (Oct. 21, 1947-Jan. 18, 1948) (hereafter cited as the Hashimoto
       Trial), NA, Sheet No. 53-54.
42   "Testimony of Hashimoto Tadashi," the Hashimoto Trial, Sheet No. 9, 35.
43   Ibid., Sheet No. 6, 32.
44   "Form of Statement by an Accused Person," in the Hashimoto Trial, 2.
45   "Military Court for the Trial of War Criminals" and "War Crimes Trial," in the Hashimoto
       Trial, no page number.

for subduing anti-Japanese elements in the region – what the IJA termed as "preserving security" to secure Japan's military presence in invaded areas – thought in fact the IJA was the main instigator, which afflicted security. The IJA's Southern Expeditionary Army promulgated a military goal of preserving "peace" and "safety" in the region as its major propaganda, emphasizing the war as a "fight for self-preservation and self-defense" and to "construct a new order of Greater East Asia" during the war.[46] Such a stance is also apparent in *The Eleventh Infantry regimental history* which presents a pretext of massacres by placing them in the larger context of war.

Images of the IJA in *The 11th Infantry Regimental History*

The language the Japanese former officers used in British courts in Southeast Asia in the early postwar period survived after several decades of the war's end. After half a century from the war's end, former members of the 11th Infantry Regiment compiled *The 11th Infantry Regimental History* in 1993. The compilation efforts began in 1977, two years after the establishment of their veterans' association, the Carp 11th Association (*Koi jūichikai*).[47] It took them more than a decade of efforts in collecting materials, including the IJA's war action reports (*sentō shōhō*) from the Malaya operations, war diaries from battles in the north of Australia, and the *War History Series* (*Senshi sōsho*) published by the National Institute for Defense Studies between 1966 and 1980.[48] While editors to *The Eleventh Infantry Regimental History* define their purpose as to record and disseminate the "historical truth" (*shijitsu*) of the war with admission of civilian massacres carried out by the hands of the Japanese Army, their accounts are narrowly written and reflect a rather unilateral aspect of Japan's war from

---

46   "*Nanpōgun meirei*" (Southern Expeditionary Group order), "*Nanpō sōsakumei dai-2 gō*" (Southern operational order no.2, November 20, 1941), in *Bōeichō Bōei Kenshūjo Senshishitsu, Marē shinkō sakusen* (Operations for the advance on Malaya) Senshi Sōsho 1, (Tokyo: Asagumo Shinbunsha, 1966), 135.

47   The association was established in 1975 for those who belonged to the regiment from the second half of the China incident (Marco Polo Bridge Incident) in 1937; Nakai Takashi, "Jobun" (Preface), and Shirai Takeo, "Maegaki" (Preface), in Koi 11-kai, *Hohei dai-11 rentai-shi*, no page number.

48   Shirai, "Maegaki", in *Koi jūichikai*, ed., *Hohei dai jūichi rentaishi*, no page number; a total of 102 volumes of war history has been published by NIDS of Japan's Ministry of Defense; and war action reports were returned from the US in 1958; see, NIDS, "Military History Documents at NIDS." Accessed July 12, 2919, http://www.nids.mod.go.jp/english/military_archives/index.html.

the IJA's point of view.[49] Moreover, *The 11th Infantry Regimental History* serves to share the recreated accounts and images of the IJA among veterans who do not necessarily share the same experiences or only know the restricted picture of its own regimental history, even within the same unit. One of its editors, Shirai Takeo, mentions how he became familiar with the whole picture of the regimental history only in the previous few years.[50] Through writing their own version of history, the regiment's former members helped recreate IJA's images, while disseminating as what Aaron W. Moore calls "their own version of the 'truth'."[51] Writing their own history helps veterans to recreate and confirm the images of the IJA in postwar Japan where people were recuperating from the defeat.

In his preface, Horie Masao, a former company leader of the 11th Infantry Artillery Unit and a former member of the House of Councilors, praises the "victory" of the defeated country. He characterizes *The 11th Infantry Regimental History* as "illustrious with glorious deeds of arms and tradition." He writes that the purpose of the regimental history is "to honor the spirits of those who offered their lives to the home country under this war flag" and "to bequeath its history and the spirit of those who hastened to join under this war flag to our descendants." He further exhibits "a strong belief that this book will be read widely and that its trace will be handed down eternally, and become food for the mind and a source of spiritual support for the people in the prefecture."[52] Its prefaces reflect the purpose behind the compilation as to record and disseminate "the truth" as part of a critical history of Hiroshima Prefecture, the regiment's hometown, and they emphasize the aspects of glory and deeds performed by the Japanese side and even their military men's spirit.

One of the editors of *The 11th Infantry Regimental History* and president of the Carp 11th Association, Nakai Takashi, was the former commander of the regiment's 5th Company and his subordinate soldiers carried out civilian massacres during March 1942.[53] In his preface, Nakai mentions that the history was compiled with the purpose of transmitting the regiment's "historical truth" and raising its awareness. Underlying this, he wishes to address a contemporary trend of a "masochistic view of history" (*jigyaku shikan*), which refers to

---

49   Nakai, "Jobun", in ed. Koi jūichikai, *Hohei dai jūichi rentaishi*, no page number.
50   Shirai, "Maegaki", in *Koi jūichikai*, ed., *Hohei dai jūichi rentaishi*, no page number.
51   Aaron William Moore, "The Problem of Changing Language Communities: Veterans and Memory Writing in China, Taiwan, and Japan," *Modern Asian Studies* 45:2 (2011), 429.
52   Horie, "Jobun" (Preface), *Hohei dai-11 rentaishi*, no page number.
53   According to Hayashi Hirofumi's investigation, Nakai himself did not participate in the killings due to his injury, but his subordinate soldiers probably killed civilians in Parit Tinggi and Joo Loong Loong; see Hayashi, *Kakyō gyakusatsu*, 164, 268.

the tendency of overestimating and highlighting the negative aspects of one's own history.[54] Shirai similarly states that "I feel somewhat hesitant to take the contemporary historical view of instantly regarding Japan's wars from the Meiji period as an invasion."[55] The 11th Infantry Regiment's massacres in the Malaya Peninsula became known to the Japanese people in 1987 when Hayashi Hirofumi divulged their massacres recorded in the 7th Company's war diaries to the media.[56] This background might have encouraged the editors to include their responses to the massacres.

In contrast to hard-core conservatives who denied the IJA's massacres, *The 11th Infantry Regimental History* does admit that the regiment participated in the mopping-up operations in Malaya, but does not mention the killing of countless civilians instigated by the regiment.[57] It further shows moderate stricture against the wartime army; however, their overall stance seems to ennoble their own war history. Nakai mentions, "Malaya was not, of course, the enemy, but they got caught up in the war between Japan and the British forces", which made "trouble" (*meiwaku*) for them.[58] The regimental history uses the word, "trouble," to characterize Japanese oppressive invasion and occupation of the peninsula.[59]

In terms of the massacres conducted by the 5th and 18th Divisions, *The 11th Infantry Regimental History* describes them in one of its chapters, "Guards of the Malaya Peninsula."[60] The regimental history retains the claim that the "guarding" was the regiment's major duty in order to remove the anti-Japanese elements and secure its military presence in the peninsula. The usage of the wartime phrase of "patrolling" seems to indicate the lack of perception regarding Japan's illegal invasion of the peninsula.[61] Under the title of guard units,

---

54 Nakai, "Jobun," in Koi 11-kai, *Hohei dai-11 rentaishi*, no page number.
55 Shirai, "Maegaki," in Koi 11-kai, *Hohei dai-11 rentaishi*, no page number.
56 Based on Hayashi's findings, Japan's *Kyōdō News* supplied the news to 42 local newspapers nationwide and this disclosure led to the 1988 visit of five survivors of the massacres to Hiroshima Prefecture, home of the regiment, through an invitation of the 'Society for Sending our Heart Out to Victims of the Asia-Pacific War and Etching Them into our Heart' (Ajia Taiheiyō sensō giseisha ni omoi o hase, kokoro ni kizamu kai). Furthermore, in the following year people from Hiroshima, though not perpetrators themselves, visited the sites of killings; see Hayashi, "The Battle of Singapore"; Hayashi, *Kakyō gyakusatsu*, 1-27.
57 Koi 11-kai, *Hohei dai-11 rentaishi*, 665-666.
58 Nakai, "Jobun," in Koi 11-kai, *Hohei dai-11 rentaishi*, no page number.
59 Koi 11-kai, *Hohei dai-11 rentaishi*, 663.
60 Ibid., 661.
61 Japan's attack on Pearl Harbour was a flagrant violation of international law; so were its invasions of British and Dutch territories and Thailand. These facts are pushed aside in regimental histories. See Yoshida Yutaka, *Ajia Taiheiyō sensō* (The Asia-Pacific War), (Tokyo: Iwanami shoten, 2007), 19-22.

the regiment conducted "purges for security" (*chian shukusei*) in the Malaya Peninsula – similar rhetoric to that used by the defendants during the war crimes trials. The regimental history also clarifies the fact that the 11th Infantry Regiment's 3rd Battalion participated in the purges along with *kenpeitai* and the 41st Infantry Regiment's 1st Battalion; nevertheless, the description of the purges goes into little detail. Moreover, the units that conducted massacres of Chinese Singaporean remains unclear, though the history describes how Chinese Singaporean men were gathered randomly and executed (*shokei*) without fair trials.[62] It is noteworthy that the regimental history integrates the estimated numbers of Chinese civilian casualties as a result of the operations: tens of thousands according to Chinese sources, and several thousand from Japanese sources. However, in contrast to its description about the massacres in Singapore, it does not mention the number of Chinese casualties conducted by the 11th Infantry Regiment in Malaya and it seems to marginalize the regiment's heinous crimes.[63]

In addition to the rather vague descriptions of its massacres, *The 11th Infantry Regimental History* imputes the reasons for these massacres, which they called "unfortunate incidents" (*fukō na jiken*), to the Dalforce, whose units of about 1,250 Chinese were summoned at the beginning of February 1942.[64] *The 11th Infantry Regimental History* highlights that the Dalforce's sudden appearance in times of Japan's encroachment on Singapore was a cause of the Japanese massacres against Chinese, while noting that the Dalforce dissolved on 13 February:

> Our military placed the fight against the United Kingdom as the first principle and it considered Malaya residents (including Chinese) friends; nonetheless, the unexpected appearance of another enemy took us by surprise, which at the same time attracted [our] extreme hostility. Why did Chinese step into the war between Japan and the UK? It would have been understandable if the volunteer army had the prospect of victory, but why couldn't they predict the consequences of the actions at the time when the Japanese military succeeded in landing on Singapore island?[65]

---

62   Koi 11-kai, *Hohei dai-11 rentaishi*, 662; *Hohei dai-11 rentaishi* also uses the phrase, "*kakyō shodan*" (Disposal of Overseas Chinese), which indicates the killing; see Hayashi, *Shingapōru Kakyō shukusei*, 201–204.

63   Koi 11-kai, *Hohei dai-11 rentaishi*, 662, 665–669.

64   Ibid., 662; Kevin Blackburn and Daniel Chew Ju Ern, "Dalforce at the Fall of Singapore in 1942: An Overseas Chinese Heroic Legend," *Journal of Chinese Overseas* 1:2 (2005), 235, 238; Hayashi, *Shingapōru Kakyō shukusei*, 207–209.

65   Koi 11-kai, *Hohei dai-11 rentaishi*, 662.

In its descriptions, the regimental history takes the stance that anti-Japanese activities undertaken by the rudimentary Chinese volunteer army was the major cause of the "unfortunate incidents." It stresses that the Dalforce "showed dauntless resistance and took antagonistic actions of providing information and irritating the Japanese army headquarters." It also notes that "there was a growing fear [among the Japanese] towards Overseas Chinese who took full control of the economy in Malaya and Singapore."[66] Perceiving the local Chinese people in the region to be a threat and hindrance to Japanese expansion and influence, the IJA justified the action it took to suppress the influence of these groups of people. In spite of its assertion, the IJA developed measures to be taken against Chinese people prior to its invasion of the peninsula, as the IJA's wartime military operational policy showed; therefore they were not impromptu ideas.[67]

The regimental history also expresses the view that the Japanese military held a sense of "hostility" or "hatred" (*tekii*) towards the Chinese, which was cultivated by representing them as anti-Japanese elements from the Japanese military's perspective from the initial stages of the war in the peninsula. The postwar regimental history stresses the critical role of the Chinese side and regards it as a cause of casualties.[68] The stance of blaming the Chinese for the IJA's involvement in massacres in the first place seems to reflect their attempt to evade war crimes responsibility of the regiment.

At the same time, *The 11th Infantry Regimental History* also criticizes the Japanese army by acknowledging that it "executed several thousands of local Chinese without being based on appropriate judgment and attributed all the causes of such situations to Chinese."[69] Additionally, the regimental history mentions the responsibility of Japanese superiors for the massacres, by particularly pointing out Lieutenant Colonel Tsuji Masanobu (25th Army's staff officer) "to be the one who was practically in charge of the massacres," as well as the 25th Army General Yamashita Tomoyuki and chief of staff General Suzuki Sōsaku's crucial role in implementing the "measurement of purge against Chinese." The regimental history states, "if they approved of massacres as operational orders, they would not have been free from responsibility for the massacres of non-combatants." *The 11th Infantry Regimental History* was sympathetic to Major General Kawamura Saburō (commander of the Singapore

---

66   Ibid., 662-663.
67   Hayashi, *Shingapōru Kakyō shukusei*, 191, 200-201, 218; see also, Renraku kaigi, "Shōwa 17-nen 2-gatsu 14-kka, Kakyō taisaku yōkō" (Outline of measures against Overseas Chinese, February 14, 1942), 0549–0552, JACAR Ref.C12120211900 (NIDS).
68   Koi 11-kai, *Hohei dai-11 rentaishi*, 661.
69   Ibid., 662.

Guard), who was executed, following the war crimes trial, for obeying his superior orders to conduct civilian massacres in Singapore, orders which were considered "sacred and inviolable"; therefore, the regimental history regards those who were executed following such trials to have encountered the "tragic fate of the death sentence."[70] *The 11th Infantry Regimental History* uses such a narrative of "sacrificial" of the convicted.

Another characteristic lies in the regiment's accounts of the absoluteness of military orders under the IJA. *The 11th Infantry Regimental History* uses a pretext of having followed such illegal orders, describing that "orders were taken as absolute truth" and "restricted imperial military men both in war and peace". The regimental history states how the absoluteness was ingrained through military education and training: for instance, the "Imperial Rescript to Soldiers and Sailors" stipulated that soldiers and officers should "regard receiving orders from superiors as immediately receiving them from the Emperor"; field manuals emphasized that "obedience needs to be second nature," as in the internal documents. The regimental history also mentions how the "Army Penal Code strictly watched over military men's disobedience and violation of orders." It asserts that "there is no doubt that the exact fulfilment of orders became a habit and second nature through the strict and repeated indoctrination of obeying orders."[71] Whereas the absoluteness of orders was also the Japanese defendants' claim during the war crimes trials, the regimental history added a narrative about military education to further justify the civilian massacres.

The 11th Infantry Regimental History also includes an account of the purges against civilians to which the 11th Infantry Regiment was assigned in Malaya in March 1942. It describes the allocations of units under the 5th Division for the mopping-up operations, stressing that there was a need to pacify anti-Japanese activities.[72] The regimental history also delineates the contexts of the activities as follows: "explosions of railways and a variety of attacks broke out, the British forces left spies and guerrilla commanders might have been hiding in mountains, and since guerrillas were not wearing formal military uniforms and were even mobilizing women, there was no way for the [Japanese] guards in the front lines to distinguish the enemy." The regimental history concludes that such circumstances gave rise to various "unfortunate incidents for both the Japanese forces and the Chinese people, which led to war crimes trials in the postwar period."[73] In the trials, the defendants mentioned these circumstances

---

70   Koi 11-kai, *Hohei dai-11 rentaishi*, 663.

71   Ibid., 664.

72   Ibid., 665-666.

73   Ibid., 669.

of alleged anti-Japanese activities, but it was undeniable that the Japanese military massacred civilians and cannot justify its invasion and the eradication of civilians.

The 11th Infantry Regimental History also notes that the IJA conducted several "mopping-up operations for security" in mountainous regions near the railway between Seremban and Tampin in the Negeri Sembilan State during March 1942. It includes a story from a Japanese officer who engaged in a mopping-up operation in a small village to which he went with his unit to investigate, as it was claimed that the village was a foothold for anti-Japanese guerrillas. In his account, the enemy initiated a skirmish against his unit in the village. The story goes on to depict a scene: "when the enemy judged that an escape would be impossible, they all of a sudden started a fire with gasoline in hutches." In the story, the fire caused "by the enemy" killed people, including a small baby, women, and an elderly person. Right before the fire, the Japanese officer heard a baby crying which "remained in [his] memory and aches [his] heart even today." In this story, the enemy, not the Japanese, instigated the sacrifice of these people – a similar justification made by Hashimoto Tadashi during the war crimes trial. The regimental history describes the scene as "horrific," but the writers does not express in the same way for the fiendish massacre perpetrated by the Japanese army in the region in their regimental history.[74] In terms of the enormous damages that the IJA inflicted upon people in the region, it even seems inappropriate to include this episode without mentioning similar stories of the IJA as perpetrators in Malaya. Such a description helps to diminish the serious offences and cruelties of the Japanese side that tortured and killed countless inhabitants and destroyed entire villages.

The 11th Infantry Regimental History does not discuss the war crimes trials against the regimental members; however, Shirai Takeo, leaves his opinion on one of the defendants. Shirai was imprisoned in the Canlubang prison together with a defendant, Hashimoto Tadashi. Shirai writes about his impression:

> [H]e had an easy-going personality, and a boy-like face appeared when he smiled; I could by no means think of him as a person who command-ed atrocious actions; he was also one of the young men who were wait-ing impatiently to return home, not knowing that there was a clause of "punishment of war criminals" in the Potsdam Declaration; I assumed that he would not have thought in the slightest of being wanted as a war criminal.... . What if the young people of the present day were to go back

---

74   Ibid.

in time and were put in such situations? That era, set under the severe
supreme command authority, is unimaginable today.[75]

Shirai saw Hashimoto's face in prison in a time of peace, not the face of when
he commanded the atrocious actions. Hashimoto's superiors gave no further
detailed instructions about what to do at the village. The military man was
said to have acted at his discretion to accommodate the operational orders of
"eliminating anti-Japanese elements."[76] Military men in battles who lacked humanity recovered a human face after the war – this was what Shirai witnessed.
Japanese brutalities confirm that people can manifest both goodness and evil-
ness. The regimental history hides the facts of the heavy casualties inflicted by
the Japanese military in the process of its expansion of the empire and acquisi-
tion of natural resources.

Justifying the Mopping-Up Operations in Regimental Histories of Untried Units

Unlike the 11th Infantry Regiment, whose members were tried, in the case
of other infantry regiments, such as the 21st, 42nd, 55th, and 56th Infantry
Regiments, deployed to the Malaya Peninsula, there is only a very limited description of the mopping-up operations against civilians. What is consistent
among the regimental histories is that civilian massacres were recounted in the
framework of the military operations. Japanese veterans used wartime military
values, particularly peremptory orders, as the pretext for having conducted the
mopping-up operations. Additionally, they integrate narratives which justify
the IJA's war conduct and evade war crimes responsibility as a result.

The 21st Infantry Regiment, which had committed civilian massacres in
Singapore in February 1942, compiled the *Hamada Regimental History* in 1973.
The regimental history records the battles during the Malaya operations, but
limited descriptions of mopping-up operations can be observed. Often, it per-
ceives the war within the frame of the Japanese "wartime propaganda," such
as Japan as a leader and liberator of Asia. For instance, considering Malaya's
rubber as a source of wealth that the British accumulated by utilizing the local
workforce, the regiment writes: "it was from these orderly rubber forests that

---

75   Shirai, "Rentai no banka" (Elegy for the regiment), *Hohei dai-11 rentaishi*, 857-858.
76   "Closing Address for the Prosecution in the Case of Lieutenant Hashimoto Tadashi," the
      Hashimoto Trial, 1–4; Hayashi, *Sabakareta sensō hanzai*, 249-250.

we fully realized our duty to 'liberate Asia'."[77] The regimental history distinguishes its military achievement of first landing Johor, south of Malaya, before participating in capturing Singapore, and it further says, "it is the capture of the Singapore Peninsula that all Japanese people were watching closely, and we acutely sensed the severity of our duties and their world-historical significance."[78] It also notes that "officers and men (*shohei*) were extremely full of esprit de corps" prior to the Battle of Singapore.[79] The Battle of Singapore has been depicted in detail as "the century's great operation" (*seiki no daisakusen*). The regimental history exhibits a sense of mission in fighting in war, connected to a large amount of propaganda about Japan's war to "liberate Asia."[80]

In contrast to the "grand victory" of Singapore, the 21st Infantry Regiment's history recounts the "guarding" role in the Malaya Peninsula, part of the mopping-up operations, to only a small extent. According the regiment's history , the regiment was assigned to "guard" Alor Setar in the Kedah state from 28 February 1942. Emphasizing that Malays had been subjugated by the British colonial policy for a long time, the regimental history characterizes Malays as "extremely favorable and friendly to the Japanese military" as they believed that the same-colored Japanese ("yellow race") defeated the former "absolute authority of the Great British Empire" and enabled their liberation.[81] The regimental history also includes a similar reasoning to other regimental units about the conditions/justification under which the Japanese military engaged in the large-scale mopping-up operations: "some of the ethnic Chinese who took control of the Malaya economy in fact held a strong anti-Japanese sentiment even if they obeyed the Japanese military on the surface, and Communists' terrorist activities became fiercer day by day." The regimental history regards the guerrilla activities as a threat to the Japanese military and the "subjugation (*tōbatsu*) of these Communist guerrillas" as "important duties during the patrolling of Malaya." The descriptions about the mopping-up operations end there, and the regimental history concludes how the regiment "distinguishes itself to be famous" through the battles in Singapore and Malaya which it considers the "limelight in the gaze of the nations". Furthermore, the regimental history even mentions that Japan's "great victory" led local people "to recognize Japanese people's superiority" and the "pacification" of local people worked

---

77   Esumi Tetsuzō, "Marē senki" (War memoir of Malaya), in Ho 21-kai, ed., *Hamada rentaishi* (The Hamada Regimental History) (Non-commercial, 1973), 391, YA, 52171.396.5i021.木.

78   Esumi, "Marē senki," in Ho 21-kai, *Hamada rentaishi*, 396-397.

79   Ho 21-kai, ed., *Hamada rentaishi*, 409.

80   Ibid., 416.

81   Ibid., 420-421.

smoothly.[82] The regiment's narratives focus on the deeds that they achieved during the battles in Malaya and Singapore, while detailed descriptions of its daily movements, including the mopping-up operations, are not included.

Similar to other regiments, the 21st Infantry Regiment records the war history in order to describe the battlefield reality from their viewpoint and pass it down to other people (not just former military members). The section "the Pacific War" particularly stresses the reasons for recording the war: "although we do not have an ability to assess and criticize the great war, for long peace to come, we have a duty to recount the true state of the war front and look in the face the reality of the past beyond positive and negative assessment". Taking the future seriously, the regimental history also notes: "[w]e think about trying to leave our records so that as many people as possible would think about and shoulder the future."[83] In the same way that they had held a sense of mission to liberate Asia, they might have wished to create a new mission to recount the war to present it to today's society.

The 21st Infantry Regiment's history also expresses its opinions about the Allied trials. Like other regiments, the 21st Infantry Regiment's history stresses that the trials were victor's justice. More importantly, the history refers to the Nanjing Massacre and various other brutalities committed against civilians that the trials revealed; however, it emphasizes that these massacres were reported with an "exaggeration" and that "many of them" were "part of operational actions." The regiment's history holds the view that their actions can be justifiable as military necessities. Furthermore, the history does not exhibit any sense of regret or sorrow towards the atrocities committed against non-combatants and only highlights aspects that they thought "unfair" to the Japanese side's legitimacy, thereby eluding their responsibility.[84]

Moreover, the 21st Infantry Regiment's history emphasizes that it "correctly describes the relationship with inhabitants" on the battleground and that they did not commit "acts to be denounced," such as "excessive behavior" that "can easily occur in the state of agitation and confusion during or immediately after battles."[85] Nevertheless, the 21st Infantry Regiment was in charge of the mopping-up operations in Singapore and Malaya; for instance, one of its former members has confessed that they killed civilians based on an operational order when they participated in the Battle of Singapore in February 1942.[86] The

---

82   Ibid., 421.
83   Ibid., 366.
84   Ibid., 515.
85   Ibid., 516.
86   Hayashi, *Shingapōru Kakyō shukusei*, 28.

regiment stresses that they had "a number of episodes regarding friendship between members of the regiment and civilians," which they claim "enriched a life of savage battles."[87] Behind the group narratives, the regiment conceals its brutality in the Malaya Peninsula.

Fifteen years after the 21st Regimental history's compilation, former members of the 42nd Infantry Regiment compiled their *The Yamaguchi 42nd Infantry Regimental History* (*Yamaguchi hohei dai-42 rentaishi*) in 1988, encouraged by other infantry regiments' ongoing compilation trend.[88] The 42nd Infantry Regimental history seems to take pride in the regiment's achievement that they "fought through until the fall of Singapore as an advance team of the 5th Division which was almost the core of the military."[89]

The 42nd Infantry Regimental history records that they took a role in "the guards and the measures of purges" in Malaya and Singapore between 16 February and 28 November 1942 in the chronological table of its war history.[90] It includes a section, "Guards of the Perak State," in which the regimental history shows their stance towards the mopping-up operations. It notes that some ethnic Chinese who resided in the Malaya Peninsula "communicated tacitly with the Chinese Eighth Route Army (the Chinese Red Army) and took part in guerrilla activities"; therefore, the Japanese military took measures to "ensure security" (*chian kakuho*) and to "completely mop up those Chinese." The Japanese military also used these kinds of justification during the war and war crimes trials. Interestingly, the regimental history further highlights that there were some infantry regiments which "carried out unnecessary purges" and the incidents "brought anxiety to civilians on the contrary."[91] It acknowledges the negative consequences of purges of civilians, but refers to those conducted by other infantry regiments, not by the 42nd Infantry Regiment. Furthermore, it remains unclear how the regiment distinguished "unnecessary" and "necessary" purges, and therefore how it justified "necessary" purges.

The Yamaguchi 42nd Infantry Regimental History describes the regiment's effort to avoid conducting "unnecessary" purges. It emphasizes that the regiment "minimized the number of mopping-up operations" by regarding "the military orders as something that would invite civilians' resistance."[92] It also mentions that the regiment did not follow the orders even when a staff officer came to

---

87   Ho 21-kai, ed., *Hamada rentaishi*, 516.

88   Yamaguchi hohei dai-42 rentaishi hensan iinkai, ed., "Atogaki" (Afterword), in *Yamaguchi dai-42 rentaishi* (Non-commercial, Yamaguchi, 1988), 874, YA, 56820.396.5i042.レ.

89   Ibid., 539.

90   Ibid., 32.

91   Ibid., 553.

92   Ibid., 553.

urge the regimental unit to obey the orders on grounds that "the thorough mopping-up operations would involve innocent civilians, which would contrarily increase their antagonism and anxiety." The regiment deemed that its persistent rejection of orders enabled safety in the region where it was assigned and the military withdrew orders.[93] Due to the hitherto unavailability of war action reports for the regiment, this aspect cannot be verified; still the way in which members of the regiment write about the mopping-up operations could tell how they were trying to distinguish themselves from other regiments that instigated "unnecessary purges." Nevertheless, it is recorded that the regiment killed and arrested suspects of anti-Japanese elements in the Malaya Peninsula in 1942.[94] The regimental history rather pays more attention to what other regiments did and how the regiment helped to avoid "unnecessary purges", thereby directing the reader's attention away from the military's responsibility for civilian massacres.

The 18th Division's 55th and 56th Infantry Regiments also have similar attitudes towards the mopping-up operations. Like the 21st and 42nd Infantry Regiments, they were also given a "patrolling" role in Malaya. They were proud of their strength in fighting major battles and surviving the war. The 55th Infantry Regiment delineates the Battle of Singapore, recounting detailed movements and conditions up to the capture.[95] The regimental history contains only limited descriptions concerning its "patrolling" role in the state of Johor, where the 18th Division conducted large-scale massacres under the divisional commander Mutaguchi Ren'ya.[96] It describes the role as "maintenance of security" (*chian iji*) and does not include the mopping-up operations against civilians, which the regiment was also part of.[97] The regimental history seems to focus on the battle history and regards the mopping-up operations as part of maintaining the "security" of the region, but obviously meaning "security" in terms of the Japanese military interests.

The 56th Infantry Regiment's history also highlights the fact that it fought as a subordinate unit of the 18th Division, emphasizing that the division was known as the "Chrysanthemum Division" and characterizing it as "the nation's

---

93   Ibid., 554.

94   Hayashi, *Kakyō gyakusatsu*, 204–205.

95   Kiku hohei dai-55 rentai senyūkai, ed., *Kikka seiretsu tari: Kiku hohei dai-55 rentai shitō no dokyumento* (Chrysanthemum cool and clean: The document of the Chrysanthemum 55th Infantry Regiment's struggles to death) (Non-commercial, Nagasaki, 1996), 89-121, YA, 80804.396.5i055.‡.

96   Hayashi, *Sabakareta sensō hanzai*, 250–251.

97   Kiku hohei dai-55 rentai senyūkai, *Kikka seiretsu tari*, 120-121.

most prominent and best military division."[98] Similarly to the 55th Infantry Regiment, their narratives are limited to the Battle of Singapore concerning the Malaya operations, and the history omits the "patrolling" duties in Malaya during which the 18th Division committed civilian massacres in the state of Johor.[99] The regimental history only describes the mopping-up operations as a "measure of purges in the Malaya Peninsula" between 16 February and 31 March 1942 in the section that summarizes the regiment's movement.[100] Concerning the Malaya operations, the capture of Singapore is the end of the narrative. It then moves on to the Burma operations, in which the regimental history stresses the struggles and suffering of the regiment on the battlefield.[101] The regimental history chose to recount the battles against the British forces during the Malaya operations for future accounts of the regiment's history.

Unlike *The 11th Infantry Regimental History*, most untried regiments seem to avoid recounting the mopping-up operations against civilians.[102] Regardless of the difference in the time when the regimental histories were compiled (1973, 1988, 1984, 1993, and 1996), the battles against the British forces in 1941 and 1942 appear to be their main focus in writing about the Malaya operations; the mopping-up operations against civilians, though conducted over a longer period, were dispelled in their infantry regimental histories. Individual veterans' opinions may differ, but the former regiments examined in this chapter seem to be unrepentant as groups that they belonged to from the wartime period.

---

98 Kiku hohei dai-56 rentai senki iinkai, ed., *Kiku hohei dai-56 rentai senki* (The Chrysanthemum 56th Infantry Regimental war memoir) (Non-commercial, Saga, 1984), v, YA, 6235.396.5i056.⨥.

99 Hayashi, *Sabakareta sensō hanzai*, 250-251.

100 Kiku hohei dai-56 rentai senki iinkai, *dai-56 rentai senki*, 985.

101 Ibid., 167-473.

102 This thesis does not encompass all units (including guard infantry regiments and the *kenpeitai*) due to its focus on infantry regiments over three regions. For some analysis of *kenpeitai* members' postwar narratives, see Hayashi, *Kakyō gyakusatsu*, 53-105; for the guard infantry regimental histories, 3rd, 4th, and 5th published a long-length history; for instance, the 5th Guard Infantry Regiment was assigned for the guarding role in the state of Johor from March to November 1942 and recorded that they participated in two mopping-up operations in April and August 1942. Like the 21st Infantry Regiment, the 5th Guard Infantry Regiment also mention anti-Japanese activities and highlighted its pacification activities. See, Konoe hohei dai-5 rentaishi hensan iinkai, ed., *Konoe hohei dai-5 rentai shi* (The 5th Guards Infantry Regimental history), 2nd vol. (Non-commercial, 1990), 459-466.

Conclusion

The regimental histories observed in this chapter were compiled from 1973 to 1996, which includes the time in the 1980s when international criticism of Japanese atrocities in Asia had heightened. Nonetheless, they similarly seem to retain the "victorious" stories of the battles during the Malaya operations, recounting them as "glorious deeds" of these regiments. They seem to value the history of the battles in which they fought and stress the importance of initial victories against the British forces in their war histories. Consequently, these regiments' involvement in large-scale civilian massacres in the Malaya Peninsula are absent in their postwar group narratives.

This chapter shows one of many examples of infantry regimental histories which were compiled in postwar Japan. The postwar production of hundreds of regimental histories attests to the fact that the defeated also writes its own version of history and war in defeat. They also helps us to understand how the groups of former military men recreated images of the fallen army and dealt with the contentious past of the wartime Japanese brutalities, whose memories still haunt other Asian neighbors today.

Abbreviations and Archives

Japan
JACAR	Japan Center for Asian Historical Records (digital archive)
NIDS	Military Archive, National Institute for Defense Studies (*Bōei kenkyūsho shiryō etsuranshitsu*)
NAJ	National Archives of Japan (*Kokuritsu kōbunshokan*)
YA	Yasukuni Archives (*Yasukuni kaikō bunko*)

United Kingdom
NA	National Archives, Kew, Richmond, Surrey

Abbreviations of following document classifications are used in the footnotes:
WO   War Office (NA's department code for specific collections)

Works Cited

Blackburn, Kevin, and Daniel Chew Ju Ern. "Dalforce at the Fall of Singapore in 1942: An Overseas Chinese Heroic Legend." *Journal of Chinese Overseas* 1:2 (2005): 233259.

Bōeichō Bōei Kenshūjo Senshishitsu. *Marē shinkō sakusen* (Operations for the advance on Malaya). Senshi Sōsho 1. Asagumo Shinbunsha, 1966.

Hayashi, Hirofumi. *BC-kyū senpan saiban* (BC-class War Crimes Trials). Iwanami Shoten, 2005.

Hayashi, Hirofumi. *Kakyō gyakusatsu: Nihongun shihaika no Marē hantō* (*Massacres Against Overseas Chinese: The Malay Peninsula Under Control of the Japanese Army*). Suzusawa shoten, 1992.

Hayashi, Hirofumi. *Sabakareta sensō hanzai: Igirisu no tainichi senpan saiban* (Adjudicated War Crimes: British War Crimes Trials against Japan). Iwanami shoten, 1998.

Hayashi, Hirofumi. *Senpan saiban no kenkyū: Senpan saiban seisaku no keisei kara Tōkyō Saiban, BC-kyū Saiban made* (Studies of War Crimes Trials: From the Formation of the War Crimes Trials' Policy to the Tokyo Trial and BC-class Trials). Bensei shuppan, 2010.

Hayashi, Hirofumi. "Shingapōru Kakyō gyakusatsu" (Massacres of Singaporean Chinese). In *Sensō hanzai no kōzō: Nihongun wa naze minkanjin o koroshita no ka* (Structure of War Crimes: Why the Japanese Military Killed Civilians), ed. Tanaka Toshiyuki, 175-205. Ōtsuki Shoten, 2007.

Hayashi, Hirofumi. *Shingapōru Kakyō shukusei: Nihongun wa Shingapōru de nani o shita no ka* (Purges of Singaporean Chinese: What did the Japanese Army do in Singapore?). Kōbunken, 2007.

Hayashi, Hirofumi. "The Battle of Singapore, the Massacre of Chinese and Understanding of the Issue in Postwar Japan." *The Asia-Pacific Journal: Japan Focus* 7, 28:4, (2009). http://apjjf.org/-Hayashi-Hirofumi/3187/article.pdf.

Kasahara, Tokushi. "Chiansen no shisō to gijutsu" (Thought and Techniques of War for Safety). In *Senjō no soshō* (Various Faces on the Battlefield). Iwanami kōza, Ajia Taiheiyō sensō 5. Edited by Yoshida Yutaka, Kurasawa Aiko, Narita Ryūichi, Tessa Morris-Suzuki, and Yui Daizaburō, 215-244. Iwanami shoten, 2006.

Kasahara, Tokushi. *Nihongun no chiansen: Nitchū sensō no jissō* (The Japanese Military's War for Security: Reality of the Sino-Japanese War). Iwanami shoten, 2010.

Moore, Aaron W. "The Problem of Changing Language Communities: Veterans and Memory Writing in China, Taiwan, and Japan." *Modern Asian Studies* 45:2 (2011), 399-429.

Orr, James J. *The Victim As Hero: Ideologies of Peace and National Identity in Postwar Japan*. Honolulu: University of Hawai'i Press, 2001.

Otsuka, Aiko. "Narratives of a Fallen Army: Japanese Veterans' Concepts of Defeat and War Crimes Responsibility in World War Two." PhD diss. University of Cambridge, 2019.

Shin jinbutsu ōraisha. *Nihon rikugun hohei rentai* (The Japanese Army Infantry Regiments). Shin jinbutsu ōraisha, 1991.

Takashima, Nobuyoshi, Hayashi Hirofumi, and Murakami Ikuzō. *Maraya no Nihongun: Neguri Senbiran-shū ni okeru gyakusatsu* (The Japanese Military in Malaya: Massacres in the Negeri Sembilan State). Aoki shoten, 1989.

Totani, Yuma. *Justice in Asia and the Pacific Region, 1945-1952: Allied War Crimes Prosecutions*. Cambridge: Cambridge University Press, 2015.

Utsumi, Aiko, and Kota Udagawa. "sensō to sabaki: Ōsutoraria saiban to hikoku'nin" (War and Justice: The Australian Trials and Defendants). *Osaka keizai hōka daigaku ajia kenkyū sentā nenpō*, 2015.

Wilson, Sandra. "War, Soldier and Nation in 1950s Japan." *International Journal of Asian Studies* 5:2 (2008), 187-218.

Yoshida, Yutaka. *Ajia Taiheiyō sensō* (The Asia-Pacific War). Iwanami shoten, 2007.

Yoshida, Yutaka. *Nihonjin no sensōkan: sengoshi no naka no hen'yō* (The Japanese Perception of War: Its Transformation in Postwar History). Iwanami shoten, 1995.

Yoshida, Yutaka. *Heishitachi no sengoshi* (Postwar History of Soldiers). Iwanami shoten, 2011.

Contributors

OLAVI K. FÄLT
is Professor Emeritus in the Department of History, University of Oulu, Finland. He has mainly published on the encounters between the West and Japan, on Japanese emperorship and nationalism, on imagology and on the history of globalization. His books include "From Exoticism to Realism. The Traditional Image of Japan in Finland in the Transition Years of the 1930's" (in Finnish, a long summary in English) (1982), "Fascism, Militarism or Japanism? The interpretation of the crisis years in the Japanese English-language press" (1985) and "The Clash of Interests. The transformation of Japan in 1861-1881 in the eyes of the local Anglo-Saxon press" (1990). His co-edited books include "Akashi Motojirô. Rakka ryûsui: Colonel Akashi's Secret Co-operation with the Russian Revolutionary Parties during the Russo-Japanese War" (1988), "Looking at the Other. Historical study of images in theory and practise" (2002) and "Imagology and Cross-Cultural Encounters in History" (2008).

JOSEPH FONSECA
is a PhD Candidate in the Department of History at the University of Calgary. His research focuses on the relationship between Japan and the Western world at the turn of the 20th century, race and empire, and the social ramifications of joint military campaigns. He is specifically focused on the growth of the Empire of Japan and its military conflicts during the Meiji and Taisho Eras.

FRANK JACOB
is Professor of Global History (19th and 20th centuries) at Nord Universitet, Bodø, Norway. Before, he held positions at Würzburg University, Germany, and the City University of New York (QCC), USA. His current main fields of research are Modern Japanese History, Revolutionary Theory and Transatlantic Anarchism. He authored or edited more than 70 books, including *The Russo-Japanese War and Its Shaping of the Twentieth Century* (Routledge 2018, paperback 2019) and *Genocide and Mass Violence in Asia: An Introductory Reader* (DeGruyter 2019, editor).

SEPP LINHART
is professor emeritus of the University of Vienna, Austria, where he taught Japanese studies from 1978 to 2012. He was visiting professor at various universities in Japan, the USA, France and Finland. From 1988 to 1991 he served

as president of the European Association for Japanese Studies, and in 2004 he was Yamagata Bantō Prize winner. He is author and editor of 40 books and author of about 200 journal articles and book chapters. His main research interest is the social and cultural history of Japan, as well as the representation of Japan in the popular culture of the West. Main books: *Ken no bunka-shi* (The Cultural History of the Game Ken, 1998), (with Sabine Frühstück) *The Culture of Japan as Seen through its Leisure* (1998), *"Dainty Japanese"* or *Yellow Peril? Japan on Western War Postcards 1900 to 1945* (2005), (with Susanne Formanek) *Written Texts – Visual Texts. Woodblock-printed Media in Early Modern Japan* (2005).

AIKO OTSUKA

completed her PhD at the University of Cambridge in 2019. Her PhD thesis examines postwar group narratives of Japanese veterans and their war crimes responsibility in World War Two. Her thesis demonstrates how wartime military values continued into the postwar period and shows that different types of defeat shaped their postwar narratives in such a way as to alleviate negative sentiments resulting from defeat, and for some group narratives, avoid accepting war crimes responsibility. During her PhD, she was a member of the European Research Council funded research project on the dissolution of the Japanese Empire, led by Professor Barak Kushner at the Faculty of Asian and Middle Eastern Studies.

HENNA-RIIKKA PENNANEN

is a Postdoctoral Researcher at the Turku Institute for Advanced Studies, University of Turku. She is also affiliated with the John Morton Center for North American Studies. Pennanen received her Ph.D. in History from the University of Jyväskylä in 2015. Her current research project focuses on U.S. threat perceptions of China and Japan. She specializes in United States-East Asia relations, the ideas of civilization and "the West," and the crisis of the liberal international order. Her recent publications include the volume *Contestations of Liberal Order: The West in Crisis?* (Palgrave, 2020), co-edited with Marko Lehti and Jukka Jouhki.

ADAM S. ROCK

received his M.A. (2014) and B.A. (2008) in History from the University of Central Florida, where he currently teaches a variety of courses on American, and World History. His research interests include the treatment of enemy prisoners of war (POW) detained within the United States during World

War II. Investigating the story of roughly 5,000 Japanese POWs held in Camps throughout California, Iowa, Wisconsin, and Texas, between 1941 and 1945, Rock uncovers significant variations in the treatment, work allowances, and reeducation programs, available to German and Japanese prisoners despite official regulations and public projections of unilateral care. His forthcoming work further examines controversial American strategies intended to influence postwar reconstruction efforts in Germany and Japan, by utilizing 're-educated' repatriates to administer and assist in Allied rebuilding programs. Ultimately Rock hopes to highlight the ever-present role POWs play in shaping both current and future conflicts.

Index